EAST SIDE
WEST SIDE

EAST SIDE WEST SIDE

Organizing Crime in New York

1930-1950

Alan Block

WITH A NEW
INTRODUCTION
BY THE AUTHOR

Transaction Publishers
New Brunswick (U.S.A.) and London (U.K.)

To Dr. Harry H. Block, Lillyan Block, and Dianne Leslie Courtney

Fourth Printing 1999

New material this edition copyright © 1983 by Transaction Publishers, New Brunswick, New Jersey 08903. Original edition © 1980 by University College Cardiff.

Library of Congress Catalog Number: 83-4773
ISBN: 0-87855-931-0 (paper)
Printed in the United States of America

Library of Congress Cataloging-in-Publication Data

Block, Alan A.
  East side, west side.

  Reprint. Originally published: Cardiff: University College Cardiff Press, 1980.
  Bibliography: p.
  Includes index.
  1. Crime and criminals—New York (N.Y.)—History. 2. New York (N.Y.)—Social conditions. 3. Organized crime—New York (N.Y.)—History. I. Title.
HV6795.N5B57 1983   364.1'06'07471   83-4773
ISBN 0-87855-931-0 (pbk.)

Contents

Acknowledgements

The study which follows enjoyed the direct support and encouragement of a number of individuals and institutions. My good friend William J. Chambliss comes first in both instances. Two of my University College, Cardiff, colleagues, Philip A. Thomas and Mike Levi also performed yeoman service. Three of my students at the University of Delaware contributed a huge amount of time and energy in their roles as research assistants. Their help and companionship were instrumental in bringing the material into somewhat manageable proportions. Sandy Richardson, Dierdre Eva Antoinette Immediato, and Laura Lembo, who are all moving into legal careers, deserve to share in whatever credit the work merits.

Without congenial surroundings, research and travel grants, and an administered teaching load nothing could ever be written. For most of the above Frank Scarpitti, chair of the Department of Sociology, University of Delaware, is directly responsible. The completion of this study coincided with a term as a visiting instructor in the Law Faculty at University College, Cardiff. Dean Lee Sheridan is responsible for giving me the time and facilities to complete this work in Cardiff and I will always be grateful.

In addition to home institutions which provide the proper setting for work, I want to acknowledge the invaluable research assistance of the staff at the New York Municipal Archives. Working under difficult circumstances, they have been invariably helpful in putting up with whatever I have requested. I particularly want to mention Lillian S. D'Aguilar, assistant director of the Archives, who was instrumental in providing the photographs in the text. In the same manner, the kindness and help I received from former Governor Thomas E. Dewey's law office—Dewey, Ballantine, Bushby, Palmer and Wood—has been enormous.

Finally, without my family I simply wouldn't have done anything. I include in this Abby Rosenberg who, while technically not family, might as well be. My children mostly stayed out of the way except to look at the pictures of dead gangsters. My wife, Marcia, on the other hand, kept it all together. The whole lot deserve combat pay for putting up with my obsession.

Introduction to the Transaction Edition

One of the major points in *East Side–West Side* is that organized crime is both a social system and a social world. The system is composed of relationships binding professional criminals, politicians, law enforcers, and various entrepeneurs. Overall, the system exhibits a high degree of continuity. There are, of course, moments when for one reason or another the system appears disrupted, when particular relationships between criminals and politicians, for instance, are revealed; but by and large, continuity is the mark of the system. The social world of organized crime, on the other hand, is often murderously chaotic because professional criminals are oriented by constant manifestations of personal power. To continue this line and to indulge in criminological ruminations, I will take this opportunity to update one of the areas of industrial racketeering discussed in this volume.

No history of organized crime in New York could avoid the waterfront;* thus chapter seven presents an analysis of waterfront organized crime on the Brooklyn piers during the 1930s and 1940s. The information utilized comes primarily from investigations carried out by a special Grand Jury and the New York State Crime Commission. Briefly, the investigations revealed that the structure of the International Longshoremen's Association (ILA), its corrupt and criminal leadership, their collaboration with the Brooklyn criminal justice system, and their collusion with certain employers (this issue was downplayed in the investigations) guaranteed organized crime domination of the Brooklyn docks. In addition, Albert Anastasia, Vincent Mangano, Sr., his brother Philip, Giaocchino Parisi, and one or two others were identified as comprising the major, most powerful, criminal syndicate on the Brooklyn waterfront. These revelations about waterfront life emerged in the early 1950s, a time when the system of organized crime experienced one of its momentary disruptions. It was also the time, as we shall see, when a particular, compelling criminology was developed, which addressed in detail waterfront organized crime. The immediate and most important consequence of the public attention that was focused on the Port was the creation of a bi-state regulatory agency, the Waterfront Commission of New York Harbor, designed to control waterfront organized crime, and established in 1953 by the 83rd Congress that voted consent to a Compact between New York and New Jersey.

A Tumultuous Decade

By the time the Waterfront Commission began its work certain patterns of criminal behavior and organization were deeply established. Nevertheless, Brooklyn's primary waterfront syndicate had undergone major personnel changes by 1953, which was a clear indication of the chaos in the social world of organized crime. For example, Parisi left New York for the quieter environs of Hazelton, Pennsylvania, where he currently resides.[1] More important, the Mangano brothers were eliminated in 1951—Vincent disappearing three days prior to his brother Philip's murder.[2] Then, from December 1952, considerable criminal justice pressure was focused on Albert Anastasia. On December 9, 1952 the Justice Department filed a "civil complaint seeking to cancel" Anastasia's citizenship in order to deport him. The government's efforts did not end until May 1956, when the Supreme Court refused to review a U.S. Appeals Court decision that "the government was not deceived into granting Anastasia's citizenship in 1943."[3] A second criminal justice move against him opened in 1954 when Anastasia was indicted on tax charges, accused of evading $11,742 in taxes for the years 1947 and 1948. The culmination of this move came on May 24, 1955 at the start of Anastasia's second tax trial, when he "entered a surprise plea of guilty" in the Camden, New Jersey, District Court.[4] A little over a week later he was sentenced to one year in jail and fined $20,000. Anastasia began his sentence in the Federal penitentiary at Milan, Michigan, on June 15.[5]

While Anastasia was concerned with his legal problems, the New York waterfront was in turmoil partly because of the waterfront investigations. The primary inquiry was carried out by the New York State Crime Commission whose recommendations for alleviating crime on the waterfront resulted in the bi-state Compact[6] and the Waterfront Commission. The manner in which the causes of organized crime were presented in the Compact is significant. The Compact developed a criminology which had important consequences especially for the Waterfront Commission. The situation in the Harbor can be seen in Article 1 of the Compact, "Findings and Declarations":

1. The state of New Jersey and New York hereby find and declare that the conditions under which waterfront labor is employed within the Port of New York district are

depressing and degrading to such labor, resulting from the lack of any systematic method of hiring, the lack of adequate information as to the availability of employment, corrupt hiring practices and the fact that persons conducting such hiring are frequently criminals and persons notoriously lacking in moral character and integrity and neither responsive or responsible to the employers nor to the uncoerced will of the majority of the members of the labor organizations of the employees; that as a result waterfront laborers suffer from irregularity of employment, fear, subjection to borrowing at usurious rates of interest, exploitation and extortion as the price of securing employment and a loss of respect for the law.[7]

The Compact goes on stating that "public loaders serve no valid economic purpose and operate as parasites exacting a high and unwarranted toll on the flow of commerce . . . and have used force and engaged in discriminatory and coercive practices including extortion."[8] Article 1 concludes, therefore, that the two states "declare that the occupations of longshoremen, stevedores, pier superintendents, hiring agents, and port watchmen are affected with a public interest requiring their regulation and that such regulation shall be deemed an exercise of the police power of the two States."[9]

The Commission was to attack racketeering through "licensing of pier superintendents, hiring agents, and stevedores," and the "registration of longshoremen and the setting up of procedures and rules governing the hiring process"[10] through Commission-established and controlled employment and information centers. As Daniel Bell put it in describing the immediate background, "The political intervention of the state and federal agencies, and the AFL, in the New York waterfront situation in 1953 and after, was based on the belief that by changing power relations in the longshore union the conditions which gave rise to racketeering might be eliminated."[11] In establishing the Commission "with broad regulatory powers over the longshoremen, the loaders, and the stevedoring concerns . . . the harbor was declared a quasi-utility."[12] With only a few exceptions, most notably the ILA, interested parties saw the Waterfront Commission with its control of hiring and attendant regulations as an immensely positive step in the control of organized crime.[13]

The creation of the Waterfront Commission was one result of the Crime Commission investigation. Also flowing from the unprecedented exposure, according to Vernon Jensen, were "the events related to the expulsion of the ILA from the AFL—with the creation of the AFL of the International Brotherhood of Longshoremen (IBL)—and the resulting bitter struggle over union representation before the NLRB,"[14] the National Labor Relations Board. In the midst of these changes, collective bargaining negotiations between the ILA and the New York Shipping Association were carried out. It was clearly an extraordinarily tumultuous and confusing period. Vernon Jensen commented:

> These three developments were observable simultaneously, but expulsion of the ILA from the AFL and the interunion struggle, for a time, substantially obliterated collective bargaining negotiations, while regulation of the industry under the Waterfront Commission, although never out of sight and appearing at first somewhat uncertain, shortly came on importantly and with great force. But once the interunion struggle quieted, the collective bargaining negotiations reemerged and ran their course, too, but now in the context of the Waterfront Commission's actions. Its regulations and program became and remained an important ongoing factor in the industry.[15]

Eventually the ILA would prevail over the International Brotherhood of Longshoremen, and would reenter the ranks of the merged AFL/CIO.

Within these struggles and others that so marked the decade, the influence of Albert Anastasia's brother, Anthony, on the ILA was considerable. By Spring 1956, for instance, he had consolidated all the Brooklyn ILA locals into one—Local 1814—over which he presided. Anthony also ran for the ILA presidency in 1959, but with little chance for success. Nevertheless, his candidacy was serious and gives some measure of his power and influence.

The ascension of Anthony Anastasia at that time raises an interesting issue. Anthony's power was directly related to the influence of his brother Albert. But in October 1957, Albert Anastasia was murdered while sitting in the Park Sheraton Hotel's barber shop. A little over a year after leaving the Federal prison in Michigan, Albert's career was over. The murder of Albert Anastasia marked the high point in the "imperial" ambitions of the infamous Vito Genovese who had planned the murder with the connivance of Joe Biondo and, more important, Carlo Gambino.[16] Anastasia's Brooklyn enterprises were for the most part taken over by Gambino. This meant that Anthony Anastasia was now responsible to Carlo Gambino, and that his authority was contingent on Gambino's favor and power.

What had transpired then in the 1950s was this: the structure of power relations on the waterfront had been deeply upset. The supposed fulcrum of racketeering, hiring and loading, was regularized by the Waterfront Commission; the ILA was thrown out of the AFL and challenged by an AFL-sponsored dual union; the manner in which the ILA had been composed was irrevocably changed with the passing of numerous semi-autonomous locals through consolidation; and the primary criminal syndicate which had controlled the Brooklyn docks to such a large extent and for so long was removed and replaced, despite the rise of Anthony Anastasia to ILA prominence.

UNIRAC

From about 1960 to mid-1970 the issue of organized crime on the waterfront receded from public view. There were no major scandals, and it appeared that the diverse elements composing waterfront society—the Waterfront Commission, the ILA, the New York Shipping Association, and indeed organized crime—had learned to accommodate each other or, at least, to battle in a quieter and more acceptable fashion. Information was developed concerning waterfront organized crime, but its significance was perhaps unclear and certainly undervalued. For instance, the Waterfront Commission both gathered intelligence and, at times, held Administrative Hearings which documented the influence of Vito Genovese and other professional criminals such as Carmine Lombardozzi and Saro Mogavero on waterfront businesses and the ILA. But because it was the Commission that did this work (surely the very work it had been created to do), no one asked whether the public interest was being served by what were, in fact, the Commission's highly circumscribed law enforcement powers. The Commission licenses certain types of waterfront businesses and workers, but it cannot prosecute anyone for anything.[17]

This long period of relative calm was over by summer 1978. The first revelations concerning contemporary waterfront organized crime surfaced in Miami, Florida. In June the Justice Department Strike Force in Miami obtained "an indictment of 22 persons charged with 70 counts of extortion, embezzlement, bribery and labor racketeering."[18] The background to the Florida investigation was complex, beginning in 1972 when "the Metropolitan Dade County Department of Public Safety received information indicating that the Dodge Island Seaport, the hub of one of South Florida's largest industries, had been infiltrated by organized crime."[19]

Among the many issues uncovered in Florida, one of the most substantial was the movement to the Miami area of certain New York ILA officials who had been associated with Manhattan Local 1826 but had been barred from working in the Port of New York by the Waterfront Commission. These individuals included Douglas Rago, James Cornelious Vanderwyde, and George Joseph Barone. As the Florida investigation proceeded, it became clear that the leaders of the several conspiracies uncovered were in New York. Around 1976 the extended investigation was taken over by the FBI and given the code name UNIRAC. The culmination of UNIRAC came in 1979 and 1980 with two major New York cases. The first involved Michael Clemente, a former official of ILA Local 856, Manhattan; Tino Fiumara "who by position, influence and reputation is a controlling figure with respect to waterfront related businesses and officials of the ILA"; Thomas Buzzanca, president of two Manhattan ILA locals; Vincent Colluci, president and secretary-treasurer of two ILA New Jersey locals and a vice-president of the ILA Atlantic Coast District; and Carol Gardner, president of another New Jersey ILA local and also a vice-president of the Atlantic Coast District. The second case dealt with Anthony Scotto, the president of Brooklyn Local 1814 and ILA vice-president for Legislative Affairs; and Anthony Anastasia, Jr., the executive vice-president of Local 1814 and the son of Anthony Anastasia.

An overview of the importance of these trials was provided by Michael S. Devorkin, the lead prosecutor in the Clemente case. He stated before the Senate Permanent Subcommittee on Investigations, that the Clemente case, as well as the others, established that waterfront union and business activities were controlled by organized crime and that "very little has changed in this industry since the 1950s and the New York Crime Commission hearings."[20] Speaking of the Clemente case, Devorkin noted that both Clemente and Fiumara were the directors exercising "control and influence over high ILA officials including the defendants Buzzanca, Colluci, Gardner, unindicted co-conspirator George Barone, Fred Field, Anthony Scotto, and others."[21] As the senior member of the enterprise Clemente, aged 73, had primary control over Manhattan piers while Fiumara held a similar position in New Jersey. Devorkin went on noting that Clemente had been a waterfront racketeer for over forty years and had been an associate of Albert Anastasia, Vito Genovese, and Joseph Profaci. Clemente's official ILA position ended in 1953 with a conviction for extortion followed by almost five years in prison. Once released Clemente exercised his former power through his protégé, Fred Field, who became the principal officer of ILA Local 856 in Manhattan.

Turning to Scotto, it was pointed out that he was president of the ILA's largest local, Brooklyn's Local 1814, and that he "exercised extortionate control akin to Clemente's and Fiumara's, in Brooklyn and Staten Island."[22] Anthony Scotto's rise to power began with his marriage to Anthony Anastasia's daughter, Marion, in June 1957. And as noted earlier, through his participation in the murder of Albert Anastasia in 1957, Carlo Gambino had assumed control of Local 1814 and exercised it through Anthony Anastasia. Therefore, when Anthony Anastasia died in 1963 "the

Anastasia family asked Gambino to appoint Scotto as Anastasia's successor."[23] In 1963 Scotto became president of Local 1814 with Gambino's permission. Devorkin also testified to tension between Scotto and Clemente during the 1960s and at least the early 1970s. Clemente, who was in the parlance of federal officials a Genovese mobster, found Scotto's political ambitions irksome and distracting. However, with Gambino as Scotto's protector there was little Clemente could do except grumble.

The Criminology of Waterfront Organized Crime

The UNIRAC probe provides an opportunity to discuss the criminology of waterfront organized crime. The fullest amplification of the criminology of the Crime Commission (which became the strategy of the Waterfront Commission) was developed several decades ago by Daniel Bell.[24] His primary point was that given the archaic waterfront facilities, the crowded tangle of Manhattan's west side piers and streets, the necessity of trucking because of the paucity of major rail lines, meant that the tasks of loading and unloading cargo from ships to piers to trucks and back was the prime structural factor that led to racketeering. Time equalled money and loading and unloading cargoes was the single most sensitive part of the waterfront process—it appeared to provide the extortionary fulcrum from which other types of conspiracies followed. Concommitant with this went the "shape," the method of hiring. Presumably, the hiring racket not only enriched particular pier bosses and their cronies, but also created an "indebted" labor force which could be used to pressure shippers for under-the-table payoffs. Beholden to the hiring boss, the workers could hardly protest their use in extortion schemes; without an effective trade union, they were faced with a host of locals and their barons. Thus, the very structure of the ILA as well as the waterfront's ecology promoted organized crime.

We should consider the sufficiency of this explanation in light of UNIRAC and intelligence gathered earlier by the Waterfront Commission. First, no explanation based on New York's physical problems (twisted city streets, ancient piers, poor rail lines) could possibly account for south Florida's situation. Extortion there would never be seen as a function of the Port's structure. Neither could it be argued that the "shape" was the original malignant force from which other racketeering abuses emerged; there was no "shape" in south Florida. Instead, south Florida's Port was a feudal enclave of New York. The actions and activities of racketeers there are an example of the national reach of New York organized crime figures who virtually controlled the ILA. Equally important are the burgeoning interests of certain waterfront employers whose Florida businesses represented extensions of their New York enterprises. Controlling the ILA in New York was imperative because "the headquarters of the International has been in Manhattan for many years, as were the headquarters of the Atlantic Coast District Council—actually the two were in the same office—and the New York District Council."[25] Without doubt, these three parts of the ILA were not only dominant but, "for many purposes, the whole union."[26] It is in the personal and political relationships among employers, ILA officials, and professional criminals (obviously overlapping categories) that extortion is grounded in Florida and in New York.

Even in New York, the traditional explanation of waterfront organized crime will not do. At most, it serves as a partial explanation for conditions prior to the Waterfront Commission, because the prime impact of the Commission was on the organization of the labor market—elimination of public loading and the open "shape" were the two major issues. Computerized and Commission-run hiring centers, a tightly controlled job registry, a contentious and complex seniority system, and the development and implementation of a Guaranteed Annual Income for waterfront workers—all worked out by the Waterfront Commission, ILA, New York Shipping Association, the Port of New York Authority, and various arbitrators and mediators—have contributed to the massive "decasualization" of the labor market.[27] There is no doubt they did materially change the structure of the labor market, and in precisely those areas which seemed to be the loci of racketeering abuse. Further, a great deal of the old physical plant of New York waterfront was abandoned, especially in Manhattan, partly because of an overall decline in waterfront industry in the Port, but more significantly because of the industry's shift to containerization. "The widespread conversion to shipping by means of huge boxlike containers which became pronounced after the mid-sixties . . . has speeded the decline in Manhattan" which, it has been projected, would have to content itself "primarily with cruise business."[28] And concerning the ILA structure in New York—another feature of the old criminology—it deserves repeating that almost all the old locals throughout the Port were consolidated by about 1960. The most conspicuous example took place in Brooklyn under the leadership of Anthony Anastasia.

The combination of labor market-environmental criminology was really addressing those segments of grossest waterfront inefficiencies—hiring and loading, and outdated, crumbling facilities. It leaves virtually untouched the business and political side of industrial racketeering—the social system of organized crime. Investigative reports and public hearings provide thousands of pages of testimony detailing political and business collusion with ILA racketeers and the more free-wheeling criminal entrepeneurs, but this overwhelming evidence has not been digested into the criminology. There is no denying the absolute viciousness of the revealed hiring and loading rackets or racketeer control of most of the ILA, but surely there is doubt that these were *the* cause of waterfront organized crime. It would be foolhardy to expect that waterfront organized crime was so unadaptable as to be controlled or diminished by strategies emanating from such a criminology.

Let us take just one issue featured in the criminology and follow its logic. Throughout this introduction I have commented upon the ILA decentralization until the late 1950s. In the criminology under discussion this was seen as a major factor in the presence of waterfront organized crime. But logically and empirically what followed from ILA decentralization was that waterfront organized crime was itself somewhat decentralized, guaranteeing strife and tension among professional criminals, as the downfall of the Manganos and Albert Anastasia indicate. Consolidation, on the other hand, meant increasing centralization of waterfront organized crime. The power of the president of Brooklyn's only local would be obviously greater than the power of one local's president out of many. Correspondingly greater would be the power of the president's patron.

The patterns of waterfront organized crime are exceptionally varied. Nevertheless, they are dependent more on the structure of private enterprise within a regulated and organized market than on the particular structure of the ILA, port facilities, and the labor market. The following examples are illustrative.

In May 1961 the trustees of the New York Shipping Association/ International Longshoremen's Association Medical-Clinical Trust Fund "decided that due to a surplus in the fund, optical services could be added to the list of benefits."[29] At a June meeting of the trustees, Anthony Anastasia suggested the services of "George Minutaglio (then operating as Gem Opticians)."[30] In August 1961 the Brooklyn Medical Center and George Minutaglio signed a contract for optical services for longshoremen. Between June and late August the name of the business was changed to George's Opticians and it moved to 361 Court Street, Brooklyn. The new premises were rented from Newbrook Enterprises, "a real estate firm in which the principals are Marion Scotto (daughter of Anthony Anastasio and the wife of Anthony Scotto); her cousin Joseph Lacqua and her uncle Leo Lacqua."[31] In the meantime, George Minutaglio picked up a partner in his firm. Joining him was Carmine Lombardozzi, an identified associate of Carlo Gambino, and one-time "labor relations consultant with waterfront firms." In a little more than four months the firm had a "net profit of $17,845.32."[32] An investigation revealed not only the real estate deal and the intrusion of Lombardozzi, but an incredible demand for glasses by Local 1814 members.

The real estate firm Newbrook Enterprises is an interesting corporation in itself. Started in 1959, the three stockholders were Marion Scotto and her relatives Leo and Joseph Lacqua. Newbrook's affairs were closely intertwined with those of two waterfront companies also owned by the Lacquas—C.C. Lumber and Court Carpentry & Marine Contractors. In violation of New York's Labor and Management Improper Practices Act, Anthony Scotto "received income from these corporations" while being president of Local 1814 and an ILA vice-president.[33] Scotto's money from C.C. Lumber and Court Carpentry reportedly came principally through Newbrook Enterprises. Also, Newbrook bought a large number of run-down properties in and around Brooklyn's Red Hook neighborhood, which were then rented to waterfront businesses for a tidy sum. In addition, Newbrook purchased the leasehold on the Englewood Country Club in fall 1964. Among the members of the club at this time were Charles Chiri, who had been associated with Joe Adonis; brothers Thomas and Pat Eboli, very close associates of Vito Genovese; Joseph Stracci, another Genovese associate primarily in the garment center; Frank Erickson, "former top lay-off bookmaker of the United States"; Dominick Alongi, "a partner of Vincent 'Chin' Gigante, the man tried for shooting Frank Costello in 1957"; James Napoli, "a major numbers bank operator"; and Anthony Provenzano, a vice-president of the Teamsters Union, who was in prison, then, for extortion.[34]

There were other cases of interest related to Scotto and Lacqua. It was reported, for instance, that Scotto was connected with the Borough Hall Travel Agency and an insurance firm named Savin Associates. The president of both companies was Joseph Lacqua, and the secretary was Scotto's cousin, Bart DiMattia, who, in 1965, was appointed secretary and business manager of the New York Shipping Association/ILA Brooklyn Medical Center.[35] Also built into these medical programs was Carlo Gambino's son-in-law, Dr. Thomas J. Sinatra.[36] The last Scotto–Lacqua deal formed part of Scotto's UNIRAC trial. Lacqua was accused of soliciting about

$75,000 in illegal payments for Scotto from William "Sonny" Montella, general manager of Quin Marine Services in Brooklyn.[37] For Scotto, his family ties, position within the ILA, and the Gambino syndicate, were complementary sources of power and therefore money—the latter generated either through apparently straightforward extortion payments or through numerous ancillary enterprises in real estate, medical-welfare, insurance, and so on. More than anything else, it seems, the Scottos and Lacquas spent time and energy putting together their several enterprises that prospered in the regulated and organized waterfront market.

The significance of private enterprises for waterfront professional criminals is further exemplified in the Erb Strapping case. Around the mid-1950s Vito Genovese became a partner in a family firm known as the Erb Strapping Co. which did primarily waterfront business. Genovese invested $249 and Arthur Erb and his sister Eleanor Erb Pica $255 for incorporation expenses. A second corporation was then formed, known as the 180 Thompson Street Corporation, to purchase the building at that address. This second corporation "was to act as landlord and Erb Strapping was to be its tenant."[38] The Erbs and Genovese each put up $5,000 for a half interest in the Thompson Street stock. When Vito Genovese went to Federal prison on narcotics charges in 1960, he transferred his Erb Strapping stock interest to his brother Michael. In April 1968, when the Waterfront Commission began investigating the company, the Erbs and Picas purchased "the 49 percent stock interest of Michael Genovese . . . for the sum of $160,000."[39] The salaries collected by first Vito and then Michael came to a total of $170,000. The other corporation was also dissolved with Michael Genovese receiving "a purchase money mortgage on the property in the sum of $50,819.25."[40]

Through the influence of Vito Genovese, the Erb Corporation became one of the largest service companies in the frozen meat and tinned meat fields in the Port of New York. In a little less than fifteen years the gross profits grew over fifteen times. Undoubtedly, some of the growth came through the employment of "non-union men . . . to perform various functions incidental to the movement of waterborne cargo at various piers and waterfront terminals in the Port of New York District and also at the defrost room in Port Newark, New Jersey, in violation of the collective bargaining agreements . . . between the applicant corporation and Local 1171 of the ILA."[41] The Corporation also saved all the fringe benefit costs such as holiday and vacation pay and company contributions to welfare and pension funds. The rather hefty legal profits of Erb Strapping were one thing; another was the strong allegation that the Erb location, 180 Thompson Street, was "the prime transshipment point for heroin smuggled into the United States."[42]

The growth case of one other corporation should suffice. Henry C. Johnson had a cleaning and maintenance company called Maintenance Associates, which was losing money in the mid-1960s according to Johnson's testimony before the Waterfront Commission.[43] Stepping in to help Johnson (and themselves) were two convicted felons, Frank D'Ambrosio, affiliated with the Teamsters, and Jack McCarthy. Maintenance Associates incorporated and D'Ambrosio and McCarthy became substantial stockholders with no financial investments. Maintenance expanded rapidly; however, the story becomes complex because there were two other closely related corporations in which the principals were also involved—International Container Repair and Inter-Fab, Inc. Through the contacts of D'Ambrosio and McCarthy, the son and daughter of Saro Mogavero— Joseph Mogavero and Marilyn Bonaventura—were brought into the three companies. There were several other individuals involved in these companies, and an almost endless series of meetings between the companies' principals and other professional criminals—including Michael Clemente, Carmine Persico, Pete De Feo, Joseph Chilli, Alphonse Persico, Saro Mogavero, and Rosario Mogavero—took place at 100 Madison Street in Manhattan.[44] The stock value of all three companies rose spectacularly as they negotiated cleaning and maintenance contracts with many waterfront enterprises. The Maintenance Associates case is similar in kind to Newbrook Enterprises, C. C. Lumber, Erb Strapping, and many others.

It is clear that waterfront companies of all types were part of the province of professional criminals providing legitimate income (undoubtedly generated by extortionary methods), vehicles for laundering illegal monies, fronts for stealing and smuggling, employment for their children and/or spouses, and contracts for those of the above involved in insurance, accounting, medical services, etc.

Change and Continuity

Earlier I quoted Michael S. Devorkin, the Clemente case prosecutor, who stated that "very little has changed in this industry since the 1950s and the New York Crime Commission hearings." In the sense that the Port was and continues to be dominated by organized crime, Devorkin is obviously right. This is so despite the very considerable changes in the Port since 1953. The most substantial are those already discussed—the consolidation of the ILA, the "decasualization" of waterfront labor, and the creation of the Waterfront Commission, which had considerable positive impact on the conditions of waterfront work. Moreover, the Commission's power to license, broadened in 1969, provided it with the power to investigate waterfront enterprises such as Erb Strapping, C. C. Lumber, and Maintenance Associates, forcing companies to find new ways to hide their organized crime partners and patrons. These were significant but ultimately limited procedures. Ironically, the Commission was probably responsible to some degree for the exportation of particular waterfront criminals (most notably those with ILA positions) to other American ports. Chasing George Barone and others out of New York was surely no boon to Miami. The point is that neither the ILA nor waterfront businesses are confined to New York, but that the Commission is.

Even within the overall continuity of organized crime in the Port, there have been considerable changes associated with the rise and fall of particular racketeers and crime syndicates. There are three major syndicates in this history—Anastasia's, Genovese's, and Gambino's. What is most surprising in this history is that the Anastasia syndicate was superseded by Gambino's, while Anthony Anastasia rose to power in the ILA followed more significantly by his son-in-law, Anthony Scotto. Anthony Scotto's career exemplifies an interesting dimension of the social system of organized crime, an instance when a known organized crime figure became a significant political figure himself. As far as the Booklyn waterfront is concerned, the public political influence of Scotto was considerable. Let me stress that very strong allegations of Scotto's organized crime activities and associates began at least in the mid-1960s,[45] so that those political figures involved with Scotto since then could, should, and probably did, know of his role in organized crime.

For almost two decades Anthony Scotto was an important political power broker in New York City and State. Former U.S. attorney and prosecutor of the Scotto case Robert B. Fiske, Jr., provided some examples of Scotto's political influence. Scotto selected the commissioner of the Department of Ports and Terminals whose department manages much of the waterfront. Securing that appointment "Scotto was able to affect the disposition of public lands in and around the waterfront, including obtaining inside information as to particular lands that would be up for lease, influencing the selection of contractors that would perform services for the government in connection with those public lands, arranging for a particular union that would be given jurisdiction over jobs at some of the

businesses operating on those public lands, and in some respects, creating
businesses that could front for him in obtaining contracts or leases for those
lands."[46] Even more startling was that New York Governor Hugh Carey
"appointed Scotto's personal attorney to the New York position on the
Waterfront Commission"[47] in 1978. That appointment elicited rather
strong political opposition and Carey withdrew it. Nevertheless, Governor Carey as well as "two former New York City mayors, a New York
State senator and the President of the AFL-CIO" testified at Scotto's trial as
character witnesses.[48]

A criminology of waterfront organized crime (indeed of organized crime
in general) must be centered on an appreciation and understanding of the
dynamics in the social system of organized crime. The relationships
characteristic of this system are neither constrained by nor contingent upon
the structure of labor markets or particular trade unions. The participants
and therefore the system are extraordinarily adaptive, increasingly expressed in a web of private enterprises that are generally but not exclusively
located in the service sector of particular economic zones of industries. The
sociology and history of organized crime must center on both the social
system and social world of organized crime—that is, must be concerned
with both continuity and chaos, the general and the particular played-out
over time.

NOTES

* Various documents cited in this introduction were kindly furnished by Paul Kelly, Esq., the
director of Law Enforcement for the Waterfront Commission of New York Harbor and
will be noted as WCNYH Papers; other documents came from the files of the New York
State Senate Select Committee on Crime through the generosity of Jeremiah McKenna,
Esq., and will be noted as NYSSC Papers.

1 Pennsylvania Crime Commission, *A Decade of Organized Crime: 1980 Report* (Pennsylvania,
1980), pp. 59, 67, 105.

2 See Thomas E. Dewey, *Personal Papers*, "The Herlands Report and Accompanying
Documents: Memorandum, Location of Vincent Mangano, May 19, 1954," in Department
of Rare Books, Manuscript and Archives, the University of Rochester Library.

3 See New York *Herald Tribune*, 10 Dec. 1952:1; New York *Mirror*, 10 Dec. 1952:3;
Philadelphia *Evening Bulletin*, 20 Sept. 1955:16; Washington *News*, 20 Sept. 1955:7; Newark
Evening News, 7 Oct. 1955:1; 21 Oct. 1955:21; 17 Nov. 1955:16; and New York *Daily News*,
15 May 1956:10.

4 See Newark *Star Ledger*, 20 Oct. 1954:3; Newark *Evening News*, 31 Mar. 1955:32; 18 Apr.
1955:27; 3 June 1955:1; Washington *News*, 23 May 1955:1; New York *Herald Tribune*, 24
May 1955:1; Washington *Star*, 4 June 1955:1.

5   Newark *Evening News*, 15 June 1955:48.
6   See New York State Crime Commission, *Fourth Report, Port of New York Waterfront*, Legislative Document no. 70 (1953).
7   U.S. House, Committee of the Judiciary, *New Jersey—New York Waterfront Commission Compact, Hearing on H.R. 6286, H.R. 6321, H.R. 6343, and S. 2383* (22 July 1953), pp. 1-2.
8   Ibid., p. 2.
9   Ibid.
10 Vernon H. Jensen, *Strife on the Waterfront: The Port of New York since 1945* (Ithaca, New York, 1974), p. 117.
11 Daniel Bell, "The Racket-Ridden Longshoremen: The Web of Economics and Politics," in *The End of Ideology* (New York, 1962). Bell was not overly sanguine about the future accomplishments of the Commission as he found the first cause of waterfront racketeering to be "spatial"—"the matrix of the problem is the dilapitated physical condition of the port" (p. 189) which translated into congestion and hence, costly delays for ships and trucks. It was the ecology of the port, accordingly, that provided a "function" for racketeers and then "shaped a pattern of accommodation between the shippers and the racketeers and led to a continuation of the system" (p. 160).
12 Ibid., pp. 184-85.
13 Author's interviews with New York City Police Department detectives (summer 1981).
14 Jensen, *Strife on the Waterfront*, p. 95.
15 Ibid., p. 96.
16 See the original FBI interviews with informant Joseph Valachi conducted by SAS Patrick J. Moynihan and James P. Flynn, filed 12/11/62, Field Office no. 92-1459; Bureau File no. 92-4281. The statement concerning Anastasia's murder is on p. 104.
17 See WCNYH Papers, The Waterfront Commission Act (with amendments).
18 U.S. Senate Permanent Subcommittee on Investigations, "Statement of George R. Havens, Chief Investigator State Attorney's Office, Dade County, Florida" (18 Feb. 1981), pp. 5-6.
19 Ibid., p. 2.
20 U.S. Senate Permanent Subcommittee on Investigations, "Statement of Michael S. Devorkin, Former Assistant U.S. Attorney, Southern District of New York" (25 Feb. 1981), p. 3.
21 Ibid., pp. 3-4.
22 Ibid., p. 8.
23 Ibid.
24 See Bell, "The Racket-Ridden Longshoremen," passim.
25 Jensen, *Strife on the Waterfront*, p. 29.
26 Ibid.
27 On "decasualization" see Jensen, pp. 118, 226, 334, 451.
28 Jensen, pp. 24-25.
29 NYSSC Papers, "George's Opticians" (27 May 1968), p. 3.
30 Ibid.
31 Ibid.
32 Ibid., p. 4.
33 WCNYH Papers, "Hearing on CC Lumber and Court Carpentry and Marine," pp. 790-833.
34 The information comes from a highly confidential document in the author's possession which is a compilation of surveillance and informant reports on Anthony Scotto, pp. 7-8.

[35] Ibid., p. 10.
[36] NYSSC Papers, "Carlo Gambino," n.d.
[37] See the "Devorkin Statement"; and "United States vs. Scotto," in WCNYH Papers (2nd Cir., 2 Sept. 1980), pp. 964-76.
[38] WCNYH Papers, "Hearing on the Erb Strapping Co., Inc.," p. 37.
[39] Ibid., p. 11.
[40] Ibid., p. 14.
[41] Ibid., p. 15.
[42] The allegation comes from a confidential source in a communication dated 10 Apr. 1980.
[43] WCNYH Papers, "Hearing on Maintenance Associates, Inc.," pp. 467-504.
[44] Ibid., pp. 241-84.
[45] NYSSC Papers, "Report on Organized Crime" (1969), pp. 255-56.
[46] U.S. Senate Permanent Subcommittee on Investigations, "Statement of Robert B. Fiske, Jr., Former United States Attorney, Southern District of New York and Alan Levine, Former Assistant United States Attorney, Southern District of New York" (25 Feb. 1981), p. 5.
[47] Ibid.
[48] Ibid., p. 6.

Chapter 1
Myth and Reality

American organized crime is a subtle and complex cultural phenomenon, a staple of the collective unconscious formed and reformed through the fictive personalities of film and television stars, their creators and real-life imitators. Its fictional uniformities signal confusion in American attitudes about business, family life, sex, violence, individualism and fraternity. Writing in 1948, film critic Robert Warshow commented that the popularity of the fictional gangster was attributable to America's need to counter a shallow and optimistic creed with a "consistent and astonishing complete presentation of the modern sense of tragedy". The gangster satisfies America's ambivalent attitude towards success by playing out to the death a deeply held belief that every attempt at success is an act of aggression that will be punished. The gangster therefore embodies what Warshow saw as the American dilemma: "that failure is a kind of death and success is evil and dangerous, is ultimately impossible".[1] Such epics as the *Godfather* indicate precious little has changed in thirty years.

And just as the fictional gangster services the American psyche by his fortunate rise and fall, so the organized criminal tends to cater to certain ideological preconceptions held by mainstream social scientists. Central to the maintenance and developments of these preconceptions is a stance toward American history which is a mixture of conspiracy theories coupled with or indeed, supported, by a seeming disregard for historical methods. Implicit in this approach and explicit in a number of studies whose thrust is policy development[2] is the idea that organized crime is a monolithic alien conspiracy. This alien conspiracy usually called La Cosa Nostra or Mafia has infiltrated and undermined significant parts of the American economy and political system. With echoes of Lincoln Steffens' moral homilies but with little of his deep fascination, the conspiracy theorists among the professional social scientists present organized crime within the context of a passion play.

Intriguing as they may be for a cultural historian, it is well to note that this trend is not only unsophisticated but also quite retrograde. Social scientists have not always insisted upon a moral context rather than a historical and sociological one in the study of organized crime. Reflect for a moment on Robert Merton's work on political structure and the function of urban

1

political bosses, as well as Daniel Bell's neglected study of the "Racket Ridden Longshoremen".[3] Both of these early works emphasize historical and sociological concerns in their schemes of the social system of organized crime. But today, while it is generally agreed that organized crime is part of a social system often characterized by reciprocal services performed by the criminal, the client and the politician,[4] little substantive historical analysis of this system has been generated.

This same basic point was made two decades ago by Eric McKitrick in his call for historical studies centred around the Merton model.[5] But in only one sense has McKitrick's hope been answered, and that by a series of publications in urban history principally focusing on the structure of municipal politics and the functions of political machines during the Progressive Era.[6] None of these have taken organized crime as their major preoccupation. They are invaluable guides detailing aspects of the social system of organized crime without coming to grips with criminal syndicates themselves. Beyond these historical works and several other exceptions it appears that McKitrick's advice had been fruitless. Certainly that is the conclusion offered by the historically-minded sociologist, William Chambliss in a recent study. Chambliss writes that the study of organized crime has been both biased and sterile overlooking the "real significance of crime syndicates". He also notes that social scientists have not consistently considered criminal syndicates "as intimately tied to, and in symbiosis with, the legal and political bureaucracies of the state". Social scientists, therefore, "have emphasized the criminality of only a proportion of those involved".[7]

The critical sense that Chambliss has in a sense rediscovered already has had a major impact in a closely related field: the study of the Mafia phenomenon within the context of Italian/Sicilian history. Carried out by a combination of anthropologists sensitive to historical issues and radical historians,[8] these studies view their task as locating the connections between the prevalence of private violence and the structure of economic and political life. For these scholars, following the path of E.J. Hobsbawm's *Primitive Rebels*,[9] mafiosi are perceived as a variety of political middlemen or power brokers whose significance is predicated upon the capacity to acquire and maintain control over the paths linking the local infrastructure of the village to the superstructure of the larger society. They have integrated Merton's notions about political structure and the functions of power brokers, as well as ecological considerations characteristic of Bell's work, with developing analyses of patron–client networks. For them organized crime or Mafia is far from a simple parable of success or a simple conspiracy, alien or otherwise, or indeed an aspect of the ineluctable tendency toward bureaucratization, one of the other favored claims advanced by conservative scholars. Rather, Mafia and syndicate criminals are among the consequences of competitive capitalism and state formation.

The point, then, is that American organized crime is the product of deep contradictions in American culture which are surely analogous to the contradictions responsible for the emergence and endurance of Mafia in Sicilian history. Contradictions which cannot be pushed aside by either ignoring history or transforming it into romance and demonology.

History and La Cosa Nostra

To give substance to the charge of historical ignorance and insensitivity in the study of American organized crime, let me relate the following rather long example. One of the most important issues in what I call the traditional histories of organized crime concerns the origins of the Cosa Nostra or as one of the latest writers, David Leon Chandler, calls it, "The Making of the Syndicate". Donald Cressey writes in "The Functions and Structure of Criminal Syndicates" that "the basic framework of the current structure of American organized crime .... was established as a result of a gangland war in which an alliance of Italians and Sicilians was victorious" in 1930–1931.[11] The culmination of this reputed war was the execution of the Mafia boss, Salvatore Maranzano and an alleged purge of old-style Mafia leaders. "The successful execution of Maranzano was the signal for the planned execution of some sixty Maranzano allies, called 'Mustaches', a reference to their traditional Sicilian ways",[12] according to Chandler whose account is not materially different than a host of other commentators. Chandler continues:

> Details of the purge are not known, even after forty years. Implemented on a national scale, it must have required extraordinary preparation and communication. Each of the sixty victims must have been kept under surveillance to establish his daily pattern. For each of the sixty, a hit team had to be organized and gunmen chosen who wouldn't betray the plan. When Purge Day arrived, the hit teams had to be delivered to their target's area. A communication liaison must have been worked out to relay the go-ahead message from New York—that Maranzano had been killed—to each of the teams.[13]

Although Chandler cites no sources in his book it is absolutely clear from the context that his source is Joseph Valachi. Chandler's story parallels the one told by Cressey in his book, *Theft of the Nation*, except for the number killed. Cressey is more conservative claiming only about forty "Italian–Sicilian gang leaders across the country lost their lives".[14]

This brings us to the first major example of historical naiveté which is composed of two seemingly contradictory parts. First is the almost total reliance on Valachi and second is the apparent disregard for Valachi's testimony before the Senate Committee Investigating Organized Crime and the Illicit Traffic in Narcotics. Valachi was closely questioned by Chairman McClellan on the very point of the Purge. When asked by the Chairman how many men were killed, Valachi responded,"four or five, Senator".[15] The Committee was obviously concerned about the number of men killed that day, for almost immediately after Valachi's statement that four or five were killed, the Chairman asked Police Sergeant Ralph Salerno to take the stand. Salerno, a recognized expert on organized crime, was asked if he had any information about other murders (besides Maranzano's and James Le Pore's who was identified by Valachi as one of the four or five victims) that took place that day. Salerno replied no. Wanting to be sure, the Committee asked Salerno the same question once again. And again, Salerno answered that he had no record of any other murders occurring that day.[16]

While all the believers in Purge Day cite figures from thirty to ninety men executed, and while all believers cite or refer to Valachi for or as evidence, Valachi testified about four or five murders. It should also be noted that Valachi's recollections about the murders were exceptionally hazy, undoubtedly because of the intervening time, but equally significant because his knowledge was based on hearsay. Clearly what has been done is to use the popular story of Valachi as a primary source in the reconstruction of the history of organized crime. [17]

There is another important and related question to be asked about the Purge story. If Valachi did not testify about it, and if he is the major source for the history of organized crime, then how did the story evolve? Certainly it seems obvious that the Senate Committee had heard of the story from the nature of their questions. There really is no mystery, however. The story of the Mafia Purge has been around since the late 1930s when it first appeared in a series of articles written by J. Richard "Dixie" Davis and published in *Collier's* magazine. In the third installment of his life and times, Davis, who had been Arthur "Dutch Schultz" Flegenheimer's attorney, recounted a story told to him by Schultz mobster, "Bo" Weinberg. In an apparent moment of trust and confidentiality, according to Davis, Weinberg who was supposedly one of the killers of Maranzano confided that "at the very same hour when Maramanenza [sic] was knocked off ... there was about ninety guineas knocked off all over the country. That was the time we Americanized the mobs". [18] Davis did add the caveat that he had been unable to check on the accuracy of Weinberg's claims about mass murder.

The unsubstantiated story of the Purge remained in limbo for approximately a decade. It resurfaced in one of the key books on organized crime published in 1951. *Murder, Inc.,* written by ex-Assistant District

Attorney (Brooklyn) Burton B. Turkus and Sid Feder, revitalized the story and transformed it into a major turning point in the history of organized crime. Turkus and Feder write: "The day Marrizano [sic] got it was the end of the line for the Greaser crowd in the Italian Society ... a definite windup to Mafia as a entity and a power in national crime." They add that "some thirty to forty leaders of Mafia's older group all over the United States were murdered that day and in the next forty-eight hours".[19] One of their primary sources for this part of their history was "Dixie" Davis's story of his conversation with Weinberg. Turkus and Feder also claim that " even more irrefutable evidence was provided ... by an eagle-beaked, one-eyed thug named Ernest Rupolo".[20] A convicted murderer turned informer, Rupolo supposedly "went into the background and modernization of the Italian Society of crime". Turkus and Feder give no details of the Rupolo story simply implying that it was consistent with the Davis account and their particular notions about the history of organized crime. Even if they had supplied particulars, however, the Rupolo story would have been no more credible than the Davis one. Rupolo, who was a rather unsuccessful informer, was not a participant in either the War or its supposed culmination, the Purge. In 1931 he was either fifteen or sixteen years old and whatever knowledge he may have had about the inner workings the underworld was at the very best based on rumor. In addition, Rupolo was something of a dope and a criminal incompetent. In 1934 he shot someone at the request of the gang. The victim survived and Rupolo went to jail serving nine years before realizing that the protection promised him by the gang was not forthcoming.[21]

There is one final personality or alleged source for the Purge story. In 1971, reporter and crime writer, Hank Messick published a biography of Meyer Lansky, one of America's most famous criminals. In it Messick recounts the story of the Purge only at this time its accuracy was based on the supposed confessions of a retired Mafia leader, Nicola Gentile. During the late 1920s and early 1930s, according to Messick, Gentile was something of a Mafia peacemaker. Messick notes that Gentile's account of the gangland war and Purge was part of a long confession given to the FBI which he, Messick, was fortunate enough to examine. "Thanks to Gentile," Messick writes, "there exists a firsthand account never before published," etc., etc.[22] For those not fortunate to have access to FBI files, however, the Gentile story can be read in an Italian paperback titled, *Vita di Capomafia* which was published in the 1960s.[23] Gentile's story is a vast history of the American Mafia overwhelmingly stuffed with the names of almost every leading gangster, the dates and places of innumerable meetings and conferences, and the trivia

5

of gangland diplomacy and violence. Gentile's devotion to detail is faithfully followed through his description of the murder of Maranzano. But then, as if in an afterthought, Gentile stated that the death of Maranzano was the signal for a massacre. But not a name, not a place, not a killing, is described or given. As far as historical evidence is concerned the Gentile account provides no more evidence for the Purge than the earlier ones.

It is one thing to question or dismiss the historical sources for the story of the Purge, it is something else to prove that it, in fact, did not happen. That is while the sources may be incompetent, the event might still have taken place. In order to investigate that question, I did a survey of newspapers in selected cities beginning two weeks prior to Maranzano's death and ending two weeks after. I looked for any stories of gangland murders that could remotely be connected with the Maranzano case. The cities chosen were New York, Los Angeles, Philadelphia, Detroit, New Orleans, Boston, Buffalo and Newark. While I found various accounts of the Maranzano murder I could locate only three other murders that might have been connected. Two of the killings were extensively reported in the Newark *Star Ledger*. The dead men were Louis Russo and Samuel Monaco, both New Jersey gangsters. Monaco and Russo were two of the men mentioned by Valachi in his testimony about the four or five murders. The other case that might be connected was found in the Philadelphia *Inquirer* on September 14. Datelined, Pittsburgh, September 13, an A.P. wire story told of the murder of Joseph Siragusa whose death was "attributed to racketeers" who "fled in an automobile bearing New York licence plates".

The killing of four or five men does not make a purge, and certainly the killing of three or four men in the New York Metropolitan area and one man in Pittsburgh does not make a national vendetta. It is also significant that all the names turned up in our survey of the historiography of the Purge story — Maranzano, Monaco, Russo, Le Pore, and perhaps Siragusa—have been accounted for. Left out are only the fictional members of the Mafia's Legion of the Damned—those unnamed and more importantly, unfound gang leaders whose massacre signalled the end of one criminal era and the beginning of another.

Earlier I asked the question that if Valachi did not testify about the Purge, and if he is the major source for this history of organized crime, then how did the story evolve. Having answered that question by our discussion of Davis, Turkus, and the others, however, we are left with another puzzle. If all the accounts of the Purge are unreliable, and if the newspaper survey is accurate, and finally, if the Purge never really took place, then how and why did various people concoct it? Did Weinberg simply want to spice up his account of the murder of Maranzano with tales of ninety other dead Italians? Did Rupolo simply want to further ingratiate himself with the Brooklyn Attorney's office, and therefore invent a story? The same question can be posed for the other principals. I think the answer is no: I believe that they believed the story that they told.

All the commentators mention that the early 1930s was a time of intense confusion in the underworld compounded by the murders of such leaders as Joe Masseria in April, 1931, and Salvatore Maranzano in September, 1931. If not an actual war, there clearly was violence and division among Italian– and Sicilian–American gangsters. One can reasonably surmise that the death of Maranzano, especially to interested outsiders and/or principals such as Weinberg and Gentile, and lower-level, young hoodlums like Rupolo, was a momentous event that both could have and should have signaled increased violence. Certainly the level of anxiety along with the need for a comprehensible framework were high. When increased violence did not follow Maranzano's death a comprehensible framework was established, not out of whole cloth, but out of the bits and pieces of events that were transformed as they were transmitted. The suggestion, therefore, is that the Purge story performed the function of reducing anxiety by magically wiping out Maranzano's followers—those who would have been expected to revenge their leader's death. Furthermore, there is evidence that suggests why criminals, especially in New York City, developed this particular story.

In the course of my newpaper search for Purge victims, I found a number of stories about Maranzano and his presumably major racket: the illegal importation of aliens. In the September 10 edition of the Newark *Star Ledger*, for example, there was a story headlined "U.S. hot on trail of ring busy smuggling aliens". Datelined New York, the story noted that the Federal government was seeking indictments "against more than a score of persons in the hope of breaking up an alien smuggling ring ... believed responsible for importing 8,000 foreigners in this country". Reportedly, nineteen men had already been indicted. "Headquarters were maintained," according to the paper, "in Montreal," while other administrative offices "were established in New York, Chicago and San Francisco". Other cities mentioned in the article included Detroit and Buffalo as trans-shipment points for the smugglers. On the following day, September 11, the *Star Ledger* headed a story "murder in N.Y. held reprisal by smugglers". The report noted that "authorities ... were convinced that Salvatore Maranzano slashed and shot by three assassins ... was the victim of the ring". The *Star Ledger* went on to say that the police were sure that the members of the ring had murdered Maranzano for supposedly informing on them.

In the Los Angeles *Times* story of the Maranzano killing it was reported that detectives had "found immigration blank forms, and Department of Justice agents expressed the belief Maranzano had been engaged ... in aiding aliens to enter the United States illegally". Finishing the Maranzano account, the L.A. *Times* wrote that "his slayers slashed a cross on his face—the sign of a traitor". Maranzano's link to alien smuggling was also reported by the New York *Herald Tribune* which stated on September 12, that "among the theories engaging the attention of investigators is one that Maranzano was marked for death in the belief that he had given evidence or was about to do so against his fellow conspirators in the smuggling racket". The *Herald Tribune* pointed out that his death "came a week after the arrest of nineteen men, ... on charges of smuggling 8,000 aliens across the Canadian and Mexican borders, at a price ranging from $100 to $5,000 a head". And finally, the *New York Times* reported on the connection between Maranzano and alien smuggling. The *New York Times* story on September 11, noted that detectives were sent to Buffalo, Chicago, Poughkeepsie, New York, and Sea Isle, New Jersey, following Maranzano's murder. "The last named point," the *Times* added, was "said to have served as a base in the smuggling operations". On September 12, the *Times* also stated that Murray W. Garrson, Assistant Secretary of the Department of Labor, admitted that Maranzano had been under surveillance for over six months.†

In what way does this material on Maranzano contribute to the development of the Purge story? First of all, it is significant that this particular racket was national, or rather international, in scope. We have a number of reports that identify locales from at least Chicago to New York as both crossing points for aliens and headquarters of the racket. In addition, there are stories which indicate that law enforcement agents were sent to a number of different cities for purposes of investigating either the murder of Maranzano or the ramifications of this murder. It is possible, if not probable, that this kind of geographical activity accounted for the notion that the purge was national. Surely something was happening all over the country because of Maranzano's death. Secondly, the murder of Maranzano, if indeed connected to the investigation of the alien smuggling racket, could have caused the enterprise to cease, at least for an important period of time. If so, his death could be interpreted as resulting in the end of the traditional Mafia which, if it existed, must have depended on the continuous importation of Sicilians.

† I have attempted to get from the Immigration Service the files on Maranzano. Unfortunately, they have been missing since late September, 1931 one week after his murder. Personal communication.

Thirdly, it can easily be imagined how the deaths of four or five important racketeers could be transmuted into a massacre of large proportions through the mechanism of rumor and hyperbole, standard fare in the secretive oral culture of the underworld.

It is possible, therefore, to explain the belief in the Purge on the part of the various underworld figures. It is also clear how the story developed. But it is by no means clear why so many scholars have bought a story which so violates historical responsibility. Without speculating on the devotion to "history as conspiracy" as an explanation, it is well to mark that the scholarly attachment to the Purge is a conspicuous example of the insensitivity to historical methods found all too often in work on organized crime. In the study of organized crime in any of its aspects, one "is not free to take his history or leave it alone. Interpretations of the present require a host of assumptions about the past". And the "real choice", therefore, "is between explicit history, based on a careful examination of the sources, and implicit history, rooted in ideological preconceptions and uncritical acceptance of local mythology".[24]

New York

As one examines organized crime literature other problems and peculiarities stand out in addition to conspiracy imagery and ahistoricism. For example, much of the literature is geographically limited concentrating on only two American cities. Often the stories and studies of organized crime and criminals are little more than vignettes about growing up tough in New York or Chicago, or exposés of the ravages of crime and corruption in each. The significant personalities who form the romantic and demonic image of the gangster are usually products of New York's Lower East Side or some comparable area in Chicago. The sagas of John Torrio and Al Capone are even more telling than most in this respect. The careers of both men form a sort of bridge of crime, corruption and violence connecting America's twin capitals of organized crime.

There are naturally, several things to note about this exclusive and limited geographical fixation. First and foremost, it must always be kept in mind that organized crime is without doubt more than the sum of illegal enterprises in either New York or Chicago, or indeed both. To believe otherwise is to fall into some variant of the conspiracy trap where evil adheres not only to certain aliens but also in America's Sodom and Gomorrah. At the same time, it would be grossly misleading to think that the crush of work oriented around New York and Chicago means that the history of organized crime in either city has been adequately examined. It has not, although the efforts of Mark

H. Haller [25] on Chicago constitute a notable beginning. As far as New York is concerned, it is dismally clear that historical studies of organized crime outside the popular genre are virtually absent and sorely needed. This despite the fact that all the real events which have been molded into the myth of the origins of La Cosa Nostra took place in the New York metropolitan area. Apparently the handicaps of conservative ideology with its devotion to conspiracy theory have left much of the history of organized crime in New York in limbo. Naturally this does not have to be the case. There is a vast amount of primary source material dealing with syndicate criminals, political and criminal justice corruption, and other aspects of organized crime in New York available in libraries and archives. The data for reliable and revealing analysis are there.

The major point of this study is to describe and analyze the social system of organized crime, and the social world of organized crime, in New York from 1930 to about 1950. Let me distinguish between the social system and social world, and indicate their significance. Social system refers to the notion that organized crime is a phenomenon recognizable by reciprocal services performed by professional criminals, politicians, and clients. Organized crime is thus understood to lie in the relationships binding members of the underworld to upperworld institutions and individuals. In defining or more accurately describing organized crime thusly unnecessary confusion arises because of the inherent difficulty in using a noun to define an action, a multifarious series of relations. Ultimately, therefore, one must keep in mind that organized crime as reciprocal services is analogous or synonymous with what Marx calls "legal relations" which could not be understood by themselves because "they are rooted in the material conditions of life, which are summed... under the name of 'civil society'; the anatomy of that civil society is to be sought in political economy".[26] Organized crime is not a modern, urban, or lower-class phenomenon; it is a historical one whose changes mirror changes in civil society, the political economy. That is why, naturally, organized crime is increasingly taken to represent a series of relationships among professional criminals, upperworld clients and politicians. I will use the term organized crime in describing the system and in dealing with criminal syndicates which are associations or organizations of professional criminals who are individuals "whose major occupational role is a criminal one, though they may have another nominal occupation as well".[27] There are times and indeed numerous examples when the fully-found system cannot be identified; when, for instance, one of the three elements—criminals, clients, politicians—is absent from some criminal conspiracy from some variant of corruption. In such cases I use the term organized criminality to differentiate between the total system and what I see as the innumerable aspects possible within that system. But more of this discussion in the conclusion of Chapter 3.

In the broadest sense an examination of the social system and social world calls for locating the connections between the prevalence of private violence and the structure of economic and political life. In locating the connections, however, we confront the social reality of private violence which is our entry into the social world of organized crime—"le milieu" of professional criminals. It is one thing to see, discuss and understand the social system, and quite another to appreciate the social life of professional criminals and the violent consequences of many of the relationships found in the social system. Private violence and all it implies is the ground upon which the social world of professional criminals is constructed. And it is a world of some complexity in and of itself, difficult to grasp let alone to plot in some systematic fashion. An environment rent by private violence is deeply chaotic. Strangely enough, as we will see, the very chaos of the social world contrasts on the surface with the extraordinary stability or better put continuity of the system. Reciprocal services—the social system of organized crime—is virtually unbroken as a general system at the same time as the participants live in a whirl of change. It is imperative to grasp both elements to fully illuminate the reality of organized crime.

Before I turn to the actual structure of this study, a few words are needed concerning the time period chosen and my methodology. I have chosen the two decades for a number of reasons, the most important being that they lie between two engines of organized crime mythology. The first is the more contemporary criminological work which takes its start from the Purge and proceeds with all the attendant silliness of La Cosa Nostra. Although this work is contemporary it has created an unfortunately lasting impression about organized crime circa 1930. The second engine was created in the early 1950s by the Federal Government. This is the famous Kefauver investigation of organized crime carried out by Senator Estes Kefauver of Tennessee and his congressional colleagues. The conclusions of the Kefauver Committee resurrected a long dormant Mafia demonology whose effects subsequently clouded future research. I have been drawn to those years then by the implicit and explicit historicist claims of the demonological literature which neatly frame the two decades.

A short word on methodology; the method I pursue is the simple one of grounding "detail upon evidence and generalization upon detail". For evidence I rely almost totally upon the minutes, memoranda, reports, hearings, summaries, transcripts, and so on of a stunning series of

11

investigations into criminal justice and assorted types of racketeering and illegal enterprises which began in the summer of 1930 with Samuel Seabury's inquiry into New York's criminal judiciary. One further word about evidence is in order: I have tried to avoid relying on any secondary source which is itself not carefully documented. In a subject plagued by unreliable works based on unsubstantiated sources, one must go as often as possible to the actual record — that host of primary source documents mentioned above.

The book is divided into two parts roughly corresponding to (1) the social system of organized crime, and (2) the social world. I say roughly because in the real world and in much of the discussion which follows these categories not only overlap but are intertwined aspects of social reality. With that in mind, however, the first part is primarily concerned with the proposition that organized crime and criminality are inextricable parts of the political history of New York. As such their significance is at least two-fold; first, by definition organized crime and criminality were an endemic part of the city's political system built, as I will show, into the political structure. At the same time and second, notions of organized crime and criminality which derived from the reports of investigators and others were images subject to manipulation by politicos of all stripes in their endless search for office and power. That is, organized crime and criminality were politicized becoming part of the political dialogue in special ways. And as they became part of that dialogue they also became agents of political change. Let me give an example. I will discuss Seabury's investigation of organized criminality in the judiciary. He exposed a veritable labyrinth of organized criminality in the lower criminal courts. The exposure itself is evidence of the social system of organized crime and will be analyzed as such. In addition, the narrative will concentrate on how and in whose interests the information about organized crime and criminality was employed in the politics of the day. It is the purpose of Part 1 then to follow the discussion of organized crime and criminality as it unfolded during the 1930s and 1940s to examine the system uncovered, and to track the significant political changes which hinged on the discussion.

The second part of this study has a theme and approach decidedly different from the first. Where politics is the guide (and power the implicit motif) in Part 1 as the system and its history are tracked, power is the explicit theme throughout Part 2. I take it as a settled issue that the historicity of organized crime in the fashion discussed above is at bottom testimony of some of the ways in which power is produced and especially distributed in urban America.[28] Questions of power, to reinforce the point, are obviously central to a world where private violence abounds. With power as a th· me, the approach focuses on associations and organizations of professional criminals. In the main I divide criminal syndicates into two types—enterprise and power syndicates. Structurally and by function I argue that there are very important differences between them. In some fundamental ways, for instance, their spheres of activity are distinct, and their modes of operation are different. Enterprise syndicates, as the term suggests, take their structure from the necessities of participating in particular illegal enterprises. Power syndicates, on the other hand, are loosely structured, extraordinarily flexible associations centered around violence and deeply involved in the production and distribution of informal power. As such their only real activity can be encompassed by the term extortion. Power syndicates and their leaders, such individuals as Arthur "Dutch Schultz" Flegenheimer, Louis "Lepke" Buchalter, Albert Anastasia, and others who were the premier entrepreneurs of violence during the period under investigation, were principally involved in various and complex extortion schemes. In fact, so important is extortion as a characteristic activity of both the profession of professional criminals, and the social life of professional criminals that it becomes a term descriptive of the social world of organized crime.

By taking seriously such ungainly neologisms as extortionary culture, and extortionary behavior, we can better appreciate the contours of "le milieu" of professional criminals as well as the nature of the connections mediated by private violence. And finally by penetrating through the meaning of power syndicates to the nature of extortion we begin to understand the existential imperatives and challenges which the social world of organized crime marches to. Ultimately perhaps this brings light to the interplay between chaos and continuity which is the dramatic heart of this history. The discussion of these issues are framed by consideration of the tensions between enterprise and power syndicates in certain vice enterprises; the functions of the power syndicates within certain zones of the city's economy; and lastly, by considering some aspects of the history of gangland murder.

NOTES

[1] Robert Warshow, *The Immediate Experience: Movies, Comics, Theater and Other Aspects of Popular Culture* (New York, 1970) 129–133.
[2] Wil Wilson, "The Threat of Organized Crime: Highlighting the Challenging New Frontiers in Criminal Law", *Notre Dame Lawyer*, 46 (1970); William S. Lynch and James W. Phillips, "Organized Crime, Violence and Corruption", *Journal of Public Law*, 20 (1971).

[3] Robert K. Merton, *Social Theory and Social Structure* (New York, 1968); Daniel Bell, "Racket-Ridden Longshoremen: The Web of Economics and Politics", *The End of Ideology: On the Exhaustion of Political Ideas in the Fifties* (New York, 1962).

[4] Joseph L. Albini, *The American Mafia: Genesis of a Legend* (New York, 1971), 63.

[5] Eric L. McKitrick, "The Study of Corruption", *Political Science Quarterly*, 72 (1957).

[6] Zane L. Miller, *Boss Cox's Cincinnat: Urban Politics in the Progressive Era* (New York, 1968). Lyle W. Dorsett, *The Pendergast Machine* (New York, 1968); James B. Crooks, *Politics and Progress: The Rise of Urban Progressivism in Baltimore, 1895 to 1911* (Baton Rouge, 1968).

[7] William J. Chambliss, "Vice, Corruption, Bureaucracy and Power", in William J. Chambliss and Milton Mankoff, eds., *Whose Law, What Order? A Conflict Approach to Criminology* (New York, 1976), 182.

[8] See Anton Blok, *The Mafia of a Sicilian Village, 1860–1960: A Study of Violent Peasant Entrepreneurs* (New York, 1974); Alessandro Pizzorno, "Amoral Familism and Historical Marginality", *International Review of Community Development*, 15/16 (1906); Jane Catherine Schneider, "Family Patrimonies and Economic Behavior in Western Sicily", *Anthropological Quarterly*, 42 (1969); Jane Catherine Schneider, "Of Vigilance and Virgins: Honor, Shame and Access to Resources in Mediterranean Societies", *Ethnology*, 10 (1971); Peter Schneider, Jane Catherine Schneider, and Edward C. Hansen, "Modernization and Development: The Role of Regional Elites and Non-corporate Groups in the European Mediterranean", *Comparative Studies in Society and History*, 14 (1972); Henner Hess, *Mafia: Zentrale Herrschaft and lokale Gegenmacht* (Tübingen, 1970); Jeremy Boissevain, *Friends of Friends: Networks, Manipulators and Coalitions* (Oxford, 1973); Alex Weingrod, "Patrons, Patronage and Political Parties", *Comparative Studies in Society and History*, 10 (1968).

[9] Eric J. Hobsbawn, *Primitive Rebels: Studies in Archaic Forms of Social Movement in the 19th and 20th Centuries* (Manchester, 1959).

[10] David L. Chandler, *Brothers in Blood: The Rise of Criminal Brotherhoods* (New York, 1975).

[11] Donald Cressey, "The Structure and Functions of Criminal Syndicates", in President's Commission on Law Enforcement and Administration of Justice, *Task Force Reports; Organized Crime* (Washington, D.C., 1967), 26.

[12] Chandler, 160.

[13] *Ibid.*

[14] Donald R. Cressey, *Theft of the Nation: The Structure of Organized Crime in America* (New York, 1969), 44.

[15] United States Senate, Hearings before a permanent subcommittee on Investigations of the Committee on Government Operations, *Organized Crime and Illicit Traffic in Narcotics* (Washington, D.C., 1964), 232.

[16] Ibid., 233

[17] Peter Maas, *The Valachi Papers* (New York, 1968).

[18] J. Richard Davies, "Things I Couldn't Tell Till Now", *Collier's, 104* (August 5, 1939), 44.

[19] Burton B. Turkus and Sid Feder, *Murder Inc.; The Story of the Syndicate* (New York, 1951), 87

[20] *Ibid.*, 88

[21] The information about Rupolo in this section comes from the *New York Times*, June 29, 1944; August 16, 1944; May 6, 1946; June 7, 1946; and June 10, 1946.

[22] Hank Messick, *Lansky* (New York, 1971), 49

[23] Nicolo Gentile, *Vita di Capomafia* (Roma, 1963).

[24] Stephen Thernstrom, " 'Yankee City' Revisited: The Perils of Historical Naivete", *American Sociological Review*, 30 (1965), 242.

[25] Mark H. Haller, "Urban Crime and Criminal Justice: The Chicago Case", *The Journal of American History*, 58 (1970); "Organized Crime in Urban Society: Chicago in the Twentieth Century", *Journal of Social History*, (Winter 1971–72); "Bootleggers and American Gambling, 1920–1950", in Commission on the Review of National Policy Toward Gambling, *Gambling in America* (Washington, D.C., 1976).

[26] Lewis S. Feuer, ed., *Basic Writings on Politics and Philosophy: Karl Marx and Friedrich Engels* (Garden City, New York, 1959), 43.

[27] Mary McIntosh, "New Directions in the Study of Criminal Organization", in Herman Bianchi, Mario Simondi, and Ian Taylor, eds., *Deviance and Control in Europe: Papers from the European Group for the Study of Deviance and Social Control* (London, 1975), 147.

[28] A fine summary of work on urban power is David Hammack, "Problems of Power in the Historical Study of Cities", *The American Historical Review*, 83 (1978).

Part 1

"Consider. Would you, in your present need, be willing to accept a loan from a friend, securing him by a mortgage on your homestead, and do so, knowing that you had no reason to feel satisfied·that the mortgage might not eventually be transferred into the hands of a foe? Yet the difference between this man and that man is not so great as the difference between what the same man be to-day, and what he may be in days to come. For there is no bent of heart or turn of thought which any man holds by virtue of an unalterable nature or will. Even those feelings and opinions deemed most identical with eternal right and truth, it is not impossible but that, as personal persuasions, they may in reality be but the same result of some chance tip of Fate's elbow in throwing her dice. For, not to go into the first seeds of things, and passing by the accident of parentage predisposing to this or that habit of mind, descend below these, and tell me, if you change this man's experiences or that man's books, will wisdom go surety for his unchanged convictions? As particular food begets particular dreams, so particular experiences or books particular feelings or beliefs. I will hear nothing of that fine babble about development and its laws; there is no development in opinion and feeling but the developments of time and tide."

Herman Melville
THE CONFIDENCE-MAN
His Masquerade

Chapter 2
Tiger Rag

When Samuel Seabury was appointed referee by the Appellate Division of the New York State Supreme Court to lead an investigation into alleged corruption in the city's Magistrates' courts, New Yorkers through decades of similar experiences had a ready symbolic framework to help assimilate the expected tales of organized crime and corruption. The outline of this framework developed in the course of the nineteenth century especially during the late 1860s, early 1870s, and the 1890s. The first period marks the time of the machinations of the so-called Tweed Ring which Leo Hershkowitz has recently and brilliantly placed into proper perspective. But even though Tweed was much more victim than culprit, his myth is central to New York history. It marks the triumph of the Tammany Tiger upon the imagination. From Tweed on, New Yorkers would have a convenient symbol of urban corruption — a metaphor summing the symbiosis of politics and crime.[1]

While the Tweed episode confirmed an image, The Lexow Committee's investigation documented the social system of organized crime through a sensational inquiry into police corruption. The Committee which had been appointed by the New York State Senate on January 30, 1894, after a dramatic series of charges leveled by the Reverend Charles Parkhurst,[2] subpoenaed patrolmen, detectives, captains, inspectors, politicians, judges, saloon owners and managers, gamblers, policy bankers, and prostitutes. What the Committee found, according to Robert M. Fogleson, is this:

> ... the police secured appointments and won promotions through political influence and cash payments. In return for regular payoffs they protected gambling, prostitution, and other illicit enterprises. Officers extorted money from peddlers, storekeepers, and other legitimate businessmen who were hard pressed to abide by municipal ordinances. Detectives allowed con men, pickpockets, and thieves to go about their business in return for a share of the proceeds. Officers also assaulted ordinary citizens with impunity.[3]

Behind all the manifestations of police corruption, indeed of organized crime in New York, stood Tammany Hall as the generator of evil through "its persuasive influence over the police department and the other parts of the criminal justice system".[4] The material uncovered by the Lexow Committee, however, brought few substantive changes to either politics, law enforcement or the social system of organized crime. In fact, the system was so engrained into both the political culture and economy of New York that a scant five years later the New York State Legislature found itself initiating another full-scale investigation into the City's affairs. This one was led by the Mazet Committee whose findings and influence were similar to its predecessor.[5]

If one were to categorize or characterize the revelations of crime and corruption up to about 1900, then clearly what was being attacked and exposed was the political structure of New York. What was constantly displayed by the Senate committees as well as press and pulpit were the wicked results of patronage, the offspring of the structure of ward politics and law enforcement. There were major faults and weaknesses in the organization of politics and criminal justice which allowed, if not promoted, organized crime and criminality.

During the first decade of the twentieth century this concentration on political structure as the root of organized crime was significantly supplemented. What was added were new ethnic stereotypes. Now, obviously, ethnicity had played a role in the formation of the demonic Tammany Tiger which for New Yorkers had a decided Irish caste. But in the twentieth century other ethnic groups were assigned criminal roles which far exceeded in pejorative terms the perceived Irish monopoly of corruption. In New York major attention focused on the most recent immigrants, Italians and Jews. One of the outstanding examples of this trend first appeared in 1897 shortly before the Mazet inquiry. Attorney Frank Moss, who had worked for the Lexow Committee and was associated with the Society for the Prevention of Crime, a Trustee of the City Vigilance Committee, and President of the New York Board of Police, wrote a multi-volume "Historiograph of New York".

In Chapter Nine, significantly titled, "New Israel: A Modern School of Crime", Moss notes that Jewish "ignorance, prejudice, stubborn refusal to yield to American ideas, religious habits and requirements, clannishness, and hatred and distrust of the Christians"[6] combine to impede the social and moral progress of the Jewish inhabitants of New York's Lower East Side. Moving specifically to criminality he writes that this Jewish district is distinctly a center of crime. Packed into this area were petty thieves and desperate housebreakers. Moss adds that the "criminal instincts that are so often found naturally in the Russian and Polish Jews come to the surface here in such ways to warrant the opinion that these people are the worst element in the entire make-up of New York life". Among the "Hebrew" contributions to organized crime, Moss recounts the tales of organized arsonists, fagins, fences, burglars, pickpockets, prostitutes and pimps. Moss saves his most pungent prose for matters of vice.

> A large proportion of the people in New Israel are addicted to vice, and very many of their women have no other occupation than prostitution ... there has grown up as an adjunct of this herd of female wretchedness a fraternity of fetid male vermin (nearly all of them being Russian or Polish Jews), who are unmatchable for impudence, and bestiality, and who reek with all unmanly vicious humors. They all called "pimps" .... They have a regular federation, and manage several clubs, which are influential in local politics.[8]

Organized vice was undoubtedly one of the most haunting spectres in American society during the first two decades of the twentieth century. In fact, anti-vice campaigns were a typical manifestation of that amalgamation known as Progressive reform. Within the partially imagined vice networks, Progressive moralists worked out their vision of urban decay: wayward, discarded children, ignorant and tending toward viciousness; abused, brutalized women abandoning themselves in licentiousness and ultimately disease; and finally, the cruel organizer, a foul foreigner who was the very antipode of American manhood.[9]

The Jewish immigrant preyed upon the imagination of Progressives as they conjured up vision upon vision of lust concretized. But this is only one of the connections made at this time by urban reformers which grounded certain immigrant groups in criminal categories. Unlike the mode within which Jewish immigrants were characterized, New York's Italian population was seen as the progenitor of violence. To make the connection even more explicit, reformers and reporters quickly turned to exploiting three favorite terms signifying Italian organized violence—Mafia, Camorra, and Black Hand. The development of these symbols has been ably told by Dwight Smith, Joseph Albini, Humbert Nelli and others in the recent past.[10] To understand the symbols attached to the caricature, however, consider the following article from the New York *Tribune* quoted by Pitkin and Cordasco in *The Black Hand: A Chapter in Ethnic Crime*.

> The city is confronted with an Italian problem with which at the present time it seems unable to cope. Citizens are waking up mornings to read "Black Hand" letters demanding extortionate sums of money, to be deposited in some out of the way rendezvous or else a pistol shot or dynamite bomb will end their days. Some of these letters have been turned over to the police, but it is believed that not one-tenth of them have been made public. Besides such threats, there have also been acts of violence and even of death. Boys have been kidnapped and held for ransom. Homes have been

wrecked with dynamite on the failure of their tenants to pay blackmail, and not long ago an Italian was murdered and thrust into a barrel and abandoned because he had aroused the vengeance of a gang of conspirators.[11]

Predatory Jews and Italians organizing vice and violence under the malign direction of Tammany was the composite of organized crime in New York until the First World War. During these formative years of the organized crime picture, several riveting incidents along with the public response to them were crucial. For instance, the reported depradations of Black Handers led to the formation in 1904 of an Italian squad within the Detective Bureau of the New York City Police Department.[12] For almost five years the squad was directed by Lieutenant Joseph Petrosino with skill and courage. But then on March 12, 1909, Petrosino was murdered in Palermo, Sicily. Petrosino, who only a month earlier was selected as "head of the new secret service branch of the police department" had been sent to Italy by New York Police Commissioner Theodore Bingham, to gather information on an estimated five thousand New York Italians who were fugitives from Italian justice. At the very least, the murder of Petrosino, writes Humbert Nelli, "inflated the reputation of *mafia* power in Sicily and Black Hand power in America, and confirmed the widespread belief that if the *mafia* decided to 'get' someone, sooner or later that person would die violently, despite any precautions he might take".[13]

For New York's Italians, the process of stereotyping was accomplished quickly with only occasional events needed to invoke and/or reinforce the Mafia, Black Hand, Camorra imagery. On the other hand, the criminal stereotyping of New York's Jews was both more complex and ultimately less successful. The themes first broadcast by Frank Moss in 1897 were once again publicly raised in the late summer of 1908. This time, Police Commissioner Bingham, stated in the *North American Review* that around fifty per cent of New York City's criminal classes were Jews. This allegation, according to Arthur A. Goren, produced an exceptionally heated debate over the course of Jewish communal life between the two major segments of New York Jewry. One segment, the so-called uptown leaders, held that the charge, though surely exaggerated, nevertheless substantiated their long-held notions about the East Side of New York: "delinquency was rising, a grim indication of the presence of moral dissolution". On the other hand, downtown Jewry saw the statement as nothing more than anti-Semitism, an attack upon the common people.[14]

Within the debate that erupted among the Jews of New York, Goren isolates several themes. For one, the Yiddish press, dominated by a "tone of rancor and self-flagellation turned to an acrimonious appraisal of the behavior of 'the magnates' ", their name for the uptown Jewish leaders, and a blistering analysis of the unmistakeable disorganization among the mass of new immigrants. In return, uptown assimilated Jews stated their distaste with the frenetic protest activity on the East Side and the role of the Yiddish press which they characterized as inflammatory. The *American Hebrew*, the most important Anglo–Jewish weekly in New York, turned in one week from castigating Commissioner Bingham to criticizing the extreme sensitivity of East Side Jews. The combined uproar in New York's Jewish community had one immediate consequence: on September 16, Commissioner Bingham withdrew his statement.[15]

But the issue of Jewish criminality did not diminish with the passing of the Bingham charge: starting in 1909 and reaching a climax during 1912, publicized disclosures of crime and vice among Jews created both dismay and alarm in Jewish communities. The conspicuous concern with crime during this period marked a new season of reform for New York City. Fed by muckraking articles, published investigations, government reports and the report of a special Grand Jury the public became privy to the "details of a vast complex of prostitution and gambling". And then in 1912, when revelations of immorality and crime seemed to have run its course, the murder of the notorious gambler, Herman Rosenthal, revitalized public concern with Jewish criminality.[16]

Shortly before the Mayoral election in 1909, *McClure's Magazine* published one of the most sensational journalistic accounts of crime in New York history. In three separate articles, *McClure's* set out to portray Tammany Hall as the leader of a massive vice operation. Also implicated along with Tammany were large numbers of Jewish criminals. One of the authors was by then the ex-Commissioner of Police Bingham, who wrote that the criminals of New York City naturally gravitated to the enclave of the downtown Jews. In discussing gambling, Bingham notes: "The game of stuss, introduced by foreign criminals into New York in the early '90s is the commonest type of gambling game among the East Side Jews".[17]

The editor of the magazine, S. S. McClure, begins his essay with praise for the Germanic races as the architects of Western civilization. In contrast to this achievement, McClure holds that the "great masses of primitive peoples from the farms of Europe, transported to this country as laborers, together with a considerable proportion of Negro slaves liberated by the Civil War" have struggled "to degrade the standards and guaranties of civilization in America". For proof, McClure turns to a description of the so-called white slave traffic in New York, linking it to Tammany Hall and the East Side immigrant Jews. Using Moss's own words, McClure writes: "There has grown up as an adjunct of this herd of female wretchedness, a fraternity of fetid male vermin (nearly all of them being Russian or Polish Jews), who are unmatchable for impudence and bestiality."[18]

The third article was George Kibbe Turner's, "The Daughters of the Poor". Turner's concern was the movement of a large alleged vice empire from Europe to the East Side of New York. He notes that around twenty-five years before, during the third great rush of immigration, which consisted of Hungarian, Austrian and Russian Jews, a large number settled in New York. In fact, Turner writes, it was the Jewish district which opened the eyes of the local slum politician to the tremendous enterprise, the business of prostitution and the traffic in women, offered him. It is also noted that the largest number of prostitutes came from immigrant Jewish families. Finally, Turner adds that the East Side Jewish pimp, along with Jewish prostitutes, were transferring to other American cities.[19]

Clearly enough, as Goren points out, these writers were playing upon the deeply felt anxieties of the period: the fear of an organized conspiracy on the part of amoral business and political interests, and the degradation of the immigrants who now appeared to control the American cities.[19] The reaction of the Jewish community to *McClure's* revelations was to a large extent cast in political terms. The Yiddish press stated that the Jews had once again been attacked for the sake of gaining base political profit. With a show of unanimity the Yiddish newspapers called for the defeat of those reform forces which had linked Tammany's fortunes to the denigration of the immigrant community. Even the Americanized community leaders who were committed to the reform forces were less than resolute in facing the issue. Their pitch, Goren finds, was to state that there was no intent in the articles to select out any group as immoral and that this notion was in reality being spread by Tammany to deceive the public and defeat reform.[20]

Following the election and for a few years afterward, the "anxiety to prove that Jewish criminality had not exceeded some permissible level seemed to have been stilled".[21] This period of relative calm abruptly ended in the summer of 1912 with the sensational murder of gambler Herman Rosenthal. Rosenthal and almost all the other principle figures in the case were Jewish, including three out of four gunmen—Jacob "Whitey Lewis" Seidenscher, Harry "Gyp the Blood" Horowitz, and Louis "Lefty Louie" Rosenberg.[22] The most sensational aspect of the Rosenthal case, the charge that Police Lieutenant Charles Becker was responsible for the murder, did not obscure the claims of Jewish venality. In fact, for New York Jewry the Rosenthal–Becker case marked some kind of watershed in their response to the accusation of Jewish criminality. It was no longer possible for Jewish apologists to view crime and criminality as something removed from the community. According to Goren, it was, in fact, the abandonment of the usual defensive posture which indicated the extent of the dismay and distress experienced by all elements of New York Jewry.[23]

Within the general acceptance of communal responsibility for criminals there were several distinct approaches. Discussion in the Yiddish press tended to focus on the children of the immigrant generation from whom, it was claimed, came most of the now acknowledged criminals. With feelings of gloom, writers placed in apposition the old country where tradition guided the young, and urban America which had no place for either God or tradition. A variation of this theme was expressed by the Socialist *Forward* which placed the blame not on America but on urbanization: Jewish crime was a factor in the large cities. Warsaw and Odessa, like New York and Chicago had their gangs of Jewish criminals. While the immigrant spokesmen had now accepted the fact of Jewish crime, they laid the blame for it on either the materialism of America or on impersonal forces such as urbanization. On the other hand, outside the immigrant neighborhoods, American bred Jews found the real cause of Jewish crime was the stultifying orthodoxy of the immigrant leaders. Unable to adjust to modern American life the immigrant religious leaders had made of both themselves and Judaism objects of hate and derision. The real culprits were those whose sole ideal was to Russianize American Judaism.[24] For the uptown Jews the problem was not the Americanization of the children, but the lack of Americanization of parents and elders in the American community.

But whatever acceptance the accusation of Jewish criminality found in the Jewish community of New York and among Gentile observers in the pre-World War I years was muted in the post war decade. What remained was the defensive posture which still cropped up from time-to-time and a developing intellectual self-censorship among American–Jewish scholars. The reasons for the disappearance of the stereotypic Jewish vice entrepreneur from public debate are many and varied. Among the factors are the general lessening of anxiety concerning immigrants with the passage in the early 1920s of immigration restriction legislation,[25] the tenacity of the Jewish community itself in resisting pejorative images through a variety of "self-defense" organizations, and the victory of Mafia imagery[26] which was ethnically exclusive having no room for Jewish mobsters. In one sense then, the perceived social bases of organized crime in New York were narrowed down in the years after World War I to Italians and Tammany Hall.

I have spent what may well be an inordinate amount of time on the Jewish stereotype and particularly the communal response, especially as the stereotype plays no public role in the 1930s and 1940s. The reasons are these. As we know, the power of Mafia imagery will grow mostly surreptitiously until it bursts forth in the early 1950s through the pronouncements of the Kefauver Committee. On the other hand, the public discussion of Jews and organized crime will not surface again—not until contemporary historians and sociologists making the most elementary calculations will re-discover the Jewish syndicate criminal. This rediscovery, of course, will not resemble the gross claims and low-spirited rantings of Moss and McClure. The point then of this excursion into ethnic stereotypes is how the loss of one masks important aspects of the social history of organized crime, while the magnification of the other—Mafia— distorts it. But more of both later.

For now we return to the first theme articulated in the nineteenth century, that of Tammany which was never far removed from discussions of organized crime and which will dominate much of the subsequent analysis. As the perceptions of ethnicity and organized crime changed during the course of the first three decades of this century, notions of Tammany wickedness remained fairly constant. However, during the 1920s there was little of the reform ethos characteristic of the pre-war years which meant that with few exceptions the corruption endemic in the city's political structure was benignly viewed.[27] Undoubtedly this laissez-faire attitude towards organized crime and criminality was framed in part by that complex known as Prohibition which immeasureably increased the numbers of both co-conspirators and clients in the social system of organized crime. While the Tiger was apparently as wicked as ever, wickedness itself was apparently much mote popular.

The high point of this process of tolerance for the machinations of Tammany politics came in 1928. That was the year when Al Smith, Tammany Hall's greatest contribution to progressive politics, was nominated for the Presidency. Tammany Hall was, it seems, reborn. It is a new Tammany which Joseph McGoldrick analyzes in the September, 1928, edition of *The American Mercury*. This intriguing essay begins:

> Now the White House is in sight. Al has been nominated for the Presidency. Naturally, the nation's interest is focused on his political parentage. Is his dam truly regenerate, as report hath it? Or has she her tongue in her velvety cheek? Has New York been bewitched by the Tiger? Is it or is it not the same old carnivorous and prehensile beast?[28]

Before answering his question, McGoldrick describes the organization. He states that the real Tammany is the Democratic organization which is comprised of the members of all the district clubs, some 50,000 voters in all. The next level is the County Committee with approximately 5,000 members. More important, he writes, is the County Executive Committee which is composed of about thirty of the district leaders. The two most significant standing committees are the Tammany Law Committee and the Steering Committee. The importance of these committees is such, McGoldrick holds, that the "Board of Aldermen has almost completely abdicated in their favor".[29] According to McGoldrick, Tammany structure is central as "it cuts through the elaborate system of governmental checks and balances, it obliterates executive and legislative distinctions, and it supplants elective discretion".[30] It turns, it seems, "topsy-turvy" formal administrative hierarchies. The structure of Tammany then is the real design of city government although it is circumscribed because its strength does not extend into all five Boroughs (counties) which have constituted Greater New York since the turn of the twentieth century.

The backbone or as McGoldrick states "the anode and the cathode of Tammany's political battery" is the district leader.

> Every night in the week, every week in the year, they can find him in his clubhouse during the entire evening, sometimes late into the night. In a little black book he enters his commissions—"contracts" he calls them. The next day he is busy about the courts, seeing clerks, district attorneys and judges, or, better still, the leaders responsible for them. He sees Commissioner this or Chief Clerk that and arranges for peddlers' and plumbers' licences, excuses from jury duty, transfers, reinstatements, the promotion of subordinates, vault permits, sewer connections, revision of assessments, and passports.[31]

All this and much more besides, McGoldrick contends, is accomplished for two reasons: money and votes. The district from whence the leader comes is the assembly district, *the* political unit in New York. In 1928 there were sixty-five of them. Within the districts, political life coalesces around the political club whose leader is the district leader. In fact, "twenty or more members of every district club hold important elective or appointive positions".[32] From dues and assorted other club levies through scores of other ways the district leader and his cronies enrich themselves and the Tammany treasury.

Still however, the question remains—is it or is it not the same old carnivorous and prehensile beast? And no is the answer offered by McGoldrick in the salad days of 1928. Take vice for instance.

> The old Tammany was a synonym for alliance with vice. Today with the Hall more completely in control than it has ever been before, and the first Tammany police commissioner in twenty-five years in office, vice conditions in New York are better than they have ever been and superior to those of any other large city in the country. Street-walking simply does not exist, Brothels are equally unknown. There is no organized or obtrusive prostitution.... Gambling has been checked. The last police commissioner even raided poker games in Tammany clubs.[33]

McGoldrick's conclusion is that Tammany governs the city well if not a bit expensively. Indeed, he argues that Tammany's greatest ally has been the general prosperity of the city itself "which has enabled it to double the budget since 1918".[34] As the city prospered so did Tammany taking a "tithe" which may after all have been its due.

This newly articulated notion of benign Tammany did not long survive, however. The chronology of its decline can be briefly sketched.[35] The Tammany Hall leader from 1924 to 1929 was George W. Olvany whose patron initially was New York Governor Al Smith. Olvany's career as leader was marked by turbulence and in 1929 he was removed as leader by a coalition of district leaders. Their major complaint, according to Herbert Mitgang, was that Olvany was simply too greedy tending to monopolize legal and other businesses which should have been more equitably dispersed throughout the political club system. The man selected and then elected to be the new Tammany leader in 1929 was John F. Curry. Curry was decidedly in the prehensile mode stating at one time that "I am the political leader of the dominant party in New York City, ... The New Tammany is a fiction".[36]

The transition from Olvany to Curry marked the ascendancy of Mayor James J. Walker's power over that of the defeated presidential candidate and ex-Governor of New York Al Smith. In fact, Curry's triumph was in large measure a victory for Mayor Walker who had pushed Curry's candidacy in the face of Smith's opposition. All these complex maneuvers within New York City had important ramifications in the broader arena of state politics. Franklin Delano Roosevelt had succeeded Smith as Governor, and was by necessity vitally concerned with maintaining Tammany support as well as keeping Tammany scandals within bounds. He could ill afford to lose democratic votes in New York City by alienating Tammany, and he had to be extremely careful to avoid being drawn into a potential quagmire of Tammany corruption which could prove even costlier to a man with presidential ambitions. The propriety of Tammany was an issue much greater than city politics.

As we have seen, Tammany within bounds is the cornerstone of McGoldrick's New Tammany. But the declawed Tiger was a fragile beast whose true nature surfaced only a few months after McGoldrick's optimistic pronouncement. The process of unmasking began during election week in 1928. The key event was not as might be expected the defeat of Smith but the murder of Arnold Rothstein, infamous gambler and suspected underworld financier of narcotics and assorted rackets.[37] Rothstein had been shot at the Park Central Hotel two days prior to the election and died on election day, November 6, 1928. Rothstein's murder was to provide a continuing source of first embarrassment and then scandal for the Walker administration and, of course, Tammany. It was not just the inability of the city's criminal justice agents to solve the murder which fueled the scandal. Equally as important was the perception that important city and Tammany officials were extremely reluctant to pursue an investigation which seemed to lead back into the maw of city politics.

In 1929 Congressman Fiorello La Guardia focused on the Rothstein case in his unsuccessful bid for the Mayoralty. On September 29, La Guardia formally accepted what he had so tenaciously fought for, the Republican nomination for Mayor. That evening he stated that he would "reorganize overlapping departments; appoint a regional planning commission; unify the transit system; clean up the police department; eliminate graft; solve the housing problem through private enterprise; and investigate the unsolved Rothstein murder".[38] Above all else, his able biographer Arthur Mann reports, was the reiterated charge that the Walker administration knew who murdered Rothstein but would do nothing "for fear of disclosing the connection between Tammany and the underworld".[39] Pointing up the connections during the campaign, La Guardia charged that Magistrate Albert H. Vitale had borrowed almost $20,000 from Rothstein. At that time Vitale was not only a City Magistrate, but was also coordinating Mayor Walker's campaign in the Italian neighborhoods of the Bronx.

Although Walker crushed La Guardia in the election the seeds of Walker's destruction and the unmasking of the "New Tammany" were deeply planted. An equation was established which linked together the underworld, the criminal judiciary, and Tammany Hall. As the Stock Market crashed and the Great Depression loomed, prosperity supposedly Tammany's greatest ally deserted the Tiger. In an increasingly bitter mood, reform groups turned their attention once more to the structure of city politics to the social system of organized crime.

Seabury and the Magistrates' Courts

The first crack in this fortress of corruption opened in the summer of 1930 when Samuel Seabury, distinguished jurist and one time political candidate for Governor, was appointed referee in an inquiry into the activities of the Magistrates' Courts of Manhattan and the Bronx.[40] Attention focused on the Magistrates because of the revelations of Vitale's interests and a subsequent scandal involving his successor to the Bench, George Ewald, who it was charged paid $10,000 for his appointment to a Tammany District Leader. Ewald resigned from the Bench and was then indicted for using the mails to defraud in a mining stock deal.[41]

Before discussing the investigation, let us look first at the formal organization of the courts. The structure and functions of the City Magistrates' Courts as they were in 1930 were created by Chapter 659 of the Laws of 1910. The courts were reorganized in 1910 following a little known investigation of them carried out by the Page Commission instituted by the State Legislature in 1908.[42] Until July 1, 1915, there were two divisions of the City Magistrates' Courts, the first encompassing Manhattan and the Bronx, the second, the other three Boroughs. According to a survey carried out by the Commissioners of Accounts and the Bureau of Municipal Research in 1915,

> Magistrate's Courts are inferior courts not of record having original criminal jurisdiction. They have power to hear, in first instance, all complaints of a criminal nature. A Magistrate may issue a warrant of arrest, subpoena witnesses and admit defendants to bail...
>
> On conviction for public intoxication, disorderly conduct tending to a breach of the peace, or vagrancy, a Magistrate may suspend sentence, impose a fine or commit the defendant to a reformatory, the workhouse, or a county jail... In case of a felony, he holds the defendant for the grand jury....
>
> Magistrates are also assigned to the night courts, one exclusively for the hearing of cases against women and the other for the hearing of cases against men and against men and women for offenses arising out of the same transaction.... All persons arrested (except for felony) too late to be arraigned in the day courts must be brought into the night courts.... The cases coming before the women's night court consist chiefly of women charged with being common prostitutes or soliciting or loitering on the public streets, of frequenting disorderly houses or of vagrancy. The Magistrates may commit such persons upon conviction to a reformatory, to the workhouse on Blackwell's Island, or may in certain instances suspend sentence or place upon probation.[43]

Finally, it is pointed out that each Magistrates' Court is presided over by one Magistrate, and that each of the District Courts (there were also Special Courts as will shortly be discussed) "has jurisdiction only over crimes" occurring in its particular district. The boundaries were set by the Mayor, the Police Commissioner and the Chief City Magistrate and had to be as close as possible to police precincts.[44]

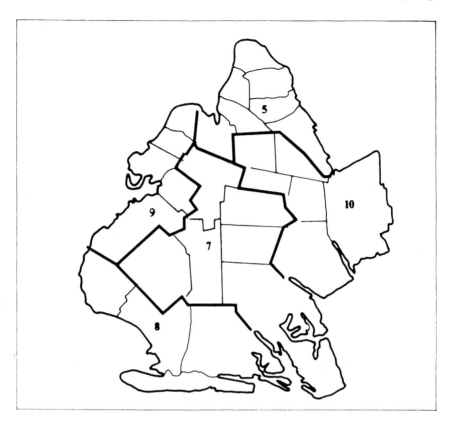

But as one can see in this map of Brooklyn in 1930 the Magistrates' Courts boundaries encompassed several police precincts. I think what the Commissioners of Accounts meant was that the Courts' boundaries should approximate Police Inspection Districts which they more nearly did.

By 1930 there were 23 District Courts and 17 Special Courts, including 3 Family, 2 Women's, 3 Traffic, 2 Night, 3 Municipal Term, 3 Homicide, and 1 Commercial Frauds Court.[45] To administer this part of the criminal judiciary there were 49 Magistrates, 1 Chief City Magistrate, 37 court clerks, 89 assistant clerks, and 182 court attendants. The scope of the Magistrates' Courts was tremendous; in 1930 alone over 500,000 New Yorkers were arraigned in this system. This represents an enormous increase: in just twenty years, 1911 to 1931, the number of defendants rose from 151,362 to 525,528.[46] These figures did not reflect the vast numbers of individuals who applied for summonses which were refused. All-in-all, the Magistrates' Courts had a commanding influence both quantitatively and qualitatively on criminal justice.

In Seabury's Final Report to the Appellate Division of the Supreme Court he remarks that the evidence gathered fell into four general and at times overlapping categories. First there was testimony bearing upon the activities of Magistrates, Court Clerks and Attendants, Assistant District Attorneys, Probation Officers, and members of the Police Department; second included material concerning the behavior of lawyers, so-called Fixers, and solicitors of bail bond business; third was evidence dealing with the disposition of cases relating to prostitution, slot machines, policy games, professional gambling, and commercial fraud; the last category dealt with the physical conditions of select Court Houses.

Seabury reports on eleven sitting or recently sitting Magistrates [47] and then adds some comments on Magistrates Vitale and Ewald whose corruption was instrumental in initiating the investigation. His immediate task was to demonstrate the tie between the Judiciary and various politicos. The tie was simple and obvious: Magistrates owed their appointments to the largesse of various District leaders. The case of Magistrate Brodsky is typical. He testified that his original appointment to the Bench was engineered by his then District Leader, James J. Hagan. Brodsky states:

> I spoke to Mr. Hagan and I mentioned the fact that I had rendered services to the organization and that I felt that I ought to get some recognition, that up to that time I had received none, that I had worked hard, and he said that if I waited a while, the first opportunity he would get, he felt I was entitled to it by reason of my experience at the Bar and the work that I had done, that I had earned some recognition, and that is the substance of the conversation we had. [48]

Turning momentarily from the Magistrates to the clerks, assistant clerks, and court attendants, Seabury shows how, in practice, the routine business of individual courts was largely controlled by the clerks and their deputies. Thus, the administration of each court depended upon the "integrity, fitness and intelligence of these administrative officers". [49] But the major function of these officers was to serve as a connecting link between the "world of politics and the lesser world of the court". [50] In the main, he finds that the clerk is a politician. A large number were captains of election districts for local Democratic clubs; others, members of their County Committee or officers in the political clubs. Just like the Magistrates, court clerks were political appointees. Assistant clerks were also elected in similar fashion even though their appointments were "said to depend only upon the competitive civil service examination".[51] At each level of court officer, the appointees were routinely beholden to the shadow government—the County political organization. The Magistrates' Courts were plums distributed by District Leaders and other politicos. Positions were quite simply rewards for party service and favors in return were expected and received. Indeed, Seabury documents numerous instances of interference in the administration of justice by the courts' patrons.

The venality of the Magistrates' Courts went much beyond the mere fact that they were first and foremost a patronage field. Partly as a consequence of relations of patronage which in these instances overwhelmed formal authority, and partly because court officers including some Magistrates saw their functions as entrepreneurial rather than legal or administrative, the Magistrates' Courts were a spawning ground of rackets and conspiracies. One of the liveliest conspiracies centered on splitting fees between certain attorneys and court officers who would steer defendants to them. Other examples include bribery of mostly assistant clerks especially in gambling cases. One reason for the preponderance of assistant clerks in these examples is that they were invariably in charge of making out complaints. The usual practice was to secure from the assistant clerk "an 0–14 form instead of a full complaint in bookmaking cases". This form was sent to a Magistrate "when the clerk who draws the complaint is in doubt as to whether the facts stated to him by the complainant are sufficient to constitute a complaint on the charge for which the defendant was arrested".[52] It was a rare Magistrate who did not defer to the 0–14. In the year before his investigation began, Seabury points out, there were 4,328 bookmaking cases brought into the Magistrates' Courts in Manhattan and the Bronx. Of that total only about 3.8 percent were held by the Magistrates for trial. [53]

Bribery was also a way of life for at least some of the nine Deputy Assistant District Attorneys assigned to various Magistrates' Courts in Manhattan. After investigating their duties in certain Manhattan courts, Seabury concludes that they did almost nothing, at least formally. One graphic example was the case of an individual who "drifted" into the Women's Court as the District Attorney's representative. For the last seven years of his service he made no report to the District Attorney and, in fact, never went to the office except to pick up his salary check. "His entire existence," Seabury recounts, "seems to have been a kind of indefinite shadow in the mind of the District Attorney, who saw him practically not at all and heard about him even less". Nevertheless, he was busy: "During all this time, he helped to throw out 600 cases and stowed away a tidy fortune in bribes".[54]

Probably the most vicious racket and certainly the one which received the most public attention involved a ring operating primarily in the Women's Court. The ring was composed of "interlocking halves, the lawyers, the bondsmen and the fixers, on the one hand, and members of the so-called Vice Squad of the Police Department and their stool-pigeons, on the other".[55] Presiding over the machinations of this ring were a number of Magistrates especially Jean H. Norris and H. Stanley Renaud. The method of the racket was to arrest falsely and illegally innocent women on various charges of prostitution. Once arrested there were any number of ways for the conspirators to make money. The police were bribed, favored lawyers and bondsmen were hired and payed exorbitant and illegal fees, clerks and the more-or-less invisible Deputy Assistant District Attorneys also received their cuts. When a woman had paid enough, charges were usually but not always dismissed. For those who refused to cooperate, conviction was the inevitable result.

The engine of corruption which was the Magistrates' Courts worked then in several ways. Payoffs in money and favors were made by the Magistrates and clerks in order to secure their appointments. Innocent people were arrested and processed through the courts paying bribes at every step hopefully to secure their release. Guilty offenders such as policy gamblers, bookmakers, and slot machine operatives were protected for a price. Clerks and assistants conspired with lawyers and bondsmen in what were by 1930 customary arrangements which included fee-splitting and bribes.

Earlier in the discussion of the "New Tammany" I noted McGoldrick's claim that the County machine turned "topsy-turvy" formal administrative hierarchies. Nothing could be clearer from Seabury's investigation than that authority and power in the Magistrates' Courts reflected the structure of county politics and the pecuniary interests of a jumble of entrepreneurs whose position in no way reflected the organizational hierarchy of the courts. Probably the most telling example of the informal power arrangements dominant in the Magistrates' Courts is found in Seabury's provocative comments on the bail bond business.[56]

To begin with, bail originally was personal. Sureties were generally required to be householders or freeholders, and the individual bailed was released into their personal custody. Security was typically household goods or real estates. With the first efforts at regulation the professional bondsmen appeared. They were shortly followed by surety companies. The activities of professional bondsmen and surety companies were not legally clear in New York until a major revision of the State Insurance Law was enacted in 1913. By the time of the investigation into the Magistrates' Courts, bail bonding had expanded significantly. There were, according to Seabury, five levels or classes in the bonding business. First there was the independent or individual bondsman who customarily put up either real estate or cash as security. This type directly solicited business in and around the courts, often hiring "chiselers" who passed out cards offering bail bonds in the corridors of the courts. The "chiseler" is the second level identified by Seabury. What made them a distinct class is that in many instances they worked independently peddling their business to various bondsmen or brokers who bargained with them for clients. The third class was the corporation: the compensated corporate surety a company organized for profit under the insurance law of the State. The fourth was the general agent. In Seabury's words, "A general agency is a sort of management company that supervises and directs the agents who are licensed by the State to represent the respective companies as bail bond agents."[57] The exact purposes of these general agencies were, however, somewhat mysterious although they were "compensated by a percentage of the territorial revenues of the bonding companies they serve". Finally, there were field agents hired "directly by the bonding company", but supervised by the general agency.[58]

As far as effective regulation of the bail bond business was concerned, Seabury finds it non-existent. There was record keeping but no checking. Bond cards were filled out by the corrupt assistant clerks in each court and then sent to the statistical bureau located in the Chief Clerk's office. But these cards were seldom tabulated and "rarely, if ever", scrutinized. Bail was also taken at police station-houses. In such cases records were also kept, but again for no purpose. The lack of regulation allowed for the following abuse in the case of independent bondsmen.

> Independent bondsmen often offer real estate as security. In many cases, however, they have in the property an equity far below the amount which they pledge. There may be liens against the property. The bondsman may have pledged the value of the property many times over. Inasmuch as there is no exchange of information between the Federal Courts, the Court of General Sessions, and the Magistrates' Courts, it is impossible to know in how many different places the same property has been pledged. At the present time there is no provision for investigation into the actual value of real estate which is offered as security.[59]

What is clearly more important, however, than the problems of keeping tabs on bonded property or whether or not bonded property was real property and so on, is the inescapable fact that bondsmen became an integral part of the administration of court business. The bondsman played the part, as Seabury puts it, of a general factotum, arranging the details and paths through the labyrinth of justice. In numerous cases the bondsman acted as a kind of general agent for a defendant, frequently hiring the lawyer, shepherding the witness, and taking care of the payoffs necessary to fix the case. While doing so, of course, the bondsman and his co-conspirators in the police, courts, and legal profession bilked every dollar they could from their clients. For the innocent the bondsman was the capstone of the justice racket; for the guilty he managed corruption, acting as a kind of "clearing house between the underworld and the realm of lawfulness".[60]

As corruption managers some bondsmen had become major criminal justice entrepreneurs. Perhaps the best example from Seabury's investigation is Anthony Iamascia who reportedly handled 95 percent of the bail bond business in the Bronx.[61] Iamascia worked independently and as an agent for the Greater City Surety and Indemnity Corporation as well as the Capitol City Surety and Indemnity Company. While bail bonding consumed all his time, Iamascia was nevertheless a full time city employee. He worked as an assistant supervisor for the Department of Public Markets. In many ways, Iamascia's career is a microcosm of an aspect of the social system of organized crime: the city sinecure representing the power of the Bronx County machine over the formal structure of government and administration, corrupt bail bonding serving as the tangible link between the underworld and criminal justice, and the drive to monopolize what was a highly competitive enterprise.[62]

The investigation of the Magistrates' Courts began in earnest in the early fall of 1930 and lasted as far as public and private hearings went until October 26, 1931. Seabury's Final Report was issued at the end of March 1932. But long before it was completed the significance of this particular investigation had its major effect upon the political history of New York. To put it briefly, the scandals uncovered in the Magistrates' Courts created enormous pressure for other investigations into municipal government. As examples of official misconduct accumulated during the enquiry, the public began to wonder how far the corruption extended. Soon it was asked why a special referee had to be appointed to lead this investigation. Finally this question was posed: "Where had the District Attorney been all this time?"[63] Responding to the growing public clamour, Governor Roosevelt on March 10, 1931, selected Seabury who was still conducting the initial investigation, to examine charges against New York County District Attorney Thomas C. T. Crain. But the excursion into the District Attorney's office was small beer compared with Seabury's next assignment which came less than two weeks later. The pressure of scandal had finally produced on March 23, 1931, a joint Senate and Assembly resolution calling for a committee to investigate the departments of the government of New York City. The Joint Legislative Committee was chaired by Samuel H. Hofstadter and its counsel was Samuel Seabury. As I will describe in the next chapter, Seabury's roles as investigator and reformer are crucial in the subsequent political history of New York. He was, as Herbert Mitgang calls him, "The Man Who Rode the Tiger".

Before turning to the even more startling and significant inquiries which flowed from Seabury's work on the judiciary, reflect on what is already established. The administration of justice at least at the level of the Magistrates' Courts was at the beck and call of assorted politicos. Criminal courts were dominated by criminal conspiracies and conspirators. With justice for sale, brokers such as bail bondsmen came to the fore as major factors in court administration. Perhaps nothing is quite so astonishing as the fact that the business of bail bonding which specialized in criminal conspiracies, whose clientele consisted often of professional criminals, occupied such a central role in criminal justice. With all this, however, there was still·little consideration of organized crime beyond the parameters of the criminal judiciary. Because of the nature of the investigation, the principals involved were criminal justice officers and assorted fixers and steerers—the court house crowd. Strong allegations were made about certain politicians and mostly fleeting references to professional criminals. The most substantial comments dealt with two policy bankers, Jose Enrique Miro and Wilfred Bender. Miro's known deposits from policy in a three year period were $1,251,556; Bender's in five years totalled $1,753,342.[64] What was germane to the investigation was their relations with court officers, lawyers and bondsmen, however, and not policy gambling in Harlem.

There is one final issue to highlight in this first stage of the Seabury investigations. We know that New Yorkers accepted certain notions about organized crime during the course of the 20th century. These notions included both structural and ethnic parts. The less phantasmagoric aspects were naturally the structural, although they too were often laced with ethnic considerations. More importantly, even when the emphasis was placed on the structure of city government as the generator of corruption and protector of organized crime, the shadow of the county machine was invoked in anthropomorphic terms. The existence of crime and corruption was laid at the door of the Tammany Tiger. If the level of corruption was high then the Tiger was prehensile; if low it was benevolent. Organized crime and corruption under these terms was a function of the morality and consciousness of the Tammany masters. That is the message of McGoldrick's mistaken analysis, as it was the major interpretative framework to emerge from the first Seabury investigation.

NOTES

[1] Leo Hershkowitz, *Tweed's New York: Another Look* (Garden City, New York, 1977), xiii–xx.

[2] For the Lexow material consult New York State Senate, *Report and Proceedings of the Senate Committee Apoointed to Investigate the Police Department of the City of New York.* (Albany, 1895). On the background to the investigation see William T. Snead, *Satan's Invisible World Displayed or, Despairing Democracy: A Study of Greater New York* (New York, 1898); and Gustavus Meyers, *The History of Tammany Hall* (New York, 1901).

[3] Robert M. Fogelson, *Big-City Police* (Cambridge, Massachusetts, 1977), 3.

[4] *Ibid.* 4.

[5] New York State Assembly, *Final Report of the Special Committee of the Assembly Appointed to Investigate the Public Officers and Departments of the City of New York and the Counties Therein Included* (Albany, 1900).

[6] Frank Moss, *The American Metropolis from Knickerbocker Days to the Present Time: New York City Life in All its Various Phases* (New York, 1897), 159.

[7] *Ibid.*,160–161.

[8] *Ibid.*,235–236.

[9] See Alan Block, "Aw! - Your Mother's in the Mafia: Women Criminals in Progressive New York, *Contemporary Crises*, 1 (1977); Howard B. Woolston,· *Prostitution in the United States: Prior to the Entrance of the United States into the World War* (Montclair, New Jersey, 1969); Edwin R.A. Seligman, ed., *The Social Evil: With Special Reference to Conditions Existing in the City of New York.* (New York, 1912); Willoughby Cyrus Waterman, *Prostitution and its Repression in New York City, 1900–1931* (New York, 1932); David J. Pivar, *Purity Crusade: Sexual Morality and Social Control, 1868–1900* (Westport, Connecticut, 1973); Roy Lubove, *The Progressive and the Slums: Tenement House Reform in New York City, 1890–1917* (Pittsburgh, 1963); and Egal Feldman, "Prostitution, the Alien Woman and the Progressive Imagination," *American Quarterly*, XI (1976).

[10] Dwight C. Smith, Jr., *The Mafia Mystique* (New York, 1975); Joseph L. Albini, *The American Mafia: Genesis of a Legend* (New York, 1971); Humbert S. Nelli, *The Business of Crime: Italians and Syndicate Crime in the United States* (New York, 1976).

[11] Thomas Monroe Pitkin and Francesco Cordasco, *The Black Hand: A Chapter in Ethnic Crime* (Totawa, New Jersey, 1977), 54–55.

[12] Nelli, 93–94.

[13] *Ibid.*, 95–97.

[14] Arthur A. Goren, *New York Jews and the Quest for Community: The Kehillah Experiment, 1908–1922* (New York, 1970), 24.

[15] *Ibid.*, 28–29, 35.

[16] *Ibid.*, 134–137.

[17] General Theodore A. Bingham, "The Organized Criminals of New York", *McClure's Magazine*, 34 (1909), 64.

[18] S. S. McClure, "The Tammanyzing of a Civilization", *McClure's Magazine*, 34(1909), 117–118.

[19] George Kibbe Turner, "The Daughters of the Poor: A Plain Story of the Development of New York City as a Leading Center of the White Slave Trade of the World Under Tammany Hall," *McClure's Magazine,* 34(1909), 47, 49–52.

[20] Goren, 138–144.

[21] *Ibid.*, 148.

[22] Andy Logan, *Against the Evidence: The Becker–Rosenthal Affair* (New York, 1972), 83.

[23] Goren, 154–155.

[24] *Ibid.*, 155–158.

[25] John Higham, *Strangers in the Land: Patterns of American Nativism, 1860–1925* (New York, 1968), 308–330.

[26] See Smith, *The Mafia Mystique*, especially in Chapter 5.

[27] One of the exceptions occurred in 1921 when the State Legislature set up another Joint Legislature Committee to Investigate the Affairs of the City of New York. The Committee known as the Meyer Committee looked into:
   1. Mandatory Legislation Affecting the City of New York.
   2. The Administration of the Police Department.
   3. Department of Licenses.
   4. Department of Markets.
   5. Department of Public Welfare.
The Committee's *Report and Summary* issued March 14, 1922, described abuses, irregularities and alleged corruption. But it had very little impact.

[28] Joseph L. McGoldrick, "The New Tammany", *The American Mercury*, XV (1928), 1.

[29] *Ibid.*, 2.

[30] *Ibid.*

[31] *Ibid.*, 5.

[32] *Ibid.*, 6.

[33] *Ibid.*, 9.

[34] *Ibid.*, 12.

[35] Herbert Mitgang, *The Man Who Rode the Tiger: The Life of Judge Samuel Seabury and the Story of the Greatest Investigation of City Corruption in this Century* (New York, 1963), 163–171.

[36] *Ibid.*, 165.

[37] Rothstein sorely needs a fresh examination. For what there is now consult Leo Katcher, *The Big Bankroll: The Life and Times of Arnold Rothstein* (New York, 1958).

[38] Arthur Mann, *LaGuardia: A Fighter Against His Times, 1882–1933.* (Chicago, 1969), 271.

[39] *Ibid.*, 227.

[40] See Norman Thomas and Paul Blanshard, *What's the Matter With New York: A National Problem* (New York, 1932); and Raymond Moley, *Tribunes of the People: The Past and Future of the New York Magistrates' Courts* (New Haven, 1932).

[41] New York State Supreme Court, Appellate Division — First Judicial Department, In the Matter of the Investigation of the Magistrates' Courts in the First Judicial Department and the Magistrates Thereof and of Attorneys-at-Law Practising in Said Courts, *Final Report of Samuel Seabury, Referee* (New York, 1932), 54–55.

[42] *Ibid.*, 14.

[43] New York City Commissioners of Accounts and New York Bureau of Municipal Research, *Government of the City of New York: A Survey of its Organization and Functions Prepared for the Constitutional Convention, 1915* (New York, 1915), 1091.

[44] *Ibid.*

[45] New York State Supreme Court, 18.

[46] *Ibid.*, 19.

[47] The Magistrates discussed in Seabury's *Final Report* are:
August Dreyer
Edward Weil
Francis X. McQuade
Maurice Gottlieb
Earl A. Smith
Henry M. R. Goodman
Jessie Sibermann
Louis B. Brodsky
Jean H. Norris
George W. Simpson
Abraham Rosenbluth

[48] *Ibid.*, 42.

[49] *Ibid.*, 56.

[50] *Ibid.*, 51.

[51] *Ibid.*, 63.

[52] *Ibid.*, 67.

[53] *Ibid.*, 65.

[54] *Ibid.*, 79.

[55] *Ibid.*, 125.

[56] *Ibid.*, 103–124.

[57] *Ibid.*, 105.

[58] *Ibid.*, 106.

[59] *Ibid.*, 104.

[60] *Ibid.*, 107.

[61] *Ibid.*, 112.

[62] Perhaps one of the reasons for Iamascia's prominence in bail bonding and his serving as a link between the underworld and criminal justice was the criminal activities of his alleged brother, Danny Iamascia. According to journalist, Paul Sann, Danny Iamascia was a member of the Dutch Schultz mob with important connections to ex-Magistrate Vitale. Danny Iamascia was killed in a gun battle with police in 1931. Sann, *Kill the Dutchman: The Story of Dutch Schultz* (New Rochelle, New York, 1971), 132.

[63] Specifically, a call for governmental action issued from the City Club of New York which charged the District Attorney with conduct "incompetent, inefficient, and futile", with failure to expose graft and other crimes and with an overall failure of purpose or activity. Joining with the City Club was the City Affairs Committee of New York whose members included Bishop Francis J. McConnell, Rabbi Stephen S. Wise, and John Dewey of Columbia University. Mitgang, 205.

[64] New York State Supreme Court, 137–138.

Chapter 3
Broadway Lament

With the opening of a new and perilous decade, public attention focused on more than corruption in the criminal judiciary fascinating as that was. By 1930 racketeers and racketeering variously defined were clearly recognized as a major social and, therefore, criminal justice problem in New York. For instance, in the late spring the Police Department's annual report was issued and, according to *The New York Times*,[1] was notable for its unusual frankness concerning racketeers and racketeering. The story which superbly defined racketeering as organized extortion went on to relate some short summaries of racketeering in the following trades:

   (a) the laundry industry in Brooklyn;
   (b) the milk industry in the Bronx;
   (c) construction trades across the city; and
   (d) the taxicab industry

Later in the summer it was reported that the Kings County (Brooklyn) Grand Jury had issued a warning that racketeering was increasing in scope and power.[2] That report was followed on August 28, with a statement from Brooklyn District Attorney George E. Brower that racketeers were working in the ice, laundry, window–cleaning, and milk trades. They were also reportedly in control of the slot-machine business.[3] And finally, in November, it was noted that the New York County (Manhattan) District Attorney Thomas C. T. Crain had declared "war" on racketeers. As part of his declaration Crain called for assistance from the Bar and various business leaders without "whose help he confessed he could not successfully cope with the menace". Crain added:

> It is the occupation and profitable calling of an increasing army of vicious and dangerous men. These constitute a more or less organized force under chosen leaders and with specified and recognized fields of activity. They levy tribute on the timid, and paralyze the administration of the criminal law by terrorizing their victims and intimidating witnesses.[4]

It was, of course, one of the major contentions of such renascent reform organizations as the City Club and the City Affairs Committee that Crain's call for aid was largely ceremonial. In addition, they agreed with that part of Crain's statement which held that "he could not successfully cope with the menace". Besides his general ineptness in handling the racketeering situation, the reform organizations also viewed the recently elected (1930) District Attorney with deep suspicion as Seabury piled up more and more evidence in the Magistrates' Courts inquiry. At last, on May 7, 1931, the City Club of the City of New York filed formal charges against Crain with Governor Roosevelt. As noted in the preceding chapter, Roosevelt quickly appointed Seabury a Commissioner under Section 34 of the Public Officers Law to investigate the charges and report to the Governor.

For narrative purposes let me state now that the charges against Crain were not sustained by Seabury. His conclusion was that Crain had acted diligently, was attentive to his office, and tried faithfully to discharge his duties. But he adds:

> Truth compels the conclusion that in many instances he busied himself ineffectively, and that he did not grasp or act upon opportunities for high public service which some of the matters referred to above presented to him. I am satisfied that wherever he failed, and I think he did fail in many cases to do all that should be done, his failure was not due to any lack of personal effort or any ignoble motive.[5]

Damning with very faint praise, indeed, Seabury's report issued on August 31 prompted Roosevelt to dismiss the charges. While vindicating Crain's integrity, Seabury did manage to lambast his performance and to increase public awareness of racketeering and the trough which was the District Attorney's office. And that was precisely his point, according to his biographer. Apparently Seabury and his staff were well aware that if they recommended Crain's removal and it was accomplished, Tammany was going to run him in the coming election in any case. And they believed that Crain would win because of Tammany's still considerable strength in Manhattan. Seabury chose the more practical path of presenting the damaging evidence without recommending removal in order to avoid "looking silly" after the election.[6]

And what of racketeering? Broadly speaking, Seabury had very little to say. He limited himself to three examples of the racketeering "situation" and then commented on the results of Crain's so-called "war".[7] His critical points were didactic: this is what the District Attorney had done, this is what he could have and should have done.

His first example concerned racketeering in the Fulton Fish Market. The crux of racketeering in this enormous fish market lay in the relations between wholesale fish distributors and the representative of the workers' union local.

The employers' representative was J. W. Walker, a director of Middleton Carman & Company which distributed fish to restaurants, hotels, and steamships. The workers were members of the United Sea Food Workers' Union, Local 16975, which was led by the notorious Joseph "Socks" Lanza. Every two years, at the end of November, the union contract expired. A short time prior, Lanza and Walker began their negotiations with Lanza demanding higher wages and Walker arguing that it could not be done. This ritual was followed by a deal between Lanza and Walker in which Lanza would be paid a negotiated amount of money for returning a contract with no wage increase. In this particular case Lanza received $5,000. In order to raise the money, Walker assessed the other distributors $82 for each of their employees. Although not commented on by Seabury who implicitly at least viewed this relationship as one of extortion against the employers, it is clear that the deal meant that labor costs would be raised only around 78 cents a week per man for two years. Obviously, the employers found it financially beneficial to deal with Lanza rather than a bona fide trade unionist.

The situation was roughly comparable in Seabury's next example which he titled in his report "racketeering in the millinery trade". In this section he recounted how in 1927 Isidore Fogel, President of the Chelsea Hat Company, was faced with a demand for unionization of his shop. Fogel was next visited by an underworld broker known as "Little Augie" who told Fogel that for $2,000 he would prevent unionization. A deal was struck but before consummated "Augie" was murdered. Shortly after that another underworld broker known as "Tough Jake" Kurzman took over the deal with some modification. Kurzman was paid $100 a month to prevent unionization. Other employers in the millinery trade who were reportedly victimized by Kurzman (although that interpretation is again seriously open to question) include the Belleclaire Hat Company and Furst & Maultzman, Inc. According to Seabury, Kurzman received payments of approximately $10,000 a year from several manufacturers to secure labor peace or more accurately, to prevent unionization and wage increases.

The final story of racketeering reported on by Seabury in his summary of District Attorney Crain's efforts was dynamically similar to the others. It involved another part of New York's garment trades this time the cloth shrinking trade in which the workers' union had been destroyed and then replaced by one under the control of racketeer Joseph Mezzacapo. The pattern was not new: Mezzacapo was paid for "sweetheart contracts" and also bilked the union members with periodical collections. Mezzacapo had done quite well, Seabury stated, amassing $332,000 in just one account in five years. What was different in the Mezzacapo story, however, was that a complaint had been lodged by one of the workers, Benjamin Krivis, with the District Attorney. Remarkably, all that Crain had done was to write Mezzacapo (to what end it is not known) and to try and find employment for Krivis who had been fired by the Loyal Excelsior Shrinking Corporation after he had complained to the District Attorney.

Seabury finished his excursion into racketeering by noting the overall futility of Crain's tenure even in the areas designated by the District Attorney as racketeer prone. In so doing Seabury indicated how deeply racketeering pervaded the economic structure of New York City. The "industries" acknowledged by Crain to be corrupted include: bead, cinder, cloth shrinking, clothing, flower shops, Fulton market, funeral, fur dressing, grape, hod carriers, kosher butchers, laundry, leather, live poultry, master barbers, millinery, musical, night patrol, neckwear, news-stand, operating engineers, overall, paper box, paper hangers, shirt makers, and window cleaners. Each of these, it appears, was subject to conspiracies and extortion. At the very least one suspects that vast numbers of employees found their union dues wasted in the trap of " sweetheart contracts" and other anti-labor conspiracies. Out of all this only five particular cases "were presented to the September (1930) Additional Grand Jury". And because of the manner of presentation, indictments were found in only two of the affected industries, the cinder and window cleaners. And even these were originally "dismissed on motion". It was a sad, biting and revealing summary.

The Main Event

In the early years of the 1930s, nothing—not the machinations of "Socks" Lanza, "Tough Jake", or Joe Mezzacapo, not the ruminations and fulminations about racketeering, not the obvious inadequacies of District Attorney Crain, and not the investigation of the Magistrates' Courts—could compete for public attention and significance with the city-wide investigation of the Hofstadter Committee whose Counsel was Samuel Seabury. The public hearings of the Committee began in the fall of 1931 and in a real sense its work only ended on September 2, 1932, when Governor Roosevelt announced the resignation from office of New York's Mayor James J. Walker.

There is, it seems in retrospect, a design or rhythm to this momentous investigation. In Seabury's first *Intermediate Report* released on January 25, 1932, the inquiry highlights certain aspects of city and county government, types of illegalities, and key political personalities. The investigation moves from Manhattan to Richmond, Brooklyn, Queens and back to Manhattan. It establishes a series of concentric circles of corruption leading inward toward the Mayor. At the same time as this geography was mapped, Seabury and his exceptionally able staff also developed a sociology of corruption laying out the deals and conspiracies endemic in parts of the city's bureaucracies. This sociology seems to have functioned in much the same manner as the geography: moving from position to position in a vertical ascent toward the Mayor. Ever closer, ever higher the Hofstadter Committee closed complementary rings around Mayor Walker.

One of the first positions and areas reported on by Seabury was the Richmond County Office of Borough President. Borough Presidents were the chief executive officers of the boroughs (counties) elected for 4 year terms. They were also members of the Board of Estimate and Apportionment (the most important governing body in the city) and the Board of Alderman. In general, their control extended over public improvements of highways, sewers and public buildings in their respective boroughs. The Richmond incumbent was John A. Lynch and his problem centered around his part in the awarding of a franchise in the summer of 1927 to the unprepared and incompetent Tompkins Bus Corporation. The franchise which permitted the Tompkins Corporation to operate buses over eighteen routes in Richmond was a form of repayment made by Lynch to the head of the bus company who had assumed several major debts owed by the Borough President.[8]

From Richmond, Seabury went to Queens and there discovered John Theofel, the Democratic leader of Queens County. Following a familiar pattern, Theofel while county leader also held a city sinecure. Seabury notes: "Since July, 1930, Theofel has been Chief Clerk of the Queens County Surrogate's Court. He was appointed to that office by Surrogate Hetherington, having previously been Deputy County Clerk of Queens County".[9] Prior to that Theofel was a "hotel keeper". The Surrogate's Court, according to the Commissioners of Accounts survey, is concerned with wills, grants and revokes "letters testamentary and letters of administration to control the conduct and settle the accounts of executors, administrators and testamentary trustees", enforces payments of debts and legacies and the distribution of estates, and so on.[10] About all this Theofel knew next to nothing. What he was both familiar with and remarkably adept at was, of course, entrepreneurial politics. His appointment as Chief Clerk was a repayment of a political favor; he dictated the appointment and tenure of Assistant District Attorneys; he had an interest in an automobile agency "from which Queens County Public Officials Must Buy Their Cars"; and he controlled campaign contributions thereby materially increasing his personal wealth. Focusing on the last, Seabury reports: "From 1924 to November,

1930, during all of which time Theofel was either treasurer or chairman of the campaign funds, and his income from salary and other sources did not exceed $11,500 a year, his net worth increased from $28,650 to $201,000".[11]

Theofel was also linked by Seabury to the activities of Joseph T. Quinn the Democratic co-leader in the Second Assembly District, Queens County. Quinn had been Sheriff of Queens and at the end of his term Theofel appointed him Deputy Commissioner of the Department of Sanitation. Seabury's investigation of Quinn centered on his activities as Sheriff during which time he received "protection money" from John M. Phillips who was "actively interested in racing in Queens County". Apparently the Sheriff was in charge of law enforcement at the tracks in Queens. From 1927 to 1929 while Quinn was Sheriff not one of "his five regular and seven special Deputy Sheriffs ever reported a single violation of law at the race tracks".[12]

In his *Second Intermediate Report* (December 19, 1932) Seabury includes a section on the Bronx. The focus in the Bronx was primarily on William J. Flynn, Commissioner of Public Works, "and, with respect to a great many daily duties, Acting Borough President".[13] As remarked on earlier, Borough government was centered on streets, sewers and public buildings. A line chart shows the Commission Of Public Works directly below the office of the Borough President. Under the Commissioner are such Bureaus as sewers, topography, buildings, permits, engineering construction, highways, audits, accounts and supplies, and street cleaning.[14] Flynn's particular crime was to thwart a legitimate builder from erecting a public garage through a series of adroit and at best, quasi-legal maneuvers, and then to acquire adjacent property in order to build his own public garage. In addition, Flynn hounded the original garage proponent through a series of irrelevant and scandalous charges brought in the city's civil courts. And finally, Seabury recounts the amassing of Flynn's fortune.

> When Flynn became Commissioner of Public Works in 1918, he owned one piece of real estate, consisting of a two-family house, which he and his family occupied. His total worth at that time did not exceed $50,000. From then on, up to the end of 1931, he had deposited in various banks, eliminating transfers between them, a total close to $650,000. His equities in real estate had increased, in this same period, to about $400,000.[15]

In his Reports, Seabury presents example after example of his theme that political influence and corruption are endemic in the political structure of New York. Looking at the Board of Standards and Appeals which dealt with requested variations of zoning regulations, Seabury turned up the remarkable case of Dr. William F. Doyle. A practising veterinarian for over three decades, Doyle in 1916 began representing clients petitioning the Board for zone variances. Doyle's methods were simple and familiar: he split his exorbitant fees with key members of the Board. Within a few years he had banked a minimum of $1,000,000.[16]

From the Board of Standards and Appeals, Seabury moved to the Bureau of Weights and Measures which was "charged with the duty of preventing short weights and measures and similar frauds in the wholesale and retail business, and for the protection of the public against such impositions".[17] At the time of Seabury's investigation, the Commissioner of the Bureau was Joseph P. McKay who had been appointed by Mayor Walker in 1926 upon the request of the then Democratic leader of Richmond, David S. Rendt. After four years, however, the Bureau's work was so notoriously careless, indolent and negligent that the notoriously negligent and indolent Mayor Walker instructed the Commissioner of Accounts to investigate the Bureau. This investigation revealed an appalling amount of neglect within the Bureau. Checking on seventeen of the Bureau's inspectors (called sealers), the Commissioner of Accounts reported on 1,347 businesses inspected by the sealers and found: 1,384 irregularities. These included 457 establishments that had no certificates of inspection; 56 which were inspected but had no certificate; 142 which were given the Bureau's seals for their scales that had no date; 262 which had scales but no seals; 143 which had clear civil violations; 146 businesses whose measuring equipment should have been either condemned or confiscated; 94 places reported as inspected but not visited by the sealers; and finally, 37 establishments supposedly inspected which no longer existed.[18] In addition to this summary which the Commissioner of Accounts presented to Mayor Walker, he included material on short weights in city coal deliveries and on Bureau staff members who were absent *with* pay anywhere from two to four years.

Seabury's conclusion is two-fold: the Bureau was a sink of corruption, and the mayor did nothing after receiving the Commissioner of Accounts' report. In fact, it is pointed out, the Commissioner of the Bureau of Weights and Measures received an increase in salary three weeks after the Mayor received the scathing denunciation of the Bureau.[19]

Another aspect of city governance covered was the administration of the City Trust Fund, a special appropriation of over $9,500,000 for unemployment relief in 1931. For those members of the growing unemployed, unskilled jobs were to be found with the Fund paying their salaries. To qualify, individuals had to be residents and voters in the city for at least the prior two years, unemployed and *have* dependents. The Fund was to be administered by the Department of Public Welfare through a series of new offices located in each borough. Applications for work were opened on April

47

21, 1931 and closed on May 2, when over 20,000 people had registered and the Fund could support no more.[20] What did Seabury find? Democratic district leaders and other politicos hiring almost overwhelmingly Democratic voters, both the indigent and the employed, under the auspices of the City Trust Fund. For instance, in Richmond the Borough President had 400 voters mysteriously added to the approved list. Also in Richmond, it was determined that 253 people who were hired and working were not qualified because they either owned property, had sufficient incomes or no dependents.[21] In Manhattan months after the application deadline "the Democratic district clubs .... were furnished with blank application cards by Delaney, Secretary to the Borough President of the Borough of Manhattan; that these cards were then filled out in the Democratic district clubs and sent back to the Borough President's office, and from them jobs were assigned to applicants".[22] Like zoning, consumer protection, and public transportation, unemployment relief was an arena rife with political influence and chicanery.

As Seabury's investigators probed into seemingly every aspect of city government they uncovered some of the deals involving George W. Olvany while leader of Tammany Hall. Not surprisingly, Olvany was at least as creative in translating political power into money as any of the politicos so far mentioned. His method was simple. For an individual or corporation to secure his influence and favor it was necessary to retain the services of the law firm, Olvany, Eisner and Donnelly. To keep these matters hidden, an attorney-of-record was employed as an intermediary. Several minor examples of this type of graft were located when Seabury probed the Board of Standards and Appeals. Variances were granted for builder, Fred F. French after he secretly retained the Olvany firm. In one case the attorney-of-record was John N. Boyle, in another Frederick J. Flynn.[23]

Perhaps a better example of Olvany's and Tammany's power of "taxation" is in the case of the North German Lloyd Steamship Company. In 1922 the Lloyd, one of the largest transatlantic companies in the world, applied to the Dock Commissioner for a lease of a city pier in Manhattan. Without a Manhattan pier the Lloyd had to dock its passengers either in Brooklyn or New Jersey. Their petition was delayed for almost ten years (the lease was finally executed on May 11, 1931) as various officials within Tammany delayed approval while negotiating the proper payoff. Beginning in the early 1920s ever increasing "legal fees", the euphemism for political payoffs, were negotiated between the Bremen office of the Lloyd and representatives of Tammany. The first Tammany intermediary was David Maier who told the Lloyd it was necessary to hire "a lawyer named William H. Hickin, well connected politically in New York City", and as Seabury reports, "now President of the National Democratic Club".[24] For years negotiations went on accompanied by assurances from Hickin that the matter was fixed and the lease was forthcoming. For instance, in April 1925 the President of the steamship company "had a confidential conversation with the Secretary of Tammany Hall, Mr. Egan, and with Mr. Hickin, during which conversation both gentlemen assured him that the pier was assured for the Lloyd".[25] Almost a year later, Hickin was again telling the Lloyd the matter was fixed. He explained the last delay by noting that the construction of the pier had been put off while the city concentrated on building its subway system.

Actually, Seabury shows, the delay was caused by the opportunity presented to Olvany and others for rather large profits in the city's purchase of the pier site from its private owner, the Hudson River Navigation Corporation. Retained by the Navigation Corporation as their attorneys-of-record were Gibboney, Johnston and Schlecter although it is clear from private correspondence uncovered by Seabury's staff that the real attorneys were Olvany, Eisner and Donnelly. Part of one letter written by the President of Hudson River Navigation boldly states: "Gibboney was merely selected as a figurehead in the matter and my employment of Olvany, Eisner and Donnelly is crystallized in the letter of October 18, 1926,..."[26] Olvany's position was seemingly secure and financially enviable. He stood to be paid by the Lloyd for aiding in the lease of a city pier, and richly compensated by the owners of the pier site for inflating the price of the land and then smoothing the city's condemnation proceedings.

Unfortunately for Olvany he lost the leadership of Tammany before either deal was consummated. In fact, it was precisely Olvany's inclination to monopolize such deals as the above which caused other Tammany leaders who had their own law firms to be so disgruntled. Their feeling was that such graft should be more equitably distributed as mentioned in Chapter 2. The particular case of the pier site is a graphic example of the jealousy caused by Olvany's hoggishness. The deal was delayed because Dock Commissioner Cosgrove insisted on a piece of the action. He waylayed the condemnation proceedings until the Hudson River Navigation Corporation bought a parcel of his own real estate located in Sunnyside, Long Island. This inland real estate, it should be added, was valueless for the Corporation.[27] Such tactics and maneuvers consumed a great deal of time, and before everyone could be satisfied, Olvany was out as Tammany's leader.

For the most part Seabury's work as chief investigator for the Hofstadter Committee concentrated on that manifestation of the social system of organized crime best described as graft. It was, in fact, fairly rare of him to delve into the palpable connections between politicians, criminal justice agents and bureaucrats, and professional criminals. He believed that the totality of the system could be deduced with little effort as he documented the conspiracies, rackets and general corruption headed by Borough Presidents, assorted Commissioners and other important politicos ranging as high as Olvany. He was quite simply most outraged by administrative and governmental perversions. But when Seabury turned his attention to the positions of district leader and sheriff he laid open whatever may have remained partially hidden and obscure.

This part of the Committee's investigation concentrated on illicit activities primarily gambling found in certain key political clubs in Manhattan and Brooklyn. As I mentioned in the preceding chapter the heart of the county political organizations is the assembly district, its vital organs the district leaders and their political clubs. Seabury's staff focused on seven clubs located in five assembly districts. Five of the clubs are Democratic and two Republican; of the five Democratic ones, two were rivals for political supremacy in Brooklyn's 15th assembly district.

The clubs, their districts, leaders and leaders' governmental positions are:[28]

(1) Thomas M. Farley Association, 14th Assembly District, Manhattan, *Leader* Thomas M. Farley, Sheriff of Manhattan, Club President Peter J. Curran, Under Sheriff of Manhattan;

(2) Tammany Central Association, 12th Assembly District, Manhattan, *Leader* Michael J. Cruise, City Clerk of the City of New York;

(3) Democratic Club, 2nd Assembly District, Manhattan, *Leader* Harry C. Perry, Chief Clerk of City Court;

(4) Lincoln League Republican Club, 2nd Assembly District, Manhattan, *Leader* Jacob Rosenberg, Assistant Deputy Sheriff of Manhattan;

(5) Peoples' Regular Democratic Organization, 15th Assembly District, Brooklyn, *Leader* Peter J. McGuinness, Assistant Commissioner of Public Works in Brooklyn;

(6) Democratic Club, 15th Assembly District, Brooklyn, *Leader* James A. McQuade, Sheriff of Brooklyn;

(7) Republican Club, 6th Assembly District, Brooklyn, *Leader* John R. Crews, Commissioner of Taxes and Assessments.

The following maps show the Assembly Districts for both boroughs.

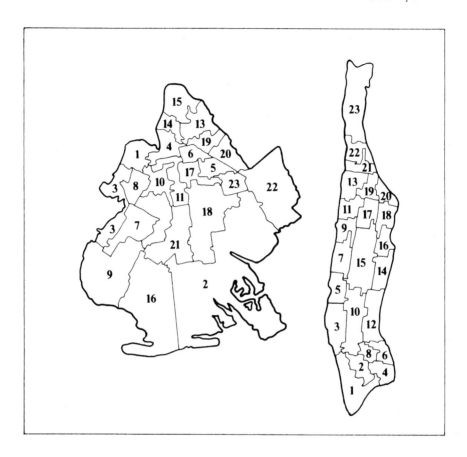

The prime task of Seabury's discussion of the illicit activities rampant in the club system is to display the role of the clubs in the social system of organized crime. Professional gamblers ran a variety of games (mostly craps) in the clubs giving either a set fee or a percentage of the action to the district leader who in turn provided protection for the gamblers. The system did not just stop there, however. The professional gamblers also had, Seabury states, their patrons, namely murderers, gunmen, and highway robbers. And they too were furnished protection by the district leaders. The relationships described by Seabury in his *Intermediate Report* look like this.

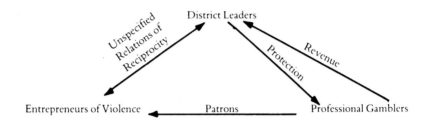

The information on them which Seabury employed in his questioning of the district leaders came from the startling activities of a short-lived special anti-gambling squad established in the Police Department under Commissioner McLaughlin in the latter 1920s. This confidential squad was organized under Captain Lewis J. Valentine who was raised to a Deputy Chief Inspector for a short period. Their mission to root out professional gambling continued under McLaughlin's replacement, Commissioner Warren.[29] Unfortunately for Valentine and his men they were too efficient and politically naive raiding the previously sacrosanct political clubs. For their effrontery they were disbanded by the next Police Commissioner, Whalen, who also reduced Valentine's rank back to Captain and transferred him to Queens. Valentine's chief assistant, Captain Keller, was sent to a precinct whose major job was to patrol a cemetery. In fact, all the members of the squad were punished by either or both a reduction in rank and the least desirable precincts in New York City.[30]

But before disbanding, the squad had relentlessly penetrated the connections between politics and crime: They had shown that "Billy Warren's gambling club" run by Warren and "Baldy" Froelich, a known associate of Arnold Rothstein, had moved its operation to Sheriff Farley's club at 359 East 692nd Street.[31] They documented that the gambling concession in the Chief Clerk Harry C. Perry's club was maintained by the notorious Johnny Baker.[32] City Clerk Cruise's gambling action was handled by two more Rothstein associates, George McManus and "Nigger Rue".[33] Another exceptionally infamous gambler, "Monkey" Reich was in charge at Commissioner Crew's club in Brooklyn.[34] And so on, in the other clubs. Each of the seven clubs was raided a number of times and anywhere from twenty to 100 gamblers were arrested. Bail was furnished by the district leaders or their associates. The cases never came to trial, however, as literally hundreds of 0–14 forms were filed in the respective Magistrates' Courts.

Being a district leader and the head of a political club with a large gambling concession had enormous financial impact. Taking their cue from the work of the anti-gambling squad, Seabury's investigators compiled all the evidence they could on the known bank deposits of five of the district and club leaders. They show: Farley $360,000; Curran $662,311; Cruise $142,800; Perry $135,061; and McQuade $510,597.

Seabury and the Hofstadter Committee were not yet finished with either New York's Sheriffs or the connections between crime, politics and criminal justice. The man who preceded Farley as Sheriff of Manhattan was Charles W. Culkin. At the time of the investigation he was an Actuary Auditor in the Pension Division of the Department of Finance and more importantly, district leader of the 3rd Assembly District in Manhattan. What primarily intrigued Seabury was Culkin's entrepreneurial activities during the entire decade of the 1920s. It is a revealing story. Prior to 1920, Culkin and James J. Hagan who was the Democratic district leader of Manhattan's 7th Assembly District (and as noted in Chapter 2, reponsible for the appointment of Magistrate Brodsky) became partners in the Monroe Lamp and Equipment Company. In 1920 Culkin and Hagan moved their business to 314 West 14th Street in Manhattan. The building was owned and partially used by a liquor wholesaler, James M. McCunn. Shortly after, McCunn became an equal partner in the lamp business. During part of Prohibition McCunn operated his business under government permits. But beginning in 1925 his permits ran out, and for the next four years he continued selling liquor illegally. The distribution of the liquor was carried out by Sheriff Culkin in crates marked Monroe Lamp.[35]

Sheriff Culkin's illicit activities were not limited to his part in bootlegging. Both Culkin and Hagan used their political positions to extort business for the Monroe Lamp. The company sold electric bulbs and similar equipment as an agent for the General Electric Corporation which set uniform prices for all their agents. To secure an advantage over other GE agents, Monroe Lamp threatened potential customers with a raft of building violations especially from the fire department if they refused to do business with Monroe. Culkin had been a Deputy Fire Commissioner. His successor in that position was Joseph M. Hannon. Significantly, Hannon had been at one time President of the Monroe Lamp. The intricacies of this racket are already somewhat confusing because of the shifting personnel, but it should be added that Hagan was Deputy Commissioner of the Department of Public Works. Once again, the racketeers were playing for very large stakes. McCunn, the bootlegger, deposited $1,310,797 from 1925 to 1931; Culkin $1,929,759; and the Monroe Lamp on a total invested capital of about $50,000 accumulated assets of $5,549,458 during the same period.[36]

The last major example in the Seabury reports explicitly concerned with documenting relationships between upperworld agents and the underworld, deals with the police and bootlegging in the borough of Queens. The evidence indicates that top police officials in Queens were approached by a man named Oxhandler who had a still. Inspector Mullarkey "said that he would permit operation for a consideration"[37] though Oxhandler would have to move his still to another location. The reason for this condition was that Inspector Mullarkey, his son, a man named Donnelly, and Peter DeVito, an infamous strikebreaker and racketeer in Queens wanted that location for their own still. Oxhandler moved his operation with the aid of Matthew Green who worked for the Sanitary Division of the Board of Health. The payoff by Oxhandler to Mullarkey was $200 a month, although it seems to have been insufficient. Oxhandler was raided by the Deputy Chief Inspector and was then told to get a bigger place and make a larger payoff. In just seven months, according to Seabury, Mullarkey deposited almost $30,000, apparently from Oxhandler's operation.[38]

Walker's Last Hurrah

At last it was Mayor Walker's turn to walk the Seabury tightrope. To a large extent all else had been preparatory. Walker was the capstone of corruption, the symbol not just of wicked Tammany but of all that was polluted and duplicitous in New York. The rings of exposure had finally closed upon the Mayor. And with a vengeance Seabury describes "the series of sinister transactions with which former Mayor Walker was connected, which led to the filing of charges against him and his resignation pending the trial thereof, in order to avoid the removal which, on the evidence before the Governor, must of necessity have followed".[39] What were the sinister transactions? They were primarily a complicated series of maneuvers in the arena of public transportation for which the Mayor was handsomely rewarded. For his part in attempting to aid in creating transportation monopolies, as well as other instances of influence peddling, Walker received almost one million dollars in skillfully hidden payoffs. Most of the money was handled by his financial agent, Russell T. Sherwood, and was deposited in various bank and brokerage accounts under names and titles designed to hide Walker's involvement. One of the schemes involved the taxicab industry, the other was the Equitable Coach Company's fantastic plan to control the city's bus services.

The major participants in the taxicab deal are Morris Mankin, President of Checker Cab Manufacturing Corporation, J. A. Sisto, the head of a brokerage firm which owned a large percentage of Checker Cab, Samuel Ungerleider, a major New York stockbroker, Russell T. Sherwood, Frank P. Walsh who was Walker's choice for chairman of a five man commission to survey the taxicab industry, State Senator John A. Hastings, a notorious grafter, and finally Mayor Walker himself.

The scheme began late in the summer of 1928 when Mankin went to Walker with a proposal to regulate competition in the industry. In April of the following year, a holding company, Parmelee Transportation, was formed by Mankin and others to "control taxicab operating subsidiaries".[40] J. A. Sisto and Company were in charge of distributing Parmelee stocks and bonds. Both Sisto and Mankin were in total agreement on the potential financial benefits for Parmelee of strong municipal regulation of taxis. In June 1929, Sisto gave Mayor Walker bonds with a market value of $26,000 which included Parmelee securities. At about the same time Samuel Ungerleider and Company held several thousand shares of Parmelee stocks and bonds as security for a large loan to J. A. Sisto and Company. Ungerleider and Company also had a "contract right" of one quarter of the profits gathered by Sisto in the marketing of Parmelee securities. In the late spring of 1929 Sherwood bought 1,000 shares of the Ungerleider Financial Corporation. Sometime in mid-May, 1930, Samuel Ungerleider and Company bought those shares from Sherwood at almost double their market value. Hasting's role in all this was to bring the conspirators together, to function as a go-between, and to serve as the malign spirit coordinating the diverse elements.

Each transaction triggered the appropriate response. In the winter of 1930 Walker called for municipal legislation. In April he appointed a special commission to make legislative recommendations. After Sherwood's Ungerleider shares were bought the commission began its work. Chairman Walsh was then in frequent contact with Mankin. The commission reported in September of 1930. They held that the "unifying of the City's taxicab service under a single franchised corporation offers manifest advantages ..." And at long last legislation was drafted into law in January, 1932, which "empowered a Board of Taxicab Control to regulate the licensing and operation of taxicabs in New York".[41] From then on no taxi or hack could lawfully operate in New York unless its owner received from the Board of Taxicab Control a certificate and license.

Much more spectacular than the graft which led ultimately to the Control Board was the sordid case of the Equitable Coach Company. The "eminence grise" for this swindle was also State Senator Hastings. The origins of this conspiracy began in 1925 when Walker entered the Democratic primary for Mayor. Hastings was a major supporter and in casting about for campaign funds secured a large contribution from a group of financial speculators in Ohio. Within two weeks of Walker's election, the Ohio group formed the Equitable Coach Company and subsequently filed under Hastings' direction for a city-wide bus franchise. The initial capitalization of the Equitable was $120,000 which was placed not in the Corporation but rather in the hands of J. Allan Smith, their New York representative. Smith banked the money in his own name and thereby created the Equitable's secret slush fund.[42]

Walker's hidden connections to the Equitable group were established by Seabury's investigators when they came across a $10,000 letter-of-credit gift to Walker from the Equitable. The day after receiving the letter-of-credit, Walker signed a franchise contract with the Equitable. This did not mean, however, that the Equitable had triumphed as will shortly be discussed. After signing the contract, Walker left for Europe and while there secured an additional $5,000 draft from the conspirators.

Although the Equitable had bought the unqualified support of Mayor Walker, it still had several hurdles to surmount. First of all, before Walker signed the franchise contract, other politicos and their business patrons had to be satisfied. For instance, Richmond Borough President Lynch was indebted to the Tompkins Bus Corporation, as noted earlier, and succeeded in removing Richmond County from the Equitable's plan. And even after the contract was signed (with certain geographic and route limitations) the Equitable still had to satisfy the State Transit Commission which had final authority to approve the contract. This the Equitable could never do for the simple reason that it had no equipment and no financial backing. Astounding as it may be, Walker had given almost total control of New York's surface transportation to a paper corporation. In his section on the Equitable, Seabury quotes part of State Transit Commissioner Godley's finding:

> The statement presented shows that instead of the applicant having any money on hand it is in debt for $600,000 for pre-organization expenses and it purposes to pay this off and obtain capital necessary to finance the enterprise by the public sale of securities through the medium of an extensive newspaper advertising campaign.[43]

Commissioner Godley finished his opinion by characterizing the Equitable as "an applicant who is not only a financial cripple but who is suffering from complete financial paralysis".[44]

Walker's graft was by no means limited to the two schemes detailed. He also received $250,000 gift from a joint stock trading account opened and managed by Paul Block, a newspaper publisher with an interest in a corporation which manufactured tiles suitable in subway construction. In fact, dividends and coupons and bonds and stock certificates and debentures and checks and cash and so on from all sort of companies and individuals and public utilities found their way into the financial accounts set up by Sherwood for the Mayor. These accounts diligently and creatively located and employed by Seabury and his staff signalled the end of both "the greatest investigation of city corruption in this century" and Walker. The Mayor was finished. And not even his splendid send-off to Europe after his resignation, which so infuriated Seabury that he listed all the participants in his report, could in any way provide more than temporary solace for his disgrace.

Consequences and Conclusions

There are two issues to be discussed. The first concerns the meaning of Seabury's work for such matters as the definition of organized crime. In the Introduction I suggested that organized crime is part of a social system in which reciprocal services are performed by criminals, their clients and politicians. And I would argue that the Seabury investigations provide ample proof of this system, of these relationships. At the same time, this definititon, if strictly followed, seems to preclude many of the organized conspiracies uncovered by Seabury and his staff. The definition demands three distinct entities functioning for some illicit purpose. What, then, do we call all those conspiracies composed of politicians and their upper-world patrons and clients? Are they sufficiently different from conspiracies in which all three elements are present? Part of the problem lies in the need to explain what are clearly organized crimes in which the personnel do not fulfill all the criteria. One way to handle this is to hold that criminal justice agents and politicians involved in criminal conspiracies are in reality professional criminals in which case they hold two roles. But for many reasons that seems to be confusing. Another even less satisfactory way is to hold that the Seabury examples are forms of organizational deviance. But this only obscures the system of informal power in which these conspiracies are endemic. Much the most economical solution is to treat or term conspiracies lacking one of the three elements as organized criminality. These conspiracies are not only the ones mentioned above, but also those in which one is hard pressed to find the client. One example should suffice: the vice racket in the Magistrates' Courts which had as racketeers: lawyers, bondsmen, police, professional informers, Magistrates' and so on. By no stretch of the imagination could the women framed be called clients. They were victims, pure and simple. And that racket was an expression of organized criminality.

It is obvious, of course, that the historical significance of both terms is quite the same. That is, they are manifestations of conspiracies that are slight variants of a common theme: the manner in which the city's political and economic power was dispersed and consumed. What the city had to offer was "influence" which translated into money and power. The many ways in which influence was bought and sold, manipulated and multiplied is the thread of all the organized crime and criminality so far described. Those with influence had power and potential profit over those without. Webs of influence were spun out through kinship, friendship, relations of patronage, and straight cash purchase. These webs linked together diverse statuses, county and city government, and fairly entangled almost all aspects of criminal justice changing it to an engine of corruption. So pervasive were they that an official position in city government or its equivalent appears to have been a virtual license to engage in non-violent extortion. In fact, one of the major distinctions between professional criminals such as Orgen and Kurzman, and corrupt politicians such as Farley and Olvany may be that the politicians did not need violence to provide the power for extortion.

The Seabury investigations are like a prism refracting light on both general and specific concerns. It illuminates a bit of the social history of the city noting, for instance, the predominant Irish caste in government and politics through the early 1930s; it shines on some of the methods of organized crime and criminality and of the immense profits available for conspirators; it reveals something of the thralldom within which criminal justice operated; it bares segments of the political economy of the city noting the effects on wages, for example, of certain types of racketeering as well as indicating important things about the general run of city services of vital concern to millions of working class individuals; and finally it lights up the greed of 1 Mayor, 26 district leaders including 2 Borough Presidents, 4 Assistant District Attorneys, 13 Magistrates, 1 State Supreme Court Justice, 1 State Senator, 6 Sheriffs, 3 Aldermen, 20 some odd and assorted Commissioners, 6 members of the Police Department including 1 Inspector, a large but unspecified number of businessmen and corporations including attorneys, and 32 individuals whose careers appear to have been totally criminal—bootleggers and gamblers for the most part.

The second issue is the effect of Seabury's work on the political history of New York. It is indisputable that Seabury had demonstrably weakened if not partially and temporarily destroyed the "regular" Democratic party in the city. The constant exposures, the revealed venality and brutality in city and county governments, the webs of corrupt influence fueled what was in effect the beginnings of municipal reform. The earliest achievements were naturally inextricably bound with Seabury's victories in his three investigations and were mainly of the "throw the rascals out" variety. But as the targets changed from Magistrates to other criminal justice agents to politicians and ultimately the Mayor, it became obvious that a struggle was brewing for control of the city. The issue would be governance; could the reformers known as Fusionists, a term and movement which encompassed liberal Republicans, reform Democrats, independents and others, translate the shame of the city into political power. At the center of this developing maelstrom stood Seabury, the moral custodian of reform and one of its principal strategists.

At the time of Walker's resignation in September, 1932, the reform forces had not yet coalesced. In fact, in the special election for the Mayoralty held in November to select someone to finish Walker's term, Tammany had triumphed. For that contest it had nominated Surrogate Patrick O'Brien known as an "old Tammany work horse", and he was elected. Clearly, it seems, Fusion needed a strong and commanding leader. And it was Seabury almost alone who decided that Fiorello La Guardia was just the person, and was instrumental in his selection as the Fusion nominee for Mayor in 1933.[45] Winning was still difficult, but in a three-man race La Guardia managed a plurality. In addition to the Mayoralty, Fusion won the other city-wide races and three of the five Borough Presidencies, thereby obtaining control of the all important Board of Estimate. One of the races Fusion lost, however, was the New York County (Manhattan) District Attorney's office. But as I will show, that loss in the final analysis did far more for the reformers than their opponents.

Important changes had and would occur under the La Guardia administrations. But it would be exceedingly foolish to imagine that city government in all its bewildering complexity was sanitized. It was not, although its tone and personnel in many instances were much elevated.[46] For New York's criminal justice system these changes meant a series of continuing battles as its customary operations, arrangements and accommodations were both threatened with exposure and disrupted. Struggles were waged for the control of criminal justice agencies and institutions for their more efficient and equitable performance. And in so doing, a particular methodology of criminal justice reform was worked out which took the Seabury efforts as a model. The method is supersession and special prosecuting—in essence a rival or supplementary prosecutorial system which is at the heart of the next chapter. Seabury, thus led to Mayor La Guardia on the one hand, and to special prosecutor Thomas E. Dewey on the other. Without his work the careers of both men and the political history of New York would have been quite different.

NOTES

1 *The New York Times,* May 18, 1930: III, 12.

2 *Ibid.,* August 2, 1930: 15.

3 *Ibid.,* August 29, 1930: 1.

4 *Ibid.,* November 15, 1930: 1.

5 *Ibid.,* September 1, 1931: 16.

6 Mitgang, 215.

7 *The New York Times,* September 1, 1931: 14. This is the full text of Seabury's Report on District Attorney Crain.

8 Samuel Seabury, Counsel to the Legislative Committee. In the Matter of the Investigation of the Departments of the Government of the City of New York, etc., pursuant to Joint Resolution adopted by the Legislature of the State of New York, March 23, *Intermediate Report* (New York, January 25, 1932), 28–51.

9 *Ibid.,* 128.

10 New York City Commissioners of Accounts and New York Bureau of Municipal Research, 1199.

11 Seabury, *Intermediate Report,* 141.

12 *Ibid.,* 126.

13 Seabury, *Second Intermediate Report* (New York, December19, 1932), 15.

14 New York City Commissioners of Accounts and New York Bureau of Municipal Research, 182.

15 Seabury, *Second Intermediate Report,* 52.

16 Seabury, *Intermediate Report,* 15–27

17 Seabury, *Second Intermediate Report,* 5.

18 *Ibid.,* 7–8.

19 *Ibid.,* 13.

20 Seabury, *Intermediate Report,* 105–106.

21 *Ibid.,* 107–109.

22 *Ibid.,* 116.

23 *Ibid.,* 12–17.

24 *Ibid.,* 86.

25 *Ibid.,* 93.

26 *Ibid.,* 99.

27 *Ibid.,* 101–102.

28 *Ibid.,* 52–53.

29 *Ibid.,* 55–56.

30 *Ibid.,* 79.

31 *Ibid.,* 56–57.

32 *Ibid.,* 66.

33 *Ibid.,* 69–70.

34 *Ibid.,* 77.

[35] *Ibid.*, 142–145.
[36] *Ibid.*, 145–152.
[37] *Ibid.*, 80.
[38] *Ibid.*, 83.
[39] Seabury, *Second Intermediate Report*, 138.
[40] *Ibid.*, 38.
[41] *Ibid.*, 45.
[42] *Ibid.*, 52.
[43] *Ibid.*, 67.
[44] *Ibid.*, 68.
[45] Charles Garrett, *The LaGuardia Years: Machine and Reform Politics in New York City* (New Brunswick, New Jersey, 1961), 112–113.
[46] For an enlightening account of political change in New York see Theodore J. Lowi, *At the Pleasure of the Mayor: Patronage and Power in New York City, 1898–1958* (New York, 1964).

Chapter 4
The Special Prosecutor

The consequences of the politicization of organized crime and criminality were overwhelmingly evident in the fall of 1933. Standing astride the city at last was the Little Flower, the affectionate and colorful nickname of Fiorello La Guardia, whose public stance was uncompromising war on gangsters, racketeers, and the scum who protected them.[1] Easier said than done, however, especially with the Manhattan District Attorney's office in the hostile hands of William Copeland Dodge.

La Guardia began his campaign against crime by first revitalizing the Commissioner of Accounts' Office. Chosen as Commissioner was Paul Blanshard who was directed "to probe into every city and county department and to report any evidence of graft, incompetence or political favoritism".[2] Blanshard did this with integrity and skill while always aware of the limitations on both his office and Fusion's electoral victory. As Commissioner, Blanshard could not "prosecute anybody for crime".[3] The Commissioner could investigate and expose, but the power of prosecution was reserved to the district attorneys of the five counties. The county offices including district attorneys were, however, precisely the ones which remained outside the grasp of the reformers. They were, Blanshard notes, "nests of the spoils system, reeking with incompetence and favoritism, and expensively operated by gentlemen of obvious unfitness".[4] The connection between the still powerful county machines and criminal justice is definitively spelled out by Blanshard:

> The county offices contain 834 exempt positions which are used for the most part for rewarding political henchmen. The city pays to this group of 834 exempt employees $2,300,000 a year. Since they are nearly all chosen by the direct orders of the county and district political leaders, the city is in effect sustaining the political machine by feeding its officers. The effect of the spoils system is apparent, for example, in the offices of certain district attorneys, notably the offices of District Attorney Dodge of New York County and District Attorney Geoghan of Kings County. The 102 exempt exployees under Mr. Dodge have been "working" arduously for $433,845 a year.[5]

Reform seemed to stop at the formidable frontier of county government bulwarked as usual by the accommodating district attorneys.

But in this post-Seabury world conditions were markedly different. And while Dodge was an obstacle to efficient and equitable criminal justice he was not insurmountable. Early on, in fact, the Manhattan District Attorney was entangled in a scandal reminiscent of his immediate predecessor Thomas C.T. Crain. Dodge came under fire for neglecting to investigate a major bail bond racket which was instead revealed by Commissioner Blanshard. In 1934 Blanshard received evidence of a conspiracy between a gambling syndicate and certain property owners who falsely pledged their property as bail. Acting as intermediaries between the criminals and the property owners were professional bondsmen. The gambling syndicate which included bondsmen and "bail runners" was the policy racket run by Arthur "Dutch Schultz" Flegenheimer. The function of the bondsmen and runners was primarily the protection of the syndicate's collectors who gathered the daily bets placed with certain merchants and newstand owners. In just nine months, Blanshard recounts, "77 property owners cooperating with the bail runners had committed perjury no less than 1,584 times".[6]

The evidence uncovered by Blanshard stimulated a number of civic organizations including the Society for the Prevention of Crime led by the Reverend George Drew Egbert, pastor of the First Congregational Church in Flushing, New York, to initiate another drive against organized crime. The activities of this Society along with the continuing inquiry by the Commissioner of Accounts and statements by Mayor La Guardia to the effect that he had evidence for a number of indictments which he would turn over to the appropriate county district attorneys, all coalesced into a famous dispute beginning in March, 1935, with District Attorney Dodge in the middle. Soon other groups and individuals entered the controversy which again centered on the allegation that Dodge was reluctant to press the investigation into the bail bond situation. Early in May, the Grand Jury investigating policy gambling, bail bonds and vice began withholding evidence from Dodge and his staff. Subsequently, the foreman of the Grand Jury, Lee Thompson Smith, announced that the meager success of the Jury was directly attributable to legal barriers. A week after Thompson's statement the Reverend Egbert suggested that Governor Lehman appoint a special deputy Attorney General to supersede Dodge. Other interested parties joined the demand for the supersession of Dodge.[7]

Finally, in June, 1935, Governor Lehman ordered Dodge to appoint a special prosecutor from a list of the Governor's choosing. Lehman made it clear that if Dodge did not accept this plan he would supersede the District Attorney. Recommended as candidates by the Governor were Charles Evan Hughes, Jr., George Z. Medalie, Thomas D. Thacher, and Charles H.

Tuttle. Dodge accepted the plan. But Lehman's choices for special prosecutor all announced they were unable to serve. In a joint statement they strongly urged the appointment of Thomas E. Dewey who was also supported by the New York Bar Association. At the end of June Lehman recommended Dewey to the District Attorney.[8]

To underline the New York Bar Association's disgust with Dodge and its support for Thomas E. Dewey as special prosecutor, consider its answers to a questionnaire circulated by the American Bar Association in 1934.[9]

Is the prosecutor's office in your community functioning satisfactorily in conducting investigations of either the commission of specific crimes or the conduct of public officers?

The prosecutor's office has not been functioning satisfactorily for over ten years. The new District Attorney took office the 1st of January, 1934.

Enumerate any other major defects in the prosecutor's office.

We think that the two most serious defects in the District Attorney's office have been (1) the lack of an able, courageous, politically independent and energetic District Attorney and staff, and (2) the failure of the District Attorney adequately to cooperate with the police and other investigating agencies in the investigation and detection of crime, and failing to initiate investigations through his office . . . .

Other questions put to the Bar dealt with the performance of the United States Attorney's office in New York. The Special Committee of the New York Bar answered that because of the ineffectiveness of the local criminal justice authorities the "tendency of the United States Attorney has been to take cognizance of crimes which should have been prosecuted under State Statutes and which were essentially local in character".[10] Such cases included labor extortion, election fraud, and corruption of local officials. The prosecutions were carried out under either the Federal Income Tax or Mail Fraud Statutes.

The individual responsible for much of the successful activity in the Federal Attorney's office was Thomas E. Dewey who first came to national prominence in the spring of 1931 with his appointment as an Assistant United States Attorney. In that capacity he prosecuted an income tax case against Arthur "Dutch Schultz" Flegenheimer and another against the equally notorious Irving "Waxey Gordon" Wexler.[11] It is certain that in 1934 the most prestigious members of the New York Bar including George Z. Medalie, Charles Evan Hughes, Jr., Joseph M. Proskauer, Charles H. Tuttle, and most importantly Samuel Seabury loathed the operations characteristic of Manhattan's District Attorney, and that in 1935 they all strongly supported Dewey as special prosecutor.

With Dewey's appointment as special prosecutor several exceptionally notable events had transpired. For one, Tammany's major criminal justice stronghold in Manhattan was circumvented which meant that patterns of influence would be broken and that some professional criminals would find themselves in increasing jeopardy. For another, it signified that reform-minded New Yorkers had availed themselves of an effective method in combating organized crime and criminality—supersession, although in this instance it was employed as a threat to force a special prosecutor upon the incumbent District Attorney.

At this juncture it is important to leave the narrative aside in order to discuss just what supersession and special prosecuting are. First of all, they are "legal methods" of "circumventing the corrupt prosecutor", according to scholars of the criminal law.[12] As such they have been analyzed (although not very often) as legal issues, but not historical or political ones. In general, when a local prosecutor such as Dodge "refuses to initiate prosecutive action", some states including New York "authorize the court to appoint a special prosecutor to carry on this function".[13] Apparently this power is based on what are called the inability statutes. The New York statute holds:

> Whenever the district attorney of any county and his assistant, if he has one, shall not be in attendance at a term of any court of record, which he is by law required to attend, or is disqualified from acting in a particular case to discharge his duties at any such term, the court may, by an order entered in its minutes, appoint some attorney at law residing in the county, to act as special district attorney during the absence, inability or disqualification of the district attorney and his assistant; but such appointment shall not be made for a period beyond the adjournment of the term at which made. The special district attorney so appointed shall possess the powers and discharge the duties of the district attorney during the period for which he shall be appointed.[14]

The second method for circumvention of corrupt local prosecutors involves the "substitution of State Attorney General". There are three primary ways in which a state attorney general can intervene. "Some states have *supervision* statutes which usually are construed to permit a state attorney general to conduct local prosecutions in the name of supervising the performance of the local prosecutor". Another type of statute grants "concurrent jurisdiction" to the attorney general in criminal proceedings. The third kind are supersession statutes which "specifically provide for substitution by the attorney general".[15] In New York State, writes Earl Johnson, Jr., there are two supersession procedures. The Governor "can direct the Attorney General's office to handle a trial or grand jury proceeding". In those cases the Attorney General or his deputies have the "same powers and responsibilities as the District Attorney". The other procedure is much broader. In this one the Attorney General either under the direction or with the approval of the Governor can start an "independent investigation into 'matters concerning the public peace, public safety and public justice' ". This type of supersession was challenged in 1951 when a State Crime Commission was appointed to investigate organized crime in the city. Technically the Commission was an "aid to the Attorney General" in an investigation of organized crime. The challenge was turned back in the courts which held the Commission duly constituted as an aid and stated "that the relationship between organized crime and politics constitutes a matter 'concerning the public peace, public safety and public justice' ".[16]

Beginning in 1930 New York City was the scene of several different but clearly related modes of circumventing local prosecutors. Seabury served as the model; he was a Referee, a Commissioner and lastly, Counsel to a Joint Legislative Committee mandated to investigate all the city's affairs. In each case what is significant beyond the substantive findings is that the prosecutorial functions were taken from the local officials and placed in the hands of an "outside" investigator. It took less than three years after Seabury for the City, in particular the Borough of Manhattan, to experience another version of the "outside" prosecutor in the person and office of special prosecutor Dewey. And before the end of the decade two more major attacks upon a local prosecutor would be launched. These occurred in Brooklyn where the District Attorney, William F.X. Geoghan, would be twice superseded (actually three times, but the first supersession came at his own request, a far cry from the others). There were no supersession incidents in the 1940s although it is important to remember that the second Geoghan supersession launched an investigation which lasted until 1942. The lack of supersession or special prosecuting in that decade does not mean that New York still did not feel the need to find some mechanism of circumvention. It did but chose for a number of reasons two other methods: the investigative Grand Jury and ultimately the State Crime Commission.

I mentioned before that supersession and special prosecuting have been, when analyzed, discussed as aspects of the criminal law. They have rarely been placed within any particular historical or political context even though they form a part of the political history of certain metropolitan communities vexed by the social system of organized crime. The functionality of supersession along with closely related strategies needs to be evaluated for their real world accomplishments and failures. This need is even more evident in the light of certain recommended standards enumerated in the very recent *Report of the Task Force on Organized Crime* written by the

National Advisory Committee on Criminal Justice Standards and Goals. Several of the recommended Standards deal exclusively with the office of prosecutor. One example is Standard 1.3 which comments that "Where the prosecutor's office is corrupt, the efforts of the most dedicated police agencies can be destroyed. To separate the prosecutor's office from corrupting influences, all members of that office should be barred from partisan political activity."[17] Much more interesting however, is Standard 7.2 "Statewide Authority for Supersession", which calls for the "establishment of procedure to supersede a local prosecutor in a specific case or investigation".[18] What is notable about the Committee's suggestion in this case is the merging of supersession with the call for a permanent statewide organized crime prosecutor. These are, in themselves, compelling reasons to discuss special prosecuting and supersession in Manhattan and Brooklyn.

The Rise of Dewey

The story of Dewey as Manhattan's special prosecutor cannot be separated from his much more substantial political ambitions. It is, of course, hardly startling to note that he was an exceptionally ambitious and able man. But the rapidity and audaciousness of his rise should be briefly recounted for the light it sheds on his activities as special prosecutor. He was appointed special prosecutor in the summer of 1935. Two years later, on August 14, 1937, he accepted the Republican nomination (Fusion and other political groups would follow) for New York County District Attorney. He over-whelmingly defeated his opponent. Barely half a year later, he secured the Republican nomination for Governor of New York. This time he was narrowly defeated by the incumbent Herbert Lehman. Nevertheless, he declared for the Presidency within 8 months of his loss. He failed to win the nomination, but bounced back to take the Governor's office in 1941. In many ways then, his career up to 1942 when he went to Albany was predicated upon his work as special prosecutor which laid the foundation for his successes as District Attorney and the bases for his future political career.

As special prosecutor Dewey and his marvelous staff pursued three major and extraordinarily complex long-term investigations. They centered on the activities and associates of Salvatore Lucania known as Lucky Luciano, Arthur Flegenheimer already identified as Dutch Schultz, and Louis Buchalter known as Lepke and his partner Jacob Shapiro alias Gurrah.

The most spectacular single accomplishment during Dewey's tenure as special prosecutor is the prosecution of Luciano for compulsory prostitution. According to Dewey's memoirs the investigation began in January, 1936, when rumors reached him that a "single combination" was running prostitution in Manhattan and Brooklyn.[19] Evidence was gathered which indicated that the head of the combination was Luciano who was arrested on April 1, 1936, in Hot Springs, Arkansas. Indicted with Luciano were Thomas Pennochio, David Betillo, James Frederico, Abraham Wahrman, Ralph Liguori, Peter Balitzer, Al Wiener, David Marcus, and Jack Ellenstein. By the summer of 1936 the trial was over and all the defendants were judged guilty. Luciano received the rather incredible sentence of 30 to 50 years, Betillo 25 to 40; Frederico and Pennochio 25 years; Wahrman 15 to 30; Liguori 7½ to 15; and the rest anywhere from 2 to 8 years.[20] It was a sensational victory for Dewey justifying the need and worth of a special prosecutor. The case against Luciano had other long-term effects for Dewey as his probe revealed significant connections between Luciano and one of New York's major politicos, Albert Marinelli. The material on Marinelli would prove very useful when Dewey campaigned for District Attorney.

The investigation into the affairs of Dutch Schultz is remarkable for its longevity, its complexities, and finally its irony. Schultz was murdered in October, 1935, long before the special prosecutor was prepared to prosecute. With Schultz dead the investigation divided into two parts. The first dealt with an industrial racket centered on a number of the city's restaurants. What Dewey turned up was a "conspiracy operated by means of three agencies, each on the surface legitimate, but each in reality dominated and controlled by the same defendants and their co-conspirators". The agencies are: Local 16 a "union of waiters employed in service restaurants as distinguished from cafeterias"; Local 302 a union of cafeteria employees; and a "purported employer's association first known as the Metropolitan Cafeteria Owners Service Company and later as the Metropolitan Restaurant and Cafeteria Association".[21] The dominant figures in this conspiracy, according to Dewey, were Dutch Schultz, his lawyer, J. Richard Davis, and two racketeers Jules Martin and Sam Krantz. The original indictment in this case was handed down one year after Schultz's death. The trial began in January, 1937, and ended with all of the remaining and alive defendants found guilty. At the time of trial both Schultz and Martin had been murdered, Davis had gone into hiding, and Krantz had quickly pleaded guilty. The major figures tried are Paul N. Coulcher, Aladar Reteck, Irving Epstein, Harry A. Vogelstein, Abraham Cohen, Philip Grossel, and Louis Beitcher.

The second aspect of the Schultz investigation was centered on his policy gambling operations. The antecedents to this work are particularly interesting. The first intimations of this enterprise and Schultz's connection had come from Seabury's work on the Magistrates when he disclosed the financial records of two Harlem policy entrepreneurs—Bender and Miro.

...u.c material was uncovered by Dewey himself during his tenure as a U.S. Attorney as he prepared the tax case against Schultz. And finally, Paul Blanshard focused on the same group and activity in his bail bond investigation discussed earlier. The culmination to this investigation came after Dewey's election as District Attorney. The investigators' path led ultimately to James J. Hines called by Dewey "the most powerful Democratic politician in the state".[22] Dewey's successful and novel prosecution of Hines and lawyer Davis, who was arrested in Philadelphia also in 1938, will be discussed in a subsequent chapter. For now it is sufficient to note that it was also important in Dewey's continuing search for higher office.

But as important as the Luciano and Schultz affairs were for Dewey's career and the history of organized crime, his efforts against Louis Buchalter and Jacob Shapiro were even more so. The activities and events constituting the criminal careers of Buchalter and Shapiro furnished him with a continuing source of material which he masterfully used in his campaign for District Attorney. In addition, Dewey's investigation of their usurpation of the flour trucking industry provided evidence that the criminal justice system in Brooklyn needed as much reform attention as Manhattan. And finally, with Schultz long dead and Luciano in prison for an extended stay, the most infamous racketeers in New York during the second half of the decade were Buchalter and Shapiro.

Jacob "Gurrah" Shapiro   *Louis "Lepke" Buchalter*

Dewey's active interest in the affairs of Buchalter and Shapiro, which was sufficient to drive them into hiding in the summer of 1937, was evident as early as October 1935, only a few months after Dewey had taken office. On October 11, 1935, Dewey's investigators raided the Perfection Coat Front Manufacturing Company and Leo Greenberg & Shapiro, Inc., seeking information about racketeering in the garment industry. At the same time,

Dewey was also pursuing an inquiry into Buchalter's involvement in the flour trucking industry. Late in the year Dewey's men seized the books and records of the Flour Truckmen's Association. Dewey also let it be known that he was seeking Max Silverman the labor adjustor for the Association.[23]

The next clear indication of Dewey's concern with Buchalter and Shapiro came in the spring of 1936, when Oscar Saffer, a garment manufacturer, was charged with filing a fraudulent state income tax return in 1933. Saffer was described as a Buchalter associate who had channeled over $150,000 in illegal payments to Buchalter and Shapiro. In the fall of 1936 Dewey released information on his investigation into the bakery and flour trucking racket. Max Silverman was identified as Buchalter's frontman in the closely related rackets. In January 1937, Dewey closed in on the bakery racket—an off-shoot of the flour trucking racket—arresting David Elfenbein, president of a baking company, attorney Benjamin N. Spevack, William "Wolfie" Goldis, president of Teamster Local 138 and Samuel Schorr an official of Local 138. Barent Ten Eyck, a Dewey assistant, gave an indication of the scope of the flour trucking and bakery rackets when he stated that the 1934 murder of William Snyder, former president of Local 138, was tied to these rackets.[24]

The trial in the bakery racket opened in the summer of 1937. The defendants included Goldis, Schorr, Spevack, and Harold Silverman, the son of Max Silverman, who was a fugitive. It was charged that they formed and dominated an employer association which controlled the cake and pastry branches of the industry. The purpose of the association was to restrain competition and regulate prices. The trial ended on July 20 with Spevack, Goldis, Schorr, and Harold Silverman found guilty. Following the conviction of Goldis and Schorr, Morris Diamond, a "member of the executive board of Local 138," issued a public statement holding that both men had the "complete confidence" of all elements of the union. Newspapers commented on Diamond's statement reminding their readers that Goldis only became president of the union upon the murder of William Snyder in a restaurant on the lower East Side, where among others, Max Silverman, Harold Silverman, Benjamin Spevack, William Goldis, and Samuel Schorr were present. The four convicted men were each sentenced to terms in the city penitentiary not to exceed three years.[25]

Dewey's victory in the bakery case, added to his already formidable list of victories as special prosecutor, made him a major candidate for District Attorney in Manhattan. The bakery racket also provided a key issue for his campaign in the unsolved murder of William Snyder. Dewey had been selected by the Republicans and Fusion as their candidate during the summer of 1937. On September 23, Samuel Seabury announced for Dewey calling his election "the keynote of the municipal campaign". The day after the Seabury endorsement Dewey broadcast the arrest, in Los Angeles, of Max Silverman wanted for extortion in flour trucking and complicity in the Snyder murder. Dewey disclosed, at this time, that Morris Goldis, the younger brother of William Goldis, was being held as a material witness in both cases. It was also revealed that Morris Goldis had been arrested and charged with the murder of Snyder back in 1934, but had been released when none of the witnesses could identify him.[26]

On September 27, the special Grand Jury turned in an indictment of eleven counts charging Silverman with extortion. Both Buchalter and Shapiro were included in the indictments. To make matters worse for Buchalter and the others, Dewey stated that a superseding indictment containing possibly fifty more counts, and several additional defendants would be returned before Silverman's trial began. Besides the indictment in the flour trucking racket, Buchalter and Shapiro also faced charges of extortion from garment manufacturers which had been voted by the Grand Jury in the summer of 1937.[27]

Only a few days after these legal proceedings, Max Rubin, the business agent for the Clothing Drivers and Helpers Union, Local 240 of the AFL and an important Buchalter associate, was shot and seriously wounded. The next day, at Silverman's arraignment, Dewey explained why Rubin was shot. "When William Snyder was shot and murdered, . . . Rubin was sent into Local 138, which was Snyder's union, as the agent of Lepke and Gurrah, and the partner" of Max Silverman. Dewey noted that he had been searching for Rubin for almost a year in connection with the investigation of Buchalter. Finally located, Rubin had testified before the Grand Jury. Dewey added that police protection had been offered Rubin, but he turned it down.[28]

The immediate significance of Rubin's shooting, along with the unsolved murder of William Snyder and the capture of Max Silverman, was evident in Dewey's campaign for District Attorney. Beginning with a radio address on October 3, Dewey molded these events into the rhythm of his campaign. Calling the attempted murder of Max Rubin "the frightened act of a desperate criminal underworld", Dewey chronicled the careers of Buchalter and Shapiro describing their dominance of industrial rackets. He stated that as a result of Buchalter's operations in flour trucking employers paid over $1,000,000 to the racketeers. Once in control of flour trucking, they added the pastry and pie division of the baking industry to the racket. Dewey also attacked the machine-controlled and corrupt District Attorney in Manhattan describing Dodge as a man who "would not, dare not and could not lift a finger" to stop these rackets. Finally, rolling out his own record, Dewey reminded his listeners that he had broken the cake and pie part of the racket and had sent Goldis, Schorr, Harold Silverman, and Benjamin Spevack to jail. He also pointed out that Max Silverman had been captured by his men and that Silverman, Buchalter, and Shapiro were all under indictment.[29]

Dewey developed his campaign from primarily an attack on racketeers to an assault on the politicians who acted in collusion with gangsters. In a radio broadcast at the end of October, Dewey accused Albert Marinelli, Tammany leader of half of the Second Assembly District and County Clerk of New York County, of being an associate of thieves, drug pushers, and racketeers. It was with Marinelli's aid, according to Dewey, that James "Jimmy Doyle" Plumeri, Dominick "Dick Terry" Didato, and Johnny "Dio" Dioguardi had taken over the trucking industry in downtown Manhattan. Dewey also noted Marinelli's connection with "Lucky Luciano" and pointed out that thirty-two men appointed by Marinelli as either county committee-men or election inspectors in the Second Assembly District had police records.[30]

John "Dio" Dioguardi   James "Jimmy Doyle" Plumeri

Actually what Dewey had on Marinelli implicated him in a variety of rackets. For instance, an informant claimed that Marinelli along with Vincent Mangano, Vito Genovese, Ciro Terranova, Lucky Luciano, and John Torrio were responsible for the murder of Dutch Schultz and several of his associates. Another informant stated "that one Peppy from Marinelli's club handles the numbers on the lower East Side Marinelli District and has 54 runners in this connection". A third informer held:

> That Torrio, in bad standing with certain underworld figures of whose identity he was not absolutely certain, left New York and started bootlegging operations in Philadelphia. Upon the repeal of prohibition, he opened the Continental Distillery in Philadelphia. During this period he had tied up with Lucky Luciano who was then operating a mob in Newark, New Jersey, specializing in the issuing of forged stocks and bonds. His financial assistance and connections were extremely valuable in putting Luciano in control of the

Unione Sicilione. He also during this period developed Joe Adonis in Brooklyn along the same lines.

These three thereupon selected Al Marinelli as their contact in the political field and made arrangements to aid him getting the leadership of his district in exchange for certain considerations that they felt he would be in a position to extend as leader. When Marinelli became leader, Torrio returned to New York and opened a wholesale liquor business in this city where he was known as Saunders.

This same informer went on commenting that Frank Galgano who was the "attorney for Marinelli's mob" was promised the position of General Sessions Judge. Dewey also possessed information that one of the victims of the trucking racket run by Plumeri, Didato and Dioguardi had stated that Plumeri "told him that he has nothing to worry about; that he had 67 charges preferred against him and that all he has to do is to call up Marinelli and they are killed".[31]

Dewey's exposure of Marinelli was only the prelude to his attack on Charles A. Schneider, an Assistant Attorney General and the Tammany Hall leader of the Eighth Assembly District. Apparently, Schneider had played a key role in the cover-up following the murder of William Snyder, which Dewey described in great detail. The most telling aspect of his story related how efficient police work produced the outline of a strong case against Morris Goldis. There were, for instance, two witnesses who recognized a picture of Morris Goldis as the killer. But in trying to locate Goldis, the police found that he had disappeared. Goldis did not turn up for seven weeks when he was surrendered by his lawyer to the District Attorney. The point Dewey was establishing with all this detail was obvious: during the time Goldis was a fugitive the corrupt criminal justice system of New York under the leadership of its Tammany District Attorney creaked along doing nothing except providing an opportunity for the racketeers to work on their defense which included successfully terrorizing the witnesses. Schneider, it turned out, was the attorney for Goldis. Dewey states his case: "Now it's not a crime in the State of New York for an assistant attorney general to represent a man accused of murder. But it's a shocking betrayal of the people of New York." Dewey accused Schneider of accepting money from racketeers in taking the case and withholding Goldis until the prosecution witnesses had been silenced.[32]

On November 2, the election was over and Dewey was in. He had defeated his opponent by over 100,000 votes, a plurality which exceeded Mayor La Guardia's margin in Manhattan. For the first time in twenty years Tammany had lost control of the District Attorney's office in New York County.[33]

With Dewey as District Attorney the pressure on the fugitives, Buchalter and Shapiro, intensified. And then, in the spring of 1938, Jacob Shapiro surrendered to Federal authorities. After the Federal authorities finished with Shapiro, he was prosecuted by the District Attorney of New York for extortion in the garment industry. Convicted, Shapiro died in prison. It took over a year from the time of Shapiro's surrender, before Buchalter finally turned himself over to J. Edgar Hoover and Walter Winchell and thereby ended one of the largest manhunts in New York City history. Buchalter faced three separate trials beginning with a Federal conviction for narcotics, followed by conviction in Manhattan for extortion in flour trucking, and ending with a guilty verdict in Brooklyn for murder. He died in the electric chair in 1944.[34]

Focus on Brooklyn

The 1930s reform attack on machine politics in the city which had primarily concentrated on criminal justice and organized crime in Manhattan soon moved across the river to Brooklyn. In the space of a few years, the District Attorney of Kings County would be twice superseded amid charges of bribery, obstruction of justice and other crimes in the administration of justice. The first scandal, which involved members of the Flour Truckmen's Association, concerned the handling of a homicide by the District Attorney's office; the second involved the whole issue of official corruption in Brooklyn and resulted in the retirement of the incumbent District Attorney.

The trouble in Brooklyn began on the night of March 3, 1935, when a call was received at police headquarters telling of a disturbance at a garage in Williamsburg. Arriving at the garage the police found a man running and arrested him. Inside the building, the police spotted a pool of blood and a trail of drops leading to a parked car inside of which was the still warm body of Samuel Drukman. Drukman had been bludgeoned with a sawed-off pool cue and strangled with a rope. Two men were caught hiding in the building; they were Fred Hull and Harry Luckman a nephew of Meyer Luckman who had been arrested outside. The police noticed that Harry Luckman's hands and clothing were heavily stained with blood. Hull was also found to have traces of blood on him. Near the car, police located the murder weapon which had blood stains on it. Finally, in Meyer Luckman's pocket there was more than $3,000 in cash. The arrested men were taken to the police station where they were questioned. It was learned that the Luckmans were flour truckers who appeared to enjoy a virtual monopoly in Brooklyn. Drukman was Meyer Luckman's nephew and was employed by the Luckman trucking company as a shipping clerk.

The accused were brought to Homicide Court for arraignment and then held for the Grand Jury. There presumably the State's exhibits including the bloodstained clothing, the "affidavits of toxicologists as to the blood stains", Meyer Luckman's $3,000 and a number of checks which were supposed to establish a motive for the murder were displayed to the grand jurors along with the testimony of police. Despite this evidence the Grand Jury voted not to indict and the checks, clothing and other evidence were released to the accused and they were discharged.[35]

As far as the Luckmans, Hull and the District attorney's office were concerned the case was closed. But this was an election year and opposing the District Attorney, William F.X. Geoghan,[36] was the Republican–Fusion nominee Joseph D. McGoldrick, the author of "The New Tammany" discussed in Chapter 2. The theme of McGoldrick's campaign was "murder is safe in Brooklyn". In October, McGoldrick speaking at a Methodist Church in Brownsville reopened the Drukman case alluding to some bizarre maneuvers in the District Attorney's office. The first response to McGoldrick's statements came not from his opponent but from Police Commissioner Lewis J. Valentine (the one-time leader of the Department's anti-gambling squad whose work was so helpful to Seabury) who said that four Brooklyn detectives would face departmental trials in connection with the Drukman affair. Valentine's statement which came after a conference with Mayor La Guardia and Captain John McGowan of the Homicide Squad in Brooklyn, held that the "Drukman case is a live, active case in the Police Department and has never ceased to be anything else from the night the murder was committed". Valentine added that the case would not be tried during the political campaign. Valentine's and presumably the Mayor's disinclination to press on immediately with an investigation matched an earlier decision of Governor Lehman. The Governor had been asked by McGoldrick to supersede Geoghan but he had refused to take action until the election was over.

As the campaign intensified, McGoldrick hammered at the District Attorney for failure to secure an indictment. On November 2, McGoldrick received the support of Samuel Seabury who charged that Geoghan was another in the long and dismaying list of Tammany District Attorneys. (He wasn't, of course, a Tammany product, but a representative of the Brooklyn Democratic party.) He added that whenever there was anything difficult to accomplish the Governor appointed someone to do the job for the District Attorney. The allusion to Manhattan's Special Prosecutor could hardly have been lost on many of his listeners.

On November 5, the voters in Brooklyn turned back the Republican–Fusion challenge to machine politics and re-elected District Attorney Geoghan by a substantial margin; McGoldrick carried only one Assembly District. Geoghan's victory was part of a sweep scored by the Democratic organization which, it was reported, "rivaled those of the days preceding the Seabury investigation". Commenting on the Drukman case, the triumphant District Attorney said that as far as he was concerned it was closed unless there was new evidence. Almost simultaneously with Geoghan's statement, however, the Grand Jury minutes of the Drukman case were turned over to Police Commissioner Valentine.

During the last week in November, Governor Lehman requested both Commissioner Valentine and District Attorney Geoghan to meet with him to discuss the case. By now constant rumors or allegations of bribery surrounded the affair. In addition, Geoghan had re-submitted the case to the November Grand Jury and they had announced they were investigating bribery as well as murder. The day after the Governor's request for a meeting, the Grand Jury indicted Meyer and Harry Luckman and Fred Hull for murder. During this same week Lehman asked that all records, including those of the Grand Jury which had failed to indict the Luckmans and Hull, be delivered to him. It was also reported that influential civic organizations were pressuring the Governor to replace Geoghan. Dewey made his presence felt by seizing on December 4, the records and books of the Flour Truckman's Association, of which Meyer Luckman was a director. Dewey denied that he was interested in the Drukman murder, however.[37]

In the first week of December, Governor Lehman announced that he had decided to supersede Geoghan. Also, an extraordinary term of the Supreme Court would be called and a special Grand Jury drawn. There were three distinct areas, Lehman held, which must be effectively and thoroughly investigated: first was the murder; second, charges of police bribery; and third, bribery in the District Attorney's office. A few days later, Attorney General John J. Bennett Jr., appointed Hiram C. Todd a Deputy Attorney General and placed him in charge of the investigation.[38]

Within six weeks the murder trial of the Luckmans and Hull was under way. The State's case began with the motive for the murder. Drukman, it was held, stole thousands of dollars from his uncle's flour and produce trucking business for gambling. When Meyer Luckman discovered the thefts he "openly threatened" to kill his nephew, and also "tried to choke his bookkeeper, Harry Kantor", whom he suspected of helping Drukman. Kantor fled to Chicago where he either fell, was pushed, or jumped from a window in a sanitarium and died.

The State presented a number of witnesses who testified that Drukman was a heavy gambler and loser. Money was given Drukman which was supposed to reach his uncle, but which was never turned over. Defense counsel called no witnesses. In their summations the best they could offer was a defense of District Attorney Geoghan asking for a "verdict that will be an answer forever to these interlopers that we have a prosecutor who investigated the case thoroughly". The three defendants were found guilty of murder in the second degree and sentenced to twenty years to life in Sing Sing.[39]

With the question of murder solved, Todd proceeded with the other phases of the case. By the middle of March, Todd's work on the question of bribery became evident: indicted for attempting to influence members of the April (1935) grand jury, were James J. Kleinman, the father of William W. Kleinman, an Assistant District Attorney on Geoghan's staff, and Carmine Anzalone, a Republican State Committeeman from the Fourth Assembly District, Brooklyn, Chief of the clerical staff of the Assembly. Several days later Todd brought charges of bribery and attempted bribery against Henry G. Singer a former Assistant United States Attorney active in Republican politics in the Sixth Assembly District, Brooklyn. In subsequent weeks Todd announced that he was seeking Max Silverman of the Flour Truckmen's Association in connection with bribery. Silverman, who at that time was a fugitive, was described as a close friend of William W. Kleinman the Assistant District Attorney whose father had been indicted. Eight more indictments were handed down by the middle of May. Heading the new group, charged with obstruction of justice, was Assistant District Attorney Kleinman. Joining him was Detective Giuseppe F.L. Dardis, a partner of Detective Charles S. Corbett, the man who was first responsible for charging bribery when the case seemed forgotten in the summer of 1935. Also charged were Carmine Anzalone, James J. Kleinman and Henry G. Singer. The last three men charged were Max Silverman and Jack Silverman (not related) and Meyer Luckman's brother, Isaac. Other people named in the conspiracy but not indicted included Leo P. Byk characterized as a former Brooklyn slot machine czar, Detective Charles Hemendinger who committed suicide days before he was scheduled to appear before the Grand Jury, the three convicted murderers, and two members of the March Grand Jury, predecessor of the one which had dismissed the Luckmans.[40]

At the same time the Grand Jury demanded of the Governor the removal of District Attorney Geoghan. They accused Geoghan of gross negligence and demonstrated incompetence in failing to investigate the scandal, and with associating with undesirable persons, specifically Leo P. Byk and Frank

Erickson known as a professional gambler and bookmaker. It was alleged that these two men contributed to Geoghan's reluctance to investigate the murder. Governor Lehman responded, however, that he would not act until the whole investigation was completed. This was interpreted as an indication to Todd that he must prove at least some of the allegations before the Governor would proceed against Geoghan.[41]

Todd had five of the eight men indicted for bribery and conspiracy on trial soon after the public disclosure of the charges against Geoghan. Isaac Luckman and Max Silverman were still missing and Carmine Anzalone had pleaded guilty to conspiracy becoming an important State's witness. During the trial Anzalone implicated former Chief Assistant United States Attorney Henry G. Singer in the scheme. Anzalone testified that Singer, whom he had known for several years having been an Assistant United States Marshal while Singer was a Federal prosecutor, asked him to contact a grand juror and offer him a bribe of $100 to vote against an indictment. The State's major witness was Detective Charles S. Corbett. He took the stand on June 11, and implicated William W. Kleinman, Leo P. Byk, and Detective Dardis in the conspiracy. Corbett in his free-wheeling manner also damned District Attorney Geoghan. The defense tried to counter his testimony by demonstrating he was mentally incompetent. As the prosecution neared the end of its case, other witnesses were called who stated the roles played by Jack Silverman and Max Silverman. On June 18, the defense presented its version of the bribery claiming that Detective Corbett had actively solicited money in return for throwing the case. Earlier, the defense had charged Anzalone with being one of the conspirators.

Near the end of June, the jury returned its verdict. Convicted of conspiracy to interfere with justice, a misdemeanor punishable by a maximum fine of $500 and one year in prison, were Singer, James Kleinman and Jacob Silverman. The jury was deadlocked, supposedly at ten to two for conviction, in the cases of William Kleinman and Dardis. The three convicted men were sentenced to one year in prison. Tentative plans were made for retrying Kleinman and Dardis.[42]

Todd must have had feelings of accomplishment and deep satisfaction: he had successfully prosecuted the Drukman killers, and convicted four out of six men, counting Anzalone, indicted for bribery and conspiracy. However, one year later, Todd's convictions were reversed by the Appellate Court. Concerning James J. Kleinman the Court stated there was simply no proof that he had joined with any persons to further any conspiracy. In reviewing Singer's conviction, the Court found serious reservations in the testimony of Anzalone. As to Jacob Silverman accused of influencing an April grand juror and of conspiring with Leo P. Byk to obstruct justice, the Court found a great deal of innuendo but little proof. Some of the innuendo, however, was most interesting. For example, in a conversation taking place the day the Luckmans were released from jail, secured by the tapping of Silverman's telephone, the defendant states: "Those two fellows will be out in fifteen minutes." In return he was asked if he called "that fellow to tell him about it". Silverman answered no and then adds: "Listen, those fellows won't believe what I can do so I had Frank Costello's brother, Eddie, with me and I told him to sit there and listen so that he would know that I took care of it." Silverman was also described as an associate of Lucky Luciano. The convictions were reversed and new trials ordered for Silverman and Singer. In Kleinman's case the indictment was dismissed.[43]

Following the conspiracy and bribery trial, public interest turned to District Attorney Geoghan who had been ordered by Governor Lehman to defend himself at a public hearing. The charges were prosecuted by Todd, while Geoghan was defended by Lloyd Paul Stryker. Governor Lehman, on September 17, reached his decision: Geoghan was completely exonerated of all charges. Lehman held there was no evidence that important information was "willfully or corruptly withheld from the April grand jury or that the District Attorney should have known that an attempt had been made to tamper with the April grand jury". Concerning Corbett the Governor stated that his testimony was "completely discredited". And as far as Geoghan's friendship with Byk and Erickson, Lehman said that they were "manifestly ill-advised", but that there was no evidence that corruption and neglect of duty resulted.[44]

Before ending his presentation, Todd gave his final version of the bribery conspiracy based on a letter from Commissioner Valentine to Geoghan on September 18, 1935. Valentine writes: "Acting Detective Sergeant Charles Hemendinger . . . was the go-between for members of the Police Department in the collection of money paid to the police in the Drukman case." Valentine adds that "all arrangements in connection with the bribe and fixing . . . were made at meetings in Sam Herman's restaurant". Finally, Valentine notes that Joe Adonis and Joseph Solovei "are believed to have distributed the Drukman money; that Erickson, one of the biggest bookmakers in New York . . . may have helped the Luckmans". Following the Governor's announcement of exoneration for Geoghan, members of the Grand Jury sent off a lengthy telegram to Lehman stating their shock and dismay at the "failure" to remove the District Attorney: and at the "tone and content" of Lehman's opinion. They state: "We looked to you for leadership. We looked in vain." Two days later Lehman replied to what he called their "abusive and misleading letter".

Lehman said it is both "monstrous" and "perverse" for the jurors to "assert that a man must be guilty just because a grand jury has brought charges against him". The Governor added a swipe at the actions of Todd noting his attempts to "damn by innuendo and to destroy by unsupported accusations".[45]

In the spring of 1938 an apparently relaxed Geoghan jokingly stated that he was worried because Brooklyn criminals did not seem to be committing serious crimes anymore. That was probably one of his last jokes for within five months Governor Lehman again found it necessary to supersede the District Attorney. The origin of this supersedure began with the work of the Citizens Committee on the Control of Crime in New York, Inc., which was founded in 1936 through the initiative of the Special New York County Grand Jury impanelled to hear evidence gathered by Dewey and his staff on organized crime. Dismayed by the scope of racketeering and the fearfulness of potential witnesses, the Grand Jury called for a Citizens Committee which would assure protection to witnesses and monitor the criminal courts and activities of prosecuting officials. The Grand Jury recognized that the proposed committee would have to function city-wide. Mayor La Guardia responded to the suggestion by forming the Citizens Committee and appointing Harry F. Guggenheim, the former Ambassador to Cuba, as chairman.[46]

In July, 1938, the Committee presented to Mayor La Guardia evidence of large-scale irregularities in the administration of justice in Brooklyn. In the early autumn of 1938, the Committee's negative attitude toward the criminal justice system in Brooklyn was reinforced when rumors were circulated charging obstruction of justice in two criminal cases by members of Geoghan's staff.[47]

The first case centered on Joseph Mauro who was charged with perjury. Mauro, released on bail failed to appear and was rearrested. In explaining his action Mauro claimed that he had paid $100, through an intermediary, to Assistant District Attorney William F. McGuinness to fix his case. The second criminal case involved Isidore Juffe, supposed ringleader of a fur racket in Brooklyn, who after his arrest was freed when Assistant District Attorney Baldwin claimed that he was unable to find witnesses. The newspapers reported that Juffe stated that he had paid for his release. District Attorney Geoghan's response to the news stories was that he was conducting an investigation. New York newspapers were quick to point out that this amounted to an investigation carried on by the accused.[48]

At this point Mayor La Guardia announced that the inquiry conducted by the Citizens Committee had charted thousands of cases in Brooklyn and had found innumerable irregularities. La Guardia added that the Commissioner of Investigations had been ordered to examine charges of police and prosecutorial corruption in Brooklyn. On October 10, the Commissioner submitted a petition to Governor Lehman asking for the supersession of Geoghan. Three days later, the Governor superseded the District Attorney. Named by Lehman to carry on the inquiry into official corruption in Brooklyn was John Harlan Amen.[49]

Amen's first investigation was a probe into the fur racket. The most important indictment in this phase of Amen's investigation was the one charging Assistant District Attorney Alexander R. Baldwin with accepting an $800 bribe from Isidore Juffe to prevent his prosecution in one of the fur swindles. The incidents related by Amen reveal Juffe, desperate to avoid prosecution as he already had 25 arrests and three felony convictions, shopping around for a man willing to cooperate. According to Amen, when Juffe was brought to Baldwin in the District Attorney's office for interrogation the search for a solution to his problem ended. At his trial, Baldwin characterized the whole affair as part of a diabolical plot to have Geoghan superseded. He explained his lenient treatment of Juffe by noting that Juffe was an informer who had proven helpful to the District Attorney's office. Having to choose between Baldwin's explanation and Juffe's accusation, the jury went with Baldwin. He was acquitted and subsequently reinstated as an Assistant District Attorney. Following this victory, however, Baldwin's license to practise law was suspended by the Appellate Division.[50]

The second major official of the District Attorney's office to be prosecuted by Amen was William F. McGuinness. McGuinness faced four charges, two of which related to an abortion racket. The portrait of McGuinness drawn by Amen depicted him as actively pursuing bribes of a consistently paltry nature: $50 to fix a suspected abortion; $100 to have a perjury charge dismissed in the Grand Jury where the foreman was a friend; $50 to have an extortion charge against three members of Teamsters Local 138 dropped (Local 138 was, as mentioned earlier, an integral part of Buchalter's flour-trucking racket); and $200 to undermine an investigation of a suspected abortionist. Amen presented other instances of McGuinness hustling money which were not included in the indictment. McGuinness pleaded guilty and was sentenced to Sing Sing for no longer than three years.[51]

The phase of Amen's work that seems to have received the greatest public attention was his inquiry into bail bond rackets. Public interest was first aroused with the disclosure in mid-October 1938, several days before Amen was authorized to begin his investigation, that six arrest books containing data on 7,200 prisoners had been stolen from a Brooklyn police station. Under the personal supervision of Police Commissioner Valentine an intensive investigation was started which implicated Police Lieutenant Cuthbert J. Behan. A few days later, Amen took over the investigation from Valentine.[52]

In his report to Governor Lehman, Amen describes, in general terms, how the bail bond racket operated. "A person who owns real estate may pledge it as security to obtain the release of a prisoner." In a felony case a judge determined the amount of bail necessary and whether or not the security offered was sufficient. However, in certain misdemeanor cases "where no court is open at which bail can be offered" an alternate system was sanctioned which became the area of greatest exploitation. In these cases the "desk officer in a police precinct station house" was allowed to accept bail — "the amount of bail being fixed as a matter of law". Amen adds that "to qualify as a surety a person must be the owner of property in the county in which the bail is offered"; and a person who goes bail more than twice in one month, "or for a fee, is engaged in the bail-bond business", must secure a license. Amen notes that there had been so many violations of these requirements and others that a blacklist was drawn up by the Chief City Magistrate and circulated to all police stations and Magistrates' Courts. Unfortunately, it was totally ignored.[53]

Amen continues: "In the Magistrates' Courts, members of the racket would approach a defendant's relatives and offer to arrange bail for a fee." None of the racketeers were licensed nor did any of them own property, but they did have the names of property owners who were willing to pledge their real estate as bail for a percentage of the fee. The only area of risk involved the person who pledged his property on the appearance of the defendant in court. However, as Amen points out, this was hardly a risk in Brooklyn: "although $300,000 in judgments on bail forfeitures had accumulated in Kings County between 1930 and 1940, none of the property involved had been sold". With cooperation between police officials and racketeers, the process was simplified. In many instances the "desk officer knew that the person who appeared before him as surety was using a false name, or that the deed offered was made out to someone other than the person presenting it". According to testimony taken during the investigation, "these officers received a percentage of the fee obtained by the bondsman" in return for accepting the phony bonds and releasing the prisoners.[54]

The first case reported on by Amen concerned Police Lieutenant Cuthbert J. Behan charged with stealing the arrest records from the police station because they could have implicated him in the bail bond racket. Amen's case against Behan rested partly on the testimony of two patrolmen, Edward J. Lawler and James Sweeney. Patrolman Sweeney, after appearing against Behan at a hearing, committed suicide "worried that his career in the Department would be ruined by testifying against a Superior". Behan was removed from the Force, although acquitted on criminal charges.[55]

Amen's investigation into the bail bond racket moved from police corruption to the Bench. In the autumn of 1938, Amen probed the affairs of racketeer, Louis Kassman. Kassman's importance to the over-all investigation lay in his testimony which formed part of the basis for charges of bribery and corruption against Magistrate Mark Rudich. Testimony against Rudich was also given by Jacob Nathanson, a former member of the New York State Assembly and a partner of Kassman's in his bail bond racket. Rudich was paid by Kassman for exercising judicial restraint. In the early spring of 1939, the Appellate Court removed Rudich from the Bench. This decision was unprecedented in Brooklyn. It was the "first time ,since its establishment as a judicial department in 1897 that the Appellate Division had removed from office a judge from the inferior courts under its jurisdiction".[56]

Following the Rudich affair, Amen turned to other bail bond rackets and uncovered some of the activities of Abe "Kid Twist" Reles and his associates. Reles and the others were closely associated with Buchalter and were among the most notorious racketeers and indeed killers in New York. On May 4, 1939, Mrs. Rose Gold, "69 years of age, decrepit and unable to read or write English", was charged with seventeen counts of perjury. Rose Gold was the proprietor of a candy store that was Reles's headquarters. According to Amen, Gold's involvement with Reles and his associates was fairly complex.

Abe "Kid Twist" Reles

She made frequent appearances in Brooklyn police stations posting bond for gamblers protected by Reles and the others. More importantly, Gold was the banker for Reles's extensive loan shark operation. How extensive was detailed by Amen who found in the space of a year about $400,000 deposited and withdrawn from Gold's bank account. Amen also established that all the bank transactions were carried out by Gold's daughter, Shirley Herman, whose husband worked for Irwin Steingut the leader of the Democratic minority in the State Assembly and considered one of Brooklyn's most powerful politicians. Gold was permitted to plead guilty to perjury in the second degree, a misdemeanor, and received a suspended sentence.[57]

During the course of his four-year long investigation, Amen uncovered some of Abe Reles's more durable enterprises. While gathering evidence on the gambling racket including lotteries, bookmaking, crap games and policy which flourished with the knowledge and help of corrupt police officers, Amen found, as noted above, Reles's loan shark racket. In charge of Reles's operation were Sam "The Dapper" Siegel and Louis "Tiny" Benson. Siegel managed the local neighborhood lending service which operated out of the Brownsville candy store owned by Rose Gold who, it turned out, was Siegel's mother. Benson handled the shylock racket at the dice games. Benson met with Reles "each night before the games" to receive money which was to be lent to needy participants. Benson had as much as $10,000 in cash to use at the games. By the time Amen had gathered sufficient evidence to indict Benson and Siegel on nine counts of violating the banking law, Reles had already been indicted for murder. Benson and Siegel pleaded guilty and received suspended sentences.[58]

Louis "Tiny" Benson

The Amen investigation covered such areas as the Probation Department of the Kings County Court, the Department of Correction, the Office of the Commissioner of Jurors, in addition to the bail bond, fur, gambling, and abortion rackets. In elaborating on the results, Amen placed high on the list of his accomplishments the forced retirement of District Attorney Geoghan.[59] In fact, within six months of the time the Amen investigation started, powerful political interests in Brooklyn requested Geoghan's resignation. More than half of Brooklyn's Democratic leaders met with Frank V. Kelly, the so-called Boss of the County machine to devise a strategy to remove Geoghan. But Geoghan resisted stating that he would not be the scapegoat for the crooks he had hired at the insistence of the District leaders. The future of the District Attorney's office was finally resolved that summer. Geoghan would retire at the end of his term which was over that year. In his place Brooklyn Democrats nominated County Judge, William O'Dwyer who enjoyed an untarnished reputation. Unlike Manhattan, the reform forces in Brooklyn were weak and disorganized and O'Dwyer had an easy time winning.[60] It is important to remember, though, that even with a new District Attorney in Brooklyn the Amen investigation continued for two more years.

Evaluation

Supersession and allied tactics are methods to circumvent the "normal" political system of municipalities at one of their most critical points—the criminal justice system especially the office of prosecutor. As we have seen, New York City from 1935 to 1942 was the scene of three supersession incidents including Dewey's appointment as Special Prosecutor which was not technically a supersession. The question now, of course, is how to evaluate them. First of all, it is clear that these particular developments were part of a broad reform movement which attempted with some spectacular successes to wrest political control of the city from the Democratic machines. As such, New York's supersessions are a part of the political history of the city. The prosecutors' offices were an integral unit in a web of corruption and racketeering which permeated all levels of city government as well as much of the political economy of New York.

Nothing was quite as telling in this regard as the Seabury investigations which led, one is tempted to say inexorably, to all the rest. Taking all his investigations together, Seabury and his staff implicated the range of city government in a tangled mass of mis-, mal-, and non-feasance as well as in several discrete criminal conspiracies which had all the characteristics of long-term rackets.

It was this display of public venality which paved the way for La Guardia's election and Dewey's appointment. Unlike Seabury, Dewey's work was totally focused on organized crime as commonly understood. He was out to get the infamous racketeers, to show the kind of job a real prosecutor could do if freed from the corrupt grip of the political machine. That his own political ambition showed in no way lessened his effectiveness as special prosecutor. From 1935 to 1938 when he took office as Manhattan's District Attorney, Dewey convicted Luciano and his associates for compulsory prostitution; convicted "Tootsie" Herbert and others for an industrial racket in the kosher chicken industry; convicted several remnants of Dutch Schultz's restaurant racket mob; convicted James Plumeri and Johnny "Dio" Dioguardi for extortion among garment truckers; convicted the bakery racketeers and solved the murder of William Snyder; indicted J. Richard "Dixie" Davis and others for policy; and finally, indicted Buchalter and Shapiro for extortion in the garment industry, the bakery racket, and flour trucking. But Dewey's work must be viewed within a radically different or changed context than Seabury's and the later supersessions. Dewey took office in the wake of very substantial political changes; behind him stood the revelations of Seabury and the power of a new Administration whose mission was at least partially the uprooting of the social system of organized crime. Within this climate Dewey chose to prosecute racketeers and to carefully *expose* their political protectors. Through his sensational prosecutions and timely exposés, Dewey placed Dodge and the official District Attorney's office into limbo. Dewey's election in 1937 only confirmed the situation.

Brooklyn was, as usual, another story. Much more limited in scope and certainly accomplishment was the supersession of Geoghan by Hiram Todd. In this instance the universe of crime and corruption was centered on fourteen principals including District Attorney Geoghan, Assistant District Attorney William Kleinman, 1 former Assistant U.S. Attorney, 1 former U.S. Marshal, 2 police officers, and assorted flour truckers. There were no other public officials named or charged. Aside from the three men convicted of murder, the only others to serve prison time were Max Silverman sentenced to a year for becoming a fugitive, and Jack Silverman who pleaded guilty to obstruction of justice at his second trial. Todd's major effort which centered on removing Geoghan from office was a failure. But like Dewey's, Todd's work must be seen in the light of the political history of both the State of New York and the Borough of Brooklyn. Governor of New York at this time was Democrat Herbert Lehman who could almost daily see the havoc wrought upon New York's Democratic party by an ambitious Special Prosecutor (Dewey). Lehman was surely in no mood to launch another Dewey, this time in Brooklyn which was solidly Democratic. In addition, Brooklyn had little of the reform ethos which animated Manhattan. Lehman went so far as superseding Geoghan, but he would not sustain Todd's charges unless there was unavoidable and unimpeachable proof of his guilt. With such tenuous support at the State level and almost no support locally, Todd's investigation into corruption was severely circumscribed. Unable to connect his efforts to broader segments of reform or to effectively penetrate the power of

Brooklyn's politicos, Todd's major contribution was historical—he materially weakened Geoghan's political power making him a potential liability for the Brooklyn machine. Geoghan's weakness was graphically displayed first in 1938 by the swiftness with which Lehman again superseded him (the Governor was more concerned with scandal than with appointing another Dewey), and then a short time later when the machine forced him into retirement.

This brings us to the final supersession, one which lasted longer than any of the others and one which is much more difficult to judge. The reason for its somewhat enigmatic character has to do with the change in the District Attorney's office with the election of O'Dwyer. As the new District Attorney O'Dwyer was immediately involved in a series of sensational murder cases which sent seven men to the electric chair including Buchalter and most of Reles's associates. These are the infamous Murder, Inc., cases which will be analyzed in a subsequent chapter. From 1940 to 1942 it appeared that the regular District Attorney was on his way to smashing organized crime in the most spectacular manner—prosecutions for murder. Indeed, while Amen uncovered Reles's loan shark racket, O'Dwyer had Reles informing on Buchalter, Joe Adonis, Albert Anastasia and other notorious racketeers. In the midst of these prosecutions, the Amen forays into police corruption and the problems with the Raymond Street Jail seemed mild if not inconsequential. To most observers, it appeared that the regularly elected Prosecutor was doing an exceptional job. There was no chance then for either Amen's work or Brooklyn's quasi-Special Prosecutor to become institutionalized within the formal structure of the Borough's criminal justice system. Unlike Dewey who took over the office, the Amen forces had less and less to do with the Prosecutor's office as time went on.

This meant that the educational and political value of Amen's investigation was short-circuited by O'Dwyer's successes. The vigor of the initial murder prosecutions suggested that the endemic corruption rampant throughout Brooklyn's criminal justice system had been met and overcome through the regular electoral process. How foolish a conclusion this was would not become evident until at least the mid-1940s when allegations of corruption about O'Dwyer and members of his staff would be seriously investigated. These allegations and others form the major content of the next chapter. Long before, however, Amen had finished his investigation which resulted in indictments and Grand Jury presentments charging primarily bribery against 5 members of the District Attorney's staff, 3 Brooklyn judges, 48 police officers, 39 corporations, and 94 individuals. Amen's conviction record was, outside of the private citizens who pleaded guilty and received suspended sentences and the corporations which pleaded guilty and were lightly fined, rather dismal. In fact, as one surveys the results moving from indictments and presentments down finally to departmental actions the impression is of a series of acquittals, dismissals, and departmental disciplinary actions. While unfolding with deadly accuracy the social structure of corruption and the social system of organized crime, the Amen investigation had little effect on either the structure or the system.

What finally can be said about supersession in general? First, there is no doubt that it has been an important weapon against aspects of organized crime and corruption in New York City at least up to the tenure of Maurice J. Nadjari (Special Prosecutor 1973–1976).[61] But it is also quite clear that major victories against professional criminals and their patrons and clients in the criminal justice system do not simply follow supersession. Special prosecuting is most effective when it is part of a broadly based reform movement; it is least effective when it stands alone as the culmination or climax of reform as it did in Brooklyn. Perhaps even more significant in this regard is to consider supersession as part of a continuing struggle against the political structure of select municipalities. As it circumvents the elected prosecutor, it stands apart and indeed, against the innumerable arrangements developed by political power brokers which have often been institutionalized within the criminal justice bureaucracies. Special prosecuting reveals the true nature of city politics and one of its major patronage fields—criminal justice.

But this brings us to one of the ironies of supersession and special prosecuting. As its effectiveness is proportional to reform in general, the stronger the reform movement, the more likely will it seek to totally overwhelm the corrupted. Not only are the rascals to be prosecuted, but they are to be replaced within the regular criminal justice system by the reformers through traditional political processes. When and if that happens, however, it opens to the new officers and politicos the range of extra-legal and informal channels of influence and accommodation. The only force to combat corruption then is personal morality which is always a fragile defense. The irony is that the most effective form of special prosecuting tends to lead the reformers into the traditional web of city politics where civic virtue is continuously assaulted.

NOTES

[1] One of the key indicators of La Guardia's attitude is his overhaul of the Commissioner of Account's Office. Harold Seidman in *Investigating Municipal Administration: A Study of the New York Department of Investigation* (New York, 1941) relates in Chapter 9 how "extra work required Blanshard's staff to put in 7,100 hours of overtime in 1934 and 1935. During the same period, 5,305 witnesses were examined as compared with 487 in 1932 and 1933'. Special studies were ordered by La Guardia on "the operation of pinball machines", see New York City Department of Investigation, (December 17, 1941); on the graft and waste in certain county offices, see *The Sheriffs' Offices of the Five Counties: A Study by the Department of Investigation and Accounts* (March, 1936) and *The Offices of Register and Commissioner of Records in the Five Counties of New York City* (March, 1937); and various notorious professional criminals such as gambler Frank A. Erickson, see New York City Department of Investigation, *Report MR–9025* (May 4, 1939).

  In addition to changing the Commissioner's office, La Guardia moved by a "passionate hatred of crime" turned to the Police Department instructing them to adopt a physically abusive attitude toward criminals (Garrett, 161–163). And finally, one should again consult Theodore J. Lowi's study of "Patronage and Power" in New York cited in the last chapter for an insightful analysis of the effect of La Guardia's administrations on the structure of machine politics. In the first half of the twentieth century, New York had only three reform mayors: Seth Low, John Purroy Mitchell, and La Guardia. Lowi states: "All three reform mayors spent most of their energies creating a record clear of corruption, attempting to set an example, hoping to raise the level of public expectations about local government" (p. 201).

[2] Among the abuses, crimes, rackets, and conspiracies reported on by Blanshard are the cruel bilking of the aged and destitute at the City Home on Welfare Island; the corruption involved in obtaining newsstand licenses especially by "crippled and disabled" individuals; racketeering in coal purchases and deliveries; tax dodging by "prominent politicians on the city payroll" especially Aaron L. Jacoby, Register of Kings County and former Sheriff, Hyman Schorenstein, Commissioner of Records of Kings County, and Samuel Pearlman, Clerk of the Sixth District Municipal Court of Brooklyn and Schorenstein's son-in-law; evasions of the city Sales Tax; cheating on the part of three investigators of the Emergency Relief Bureau in order to virtually steal clothing allowances from the destitute; police brutality during a shipyard strike in Brooklyn; the so-called "kick-back" racket in the city's building trades; various rackets which involved paying for city jobs and promotions, and much, much more. New York City Department of Investigation and Accounts, *Investigating City Government in the La Guardia Administration: A Report on the Activities of the Department of Investigation and Accounts* (New York, 1937).

[3] *Ibid.*, 7.

[4] *Ibid.*, 8.

[5] *Ibid.*, 9.

[6] *Ibid.*, 52.

[7] See *The New York Times*, March 1, 1935: 1; March 14, 1935: 1; March 16, 1935: 1; April 2, 1935: 1; May 8, 1935: 40; May 13, 1935: 11; May 16, 1935: 1; May 19, 1935: 1.

[8] *Ibid.*, June 25, 1935: 1; June 28, 1935: 15.

[9] *American Bar Association Journal*, XX (May, 1934), 301.

[10] *Ibid.*, 303.

[11] Thomas E. Dewey, *Twenty Against the Underworld*, Rodney Campbell, ed., (New York, 1974), 77–155.

[12] See Earl Johnson, Jr., "Organized Crime: Challenge to the American Legal System," *Journal of Criminal Law, Criminology, and Police Science* 54 (1963) especially part 2 "The Legal Weapons . . ." and part 3 "Legal Antidotes . . ." Also see "Legal Methods for the Suppression of Organized Crime (A Symposium)," *Journal of Criminal Law, Criminology and Police Science*, 48 (1957), including part 2 Marvin E. Aspen, "The Investigative Function of the Prosecuting Attorney," 48 (1958). There is one study of supersession which includes material on New York during the period under study: Morris Ploscowe and Milton H. Spiero, "The Prosecuting Attorney's Office and the Control of Organized Crime," in American Bar Association, Morris Ploscowe, ed., *Organized Crime and Law Enforcement* (New York, 1952).

[13] Johnson, Jr., 128.

[14] Quoted in *Ibid.*

[15] *Ibid.*, 129.

[16] *Ibid.*, 130. Concerning the challenge of the constitutionality of the Crime Commission see New York State Crime Commission, *First Report to the Governor, the Attorney General and the Legislature of the State of New York*, Legislative Document no. 23 (1953), 56: Pursuant to Section 63 (8) of the Executive Law, the Attorney General, at the request of the Commission, duly appointed a staff of attorneys, investigators, accountants and clerical personnel to assist the Commission in its work . . .

The legality of the appointment of the members of the Commission and the Commission's power to issue subpoenas was established by a decision of the Court of Appeals rendered on July 11, 1951. *Matter of DiBrizzi*, 303 N.Y. 206 (1951).

[17] National Advisory Committee on Criminal Justice Standards and Goals, *Report of the Task Force on Organized Crime* (Washington, D.C., 1976), 38.

[18] *Ibid.*, 144.

[19] Dewey, 190.

[20] *Ibid.*, 266.

[21] New York State Supreme Court, Appellate Division—First Department, The People of the State of New York against Paul N. Coucher, *et al.*, *Respondent's Brief*, 3. The copy of both the trial transcript and *Respondent's Brief* which I used was provided by Governor Dewey's Law Office, Dewey, Ballantine, Bushby, Palmer and Wood at 140 Broadway, New York. Their generosity is heartily appreciated.

[22] Dewey, 379.

[23] U.S. Department of Justice, Federal Bureau of Investigation, "The Fur Dress Case," *Report # 60–1501* (November 7, 1939), 9.

[24] *The New York Times*, April 30, 1936: 44; October 22, 1936: 1; January 16, 1937: 1.

[25] *Ibid.*, June 29, 1937: 1; July 7, 1937: 48; July 21, 1937: 3; August 3, 1937: 7.

Diamond's confidence in the racketeers was short-lived and ill-rewarded. He was shot to death in 1939 for giving information to Dewey about Buchalter's trucking racket in the garment industry. Turkus and Feder, 459, 493.

[26] *Ibid.*, August 29, 1937, VIII: 7; September 24, 1937: 1; September 25, 1937: 1; September 26, 1937: 3.

[27] Federal Bureau of Investigation, 20.

Also indicted with Buchalter and Shapiro were Benjamin Levine, Samuel Weiner, Irving Feldman, Joseph Miller, Abraham Friedman, Herman Yuran, Harry Greenberg, Sol Feinberg, Henry Teitelbaum, Paul Berger, David Horn, Joseph Amoroso, Joseph

Rocconbone, and Leon Scharf. At least four of these men were murdered before Buchalter's surrender.

[28] Turkus and Feder, 363–407; *The New York Times,* October 2, 1937: 1; October 3, 1937: 1, 41.

[29] *Ibid.,* October 4, 1937: 1. The text of Dewey's radio address is on page 2.

[30] *Ibid.,* October 25, 1937: 1.

[31] All of the information can be found in Thomas E. Dewey, *Personal Papers,* Series 1: Early Career, Box 90, The University of Rochester Library, Department of Rare Books.

[32] *The New York Times,* October 28, 1937: 1. The text of Dewey's radio address is on page 17.

[33] Several days after Dewey's victory, Morris Goldis was indicted for the first degree homicide of Snyder. Seven months later a superseding indictment naming Max Silverman, Samuel Schorr, William and Morris Goldis was handed down. By this time Silverman was serving a sentence for his part in another case while William Goldis and Schorr were in prison for their participation in the bakery racket. At long last, on the first of July, it was reported that Morris Goldis had confessed that he was the gunman in the killing. Both brothers were allowed to plead guilty to first-degree manslaughter. See Court of General Sessions of the County of New York—Part IV, *The People of the State of New York Against Max Silverman, Samuel Schorr, William Goldis, Morris Goldis,* Indictment # 221026.

[34] Federal Bureau of Investigation, 34, 44–45.

[35] *The New York Times,* November 17, 1937: 11.

[36] Geoghan was born in Philadelphia in 1882, where he attended St. Joseph's College receiving a B.A. in 1903 and an M.A. in 1905. From there he went to Georgetown Law School while at the same time teaching English and History at Gonzaga College. He passed the Bar in 1906 and then went to New York as an instructor in English at the College of the City of New York. He practised law at the same time. On January 1, 1923, he was appointed an Assistant District Attorney of Kings County. He became the District Attorney on January 1, 1931. Geoghan took office in a special election held after the incumbent resigned to become a Justice of the Supreme Court of New York. In the fall of 1931, Geoghan was elected to a full term of four years. See "Charges Made to Governor Herbert H. Lehman with Respect to Removal of William F.X. Geoghan from the Office of the District Attorney of Kings County, May 19, 1936," in the *Public Papers of Herbert H. Lehman, Forty-Ninth Governor of the State of New York, Second Term.* (Albany, 1940).

[37] *The New York Times,* October 23, 1935: 1; November 3, 1935: 1; November 6, 1935: 1; November 7, 1935: 16; November 25, 1935: 1; November 27, 1935: 1; November 29, 1935: 1; December 5, 1935: 1.

[38] Todd, born in Saratoga Springs, New York, and admitted to the Bar in 1900, had long experience as a Special Prosecutor. He had served as one of the counsels for the Board of Impeachment which removed Governor Sulzer in 1913, and was appointed a U.S. Attorney by President Harding in 1921. He resigned that position one year later and went to work for Attorney General Harry M. Daughtery as a special assistant working to prosecute striking western railway workers. Todd served in the same capacity in 1924 this time prosecuting Gaston B. Means and Colonel Thomas B. Felder for conspiring to obstruct justice. In 1929, Todd was appointed a Special Assistant District Attorney and took charge of the cases resulting from the failure of the City Trust Company. Subsequently, he was appointed a Special Assistant Attorney and worked on the case of former Magistrates George E. Ewald, Tammany leader Martin J. Healy, and Thomas K. Tommaney. *Ibid,* December 7, 1935: 1; December 10, 1935: 22.

[39] *Ibid.*, February 11, 1936: 7; February 18, 1936: 46; February 20, 1936: 1.

[40] *Ibid.*, February 20, 1936: 1; March 14, 1936: 1; March 17, 1936: 1; April 10, 1936: 33; May 19, 1936: 1.

[41] *Ibid.*, May 24, 1936: 1 & 2, and IV: 10.

[42] *Ibid.*, June 10, 1936: 1; June 11, 1936: 1; June 12, 1936: 2; June 13, 1936: 1; June 16, 1936: 1; June 19, 1936: 1; June 28, 1936: 1; July 1, 1936: 1.

[43] People v. Silverman, 297 N.Y.S. 449: 457–467.

[44] *The New York Times*, September 4, 1936: 1; September 5, 1936: 1; September 9, 1936: 1; September 18, 1936: 1.

[45] *Public Papers of Herbert H. Lehman*, 735–743.

[46] *The New York Times*, August 11, 1936: 1; August 12, 1936: 1.

[47] The Citizen's Committee on the Control of Crime in New York, Inc., *Crime in New York City in 1939* (New York, 1940), 18–19.

[48] John Harlan Amen, *Report of the Kings County Investigation, 1938–1942*. (New York, 1942), 8–9.

[49] *Ibid.*, 9–10.
Amen who was Grover Cleveland's son-in-law had been serving as a Special Assistant to the Attorney General of the United States for the past ten years. He recently had been "in charge of the rackets for prosecution in New York" and had launched a number of significant prosecutions under the so-called Federal anti-racketeering act. Among the cases handled by Amen were the "fish racket" where he convicted Joseph "Socks" Lanza and Louis Palermo, and the "artichoke racket". *The New York Times*, October 18, 1938: 1.

[50] Amen, 48–53.

[51] *Ibid.*, 84–87.

[52] *The New York Times*, October 22, 1938: 1; October 23, 1938: 39; October 25, 1938: 1; October 26, 1938: 2.

[53] Amen, 56–57.

[54] *Ibid.*, 58.

[55] *Ibid.*, 60–65.

[56] *Ibid.*, 65–73.

[57] *Ibid.*, 73–74.

[58] *Ibid.*, 123–125, 178–181.
"The lending policy of the shylock racket was done on a 6-for-5 basis. That is, for every $5 loaned a $6 repayment was required. The time of payment was generally six weeks. Due to the method of repaying the principal, the rate of interest was 342 per cent." *Ibid.*, 123–125.

[59] Amen also worked on a number of individual indictments which stemmed from evidence uncovered in his regular investigations. The most interesting of these cases was the indictment of Joe Adonis and Sam Gasberg for kidnapping and extortion, *Ibid.*, 177–178. Also see New York State Attorney General's Office, *a Report on the Administration by the Department of Corrections of the City of New York* (New York, 1943); Supreme Court State of New York—County of Kings, *A Presentment Concerning the Enforcement by the Police Department of the City of New York of the Laws Against Gambling*, (New York, 1942), and *A Presentment on the Execution of Bail Bonds*, (New York, 1941).

[60] *The New York Times*, May 11, 1939: 1; June 5, 1939: 36; August 26, 1939: 32; November 3, 1939: 1.

[61] A very strong case against both the work of Nadjari and of special prosecuting in general is Maurice Nessen, "No More Nadjari, No More Special Prosecuting," *Empire State Report* (February, 1977).

Chapter 5
O' Dwyer

To move from the Depression decade to the 1940s is to move from one social vista to another vastly different. The one intensely-inward looking seeking to explain the lost dream, the failed enterprise, by denouncing the "interests", the corrupt money-boys. In this sense, corruption went to the very core of sensibilities in the 1930s. In the dawning years of the next decade, however, meditation upon the navel of municipal politics and organized crime and criminality was almost impossible. No longer was the enterprise lost. On the contrary, the meaning of America was not even enterprise free or managed, but democracy and freedom. And the real enemies were tangible villains who lived and killed abroad. This was war and full employment! For a few short years organized crime and criminality were strictly bush-league political issues. But this situation would not out-last the war itself by many years. And as the euphoria of victory was replaced by the bewildering perplexities of peace, and the complexities of a new world of tension, the search for the sources of this tension, this almost unbearable anxiety, once more turned inward. Only this time it was not corruption which explained despair. This time it was conspiracy just as it had been after the last war. And when thoughts turned back to the mundane world of the city, and when charges of organized crime and criminality were once again raised, it would be in a radically new context. Conspiracy in 1950 was a world, or rather a war apart from conspiracy in 1930.

Much of the political career of William O'Dwyer, New York's major political figure of the decade, spanned this peculiar time and was centrally affected by changes in the symbolization of organized crime. As we will see, it is no exaggeration to hold O'Dwyer as the key political personality in New York during the 1940s, even though he was overshadowed by La Guardia in the early years. And it is not inappropriate to hold the meaning of his career contained within the changing perceptions of organized crime. The depths of O'Dwyer's fall can only be gauged by the interplay between the changing perception of organized crime emerging in the late 1940s and early 1950s, and his perceived betrayal of his former persona as a stalwart against syndicate criminals. In this sense, there is no comparing O'Dwyer and Walker even though both Democratic Mayors would resign the office trapped in the mire of organized crime and criminality. Walker was never a stalwart except in the pursuit of fun. No one with any savvy at all could ever feel betrayed by Walker. O'Dwyer was something quite different.

Born in Ireland, O'Dwyer migrated to the United States in 1910 and joined the Police Department in 1917. He left the Department in 1924 to pursue a private law practice. In the short period between the resignation of Mayor Walker and the special election to fill out Walker's term, the acting Mayor, McKee, appointed him a City Magistrate. His next office came in 1937 when Governor Lehman selected O'Dwyer to fill out a vacancy in the Brooklyn County Court. The following year he ran for the Judgeship and was elected for a 14 year term. From that position he moved to the office of Brooklyn District Attorney.

Almost immediately upon taking office O'Dwyer achieved fame in his investigation of the so-called Murder, Inc. mob of racketeers and killers. O'Dwyer tried to translate his success in the murder prosecutions into the Mayoralty and ran against La Guardia in 1941. He lost a rather close election to La Guardia and then in 1942 took a leave of absence from the District Attorney's office to join the Army. While in the military, according to historian William Howard Moore, "he rose to the rank of brigadier general through his work in uncovering fraud and mismanagement in the production and delivery of supplies for the Army Air Force".[1] O'Dwyer returned from military service to the prosecutor's office, but quickly resigned in August 1945 to run again for Mayor. This time he won in spite of a well publicized Grand Jury investigation managed by the interim Brooklyn District Attorney, Republican George J. Beldock appointed by Governor Dewey, which called into question O'Dwyer's handling of organized crime. In 1949 O'Dwyer vacillated between running for Mayor again or retiring, finally deciding to campaign. This perhaps unwanted victory rapidly turned dismal as Brooklyn District Attorney Miles McDonald began a major investigation into gambling and police corruption late in 1949. The evidence uncovered by McDonald was central in convincing O'Dwyer that he had had enough of New York politics and he resigned the Mayoralty in 1950 taking the post of Ambassador to Mexico which had been secured for him by Ed Flynn Democratic leader of the Bronx. O'Dwyer's tribulations were not over, however. In the spring of 1951 he returned to New York to testify before the Kefauver Committee which somewhat gleefully laid bare every shred of evidence and innuendo connecting O'Dwyer to the world of organized crime.

The Kefauver Committee had two targets in mind when it brought its road show to New York: Frank Costello and William O'Dwyer. Costello because he was reputed to be the key individual in a gangster triumvirate along with Joe Adonis and Meyer Lansky which controlled what had become in the Committee's opinion a single entity—organized crime. O'Dwyer was viewed as at least partially responsible for the success of Costello and therefore organized crime. Their importance was so great to the televised hearings that the Committee notes in its report:

> The New York hearings covered many facets, including the links between crime and politics, crime on the waterfront, large scale bookmaking and gambling operations, narcotics racketeering, operations at the Roosevelt Raceway, gambling conditions in Saratoga, the links particularly stressed both the personnel and the form of the huge crime syndicate which is primarily directed by Costello, Adonis and Lansky. Not all of these subjects were explored at the open hearings, or in the committee's investigations. Most of the subject matter, however, revolved around the testimony of two major witnesses, Frank Costello and William O'Dwyer. Both of these witnesses were questioned on a wide variety of subjects bearing on organized crime and its links with politics with the result that practically all of the information developed in the New York hearings could most expeditiously be related by reference to the testimony of these two witnesses.[2]

O'Dwyer's testimony before the Committee covers nine general topics including his work as District Attorney on the Murder, Inc. investigation, his "failure to prosecute Albert Anastasia", his attempts to block the McDonald investigation of police corruption and gambling, his relationships with Costello, Adonis, and other professional criminals, and the machinations of his friend and confidante the corrupt James Moran. The Committee's conclusion basically is that as District Attorney, for all his fine work in prosecuting notorious killers, he allowed the bosses and leaders to get away. And as the bosses of both the so-called Murder, Inc. mob and the Brooklyn waterfront were Albert Anastasia and Joe Adonis, his failure to prosecute either is evidence of O'Dwyer's corruption. In addition, his contacts or friendships with Costello and Adonis indicates how deeply enmeshed they were in municipal politics at the very least. The Kefauver conclusion holds:

> During, Mr. O'Dwyer's term of office as district attorney of Kings County, between 1940 and 1942, and his occupancy of the Mayoralty from 1946 to 1950, neither he nor his appointees took any effective action against the top echelons of the gambling, narcotics, waterfront, murder, or bookmaking rackets. In fact, his actions impeded promising investigations of such rackets. His defense of public officials who were derelict in their duties, and his actions in investigations of corruption, and his failure to follow up concrete evidence of organized crime, particularly in the case of Murder, Inc., and the waterfront, have contributed to the growth of organized crime, racketeering, and gangsterism in New York City.[3]

Prosecutor

William O'Dwyer's famous investigation into gangland murders began in a curious way with a letter sent from the City Workhouse by Harry Rudolph which implicated Abe Reles and several others in a seven-year old murder. Rudolph wrote that Reles, Martin Goldstein and "Dukey" Maffetore had murdered Rudolph's friend Alex Alpert in 1933. Apparently, Rudolph had been trying for years to tell someone in the prosecutor's office about the murder, but with little success. But the situation was different with the new administration and a murder indictment was secured from the Grand Jury. The apprehension of the three indicted men was suprisingly easy: when Reles and Goldstein heard that the police wanted to question them, they proceeded to walk in voluntarily, believing it to be of little consequence. Maffetore was arrested the same day the other two surrendered.[4]

Anthony "Duke" Maffatore

Abraham "Pretty" Levine

Harry "Happy" Maione

Frank "Dasher" Abbandando

The District Attorney's office immediately began trying to break down the arrested men hoping to get an informer. The first to talk was Maffetore who implicated his friend Abraham Levine in several crimes. Levine was arrested and subsequently pressured into talking. According to Assistant District Attorney Burton Turkus, Levine placed Harry Maione, Frank Abbandando, Louis Capone, Harry Strauss, Martin Goldstein, and Reles into an organization of murderers. And then, in March, 1940, Abe Reles turned informer and started describing a vast number of murders including the killers and accomplices.

Harry "Pittsburgh Phil" Strauss   *Martin "Bugsy" Goldstein*

On March 25, 1940, it was announced that the "mass murder inquiry ... moved closer to Louis (Lepke) Buchalter ... with the arrest and arraignment: of Albert Tannenbaum and Charles Workman".[5] Shortly after, District Attorney O'Dwyer identified Louis Capone as the liaison man between Buchalter and other important racketeers and the Brooklyn killers. In mid-April investigators for the District Attorney's office stated that they had tied Buchalter to the 1936 murder of Joseph Rosen a former garment truckman who was brutally shot in his Brooklyn candy store. Credit for this information was given to Reles and an unidentified material witness who was, in fact, Max Rubin the former Buchalter employee shot in 1937.

The first men brought to trial were Frank Abbandando and Harry Maione who were represented by former Assistant District Attorney William Kleinman. They were charged with the murder of gangster George Rudnick on May 24, 1937. Reles was the major prosecution witness; corroboration was furnished by Julie Catalano known as a worker for Maione in the bookmaking trade. Maione and Abbandando were convicted of murder in the first degree which carried a mandatory death sentence. They were not the first of the Brooklyn criminals to be executed, however. On December 31, 1940, the Court of Appeals reversed the judgement.[6] Quickly retried, both men were again convicted and in February, 1942, they were electrocuted, their delay making them the third and fourth of the killers executed. Preceding them to the electric chair were Martin Goldstein and Harry Strauss who were tried and convicted of the murder of Irving Feinstein in September, 1939.[7] Again Reles was the State's major witness testifying that the Feinstein murder was ordered by Albert Anastasia as a favor for his associate Vincent

Mangano. Reles's story was corroborated by criminals Seymour Magoon, Levine and Maffetore. In September, 1940, the accused were found guilty and were executed in June, 1941.

Julie Catalano   George Rudnick

By far the most important murder case presented by the O'Dwyer administration was the one in which Buchalter, Louis Capone and Emmanuel "Mendy" Weiss were charged with the murder of Joseph Rosen. The motivation for the murder was discussed by Max Rubin while the mechanics of the killing was developed by three other informers: Seymour Magoon, Albert Tannenbaum and Sholem Bernstein. As noted earlier the three defendants were convicted and eventually electrocuted after several years delay brought on by appeals and jurisdictional disputes between the State of New York and the Federal government over Buchalter.[8]

Emmanuel "Mendy" Weiss

The Buchalter trial opened on October 20, 1941. At that time O'Dwyer was certainly riding high as an unidentified summary of his work prepared for Mayor La Guardia indicates. Dated October 21, 1941, the three page report is simply titled "Rackets Work of Kings County District Attorney."[9] It begins with the Murder Ring Indictments:

★ People v. Goldstein, Reles and Maffatore (2/2/40)
Murder of Alexander Alpert on Nov. 25, 1933. Case is pending against
Reles and Maffetore. Alpert was obscure gangster—killed because
thought to have "talked".

★ People v. Buchalter, Weiss, Strauss, Feraco, Cohen and L. Capone
(5/28/40)
Murder of Joseph Rosen on Sept. 13, 1936. Case is now on trial. Rosen
was a potential Dewey witness "Lepke" Buchalter in the trucking racket
investigation—had Brownsville candy store.

★ People v. Maione, Abbandando and Strauss (3/29/40)
Murder of George Rudnick on May 25, 1937. Maione and Abbandando
found guilty on two trials, Strauss severed motion of D.A. Rudnick was
former triggerman for Murder Ring who turned stool pigeon.

★ People v. Abbandando and Golob (3/28/40)
Murder of John Murtha on March 3, 1935. Case is pending against Golob.
Murtha was a gangster and ex-convict.

James Feraco   *Max "The Jerk" Golob*

★ People v. Goldstein and Strauss (4/12/40)
Murder of Irving Feinstein on Sept. 4, 1939. Both found guilty—
conviction upheld. Feinstein tried to muscle in on loan shark racket,
according to papers.

★People v. Gurino, Abbandando and Maione (9/13/40)
Murder of Cesare Lattero on Feb. 6, 1939. Case is pending against Gurino.
Lattero and Siciliano were union plasterers believed to have been killed
because they refused to "eliminate" Calogero Veruso.

★ People v. Aloi, Melia, DeGregorio, Cortese, G. Capone (5/3/40)
Attempted murder of Calogero Veruso of Feb. 3, 1939. Case is pending.
Veruso was leader of group in plasterers' union which was protesting
against kickbacks to racketeers represented by G. Capone, union delegate,
brother of L. Capone.

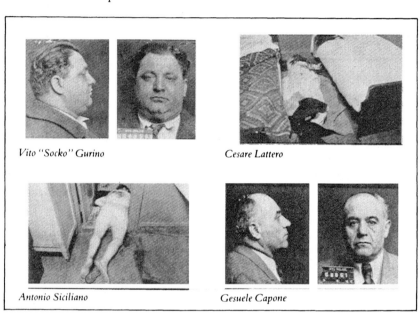

Vito "Socko" Gurino *Cesare Lattero*

Antonio Siciliano *Gesuele Capone*

★People v. Nitzberg and Shapiro (7/2/40)
Murder of Albert Shuman on Jan. 9, 1939. Nitzberg was convicted.
Believe Shapiro not yet apprehended. Shuman thought to be giving
information about Buchalter. Nitzberg, a gunman friend of Shuman, was
imported from Bronx to do job. Reles testified Anastasia O.K.'d job.

★ People v. Strauss and Goldstein. (8/21/40)
Murder of Irving Amron on Sept. 15, 1935. Defendants have been
executed.

★ People v. Strauss and Goldstein (8/7/40)
Murder of Abraham Meer on Sept. 15, 1935. Defendants have been
executed. Meer and Amron shot because they refused to split robbery
proceeds.

In addition to the above indictments the summary notes that "O'Dwyer announced on June 4, 1940 that 57 murders involving that ring had been solved." The report continues: "O'Dwyer also obtained one murder indictment against members of a smaller murder ring charged with ten killings, including those of Rubin Shapiro and Harry Halpern." This particular ring known as the Larney Mob was "headed by the Ludkowitz brothers, loan sharks and gambling racketeers, and included Mrs. Rose Pantiel". The summary then adds an interesting caveat: "Outside of his work on the murder rings, O'Dwyer appears to have accomplished little in prosecuting rackets." It mentions that he has claimed to investigate "gangster control over the International Longshoremen's Association" whose leader is the fugitive Albert Anastasia, but it clearly reserves concluding that he has.

It is very important to realize that as early as October 1941 doubts had been raised—even thought only in a private communication to Mayor La Guardia—about the performance of O'Dwyer in connection with organized crime on the Brooklyn waterfront and Albert Anastasia. As the Kefauver report indicates it is a problem that would grow and haunt O'Dwyer in the years to come. But it has always been assumed that the origin of this suspicion began several weeks later with the spectacular death of informer Abe Reles. The Reles death while not in itself responsible for the initial suspicions no doubt enormously increased them.

The Canary That Couldn't Fly

The enigmatic death of informer Abe Reles is one of the key events in the history of organized crime and politics in New York. At the least it functions to cast grave doubt on the honesty of O'Dwyer and several of his closest associates as well as serving as a seemingly tangible link to the unindicted Albert Anastasia. No one did more to develop these themes than Assistant District Attorney Burton B. Turkus the prosecutor of most of the Murder, Inc., cases and author of *Murder, Inc.* a publication discussed earlier and one which is still to be more fully explored.

To begin with, Reles's death occurred simultaneously with the murder trial of Buchalter, Weiss and Capone. Reles could offer no direct testimony at this trial, however, since he had been in jail when the murder of Joseph Rosen took place. Nevertheless, the prosecutor Turkus felt as though he had been "kicked in the stomach" when informed that Reles had died. Turkus was upset by several peculiarities surrounding the death. For one, he only learned about it when a reporter telephoned him at home: "The key witness plunges to his death right in the middle of the biggest of all Murder, Inc., trials ... and the trial prosecutor has to learn of it from an outsider."[10] For another, Turkus found the details of Reles's death, which was described as an attempted escape that failed, strange. Sometime early in the morning of November 12, 1941, "Reles had twisted two bedsheets together, tied a length of wire to them, and wrapped the wire around a radiator pipe. He had flipped his home-made rope out … had slid down it, and was trying to get into the window of the room below his own when the wire came loose." With his rope broken, Reles crashed "forty-two feet to the roof of a kitchen extension of the hotel".

Reles along with fellow informers Sholem Bernstein, Albert Tannenbaum and Mikey Syckoff "had been guarded in the Half Moon Hotel on the Coney Island waterfront". The witnesses and their special police guard had taken over the entire east wing of the hotel's sixth floor which had been altered to make it a supposedly "impregnable fortress". To fortify the area "a steel door had been erected from wall to wall, sealing off the entire section". Situated "just back of the steel door, on the outer side", was a room used only by the detectives who were supposed to be guarding the "entrance at all times".[11]

Meyer "Mickie" Sykoff   *Abe "Kid Twist" Reles*

Turkus continues noting that the death of Reles was a momentous event for Brooklyn law enforcement: "Investigations galore were started. Charges of neglect of duty were filed against the five officers on duty in the suite that morning." The mysteries surrounding the case proved to be so compelling that it was periodically reopened. Writing himself ten years after the event, Turkus comments that there still remain unanswered questions. For example, there were contradictory statements about the number of guards permanently assigned to watch the witnesses and whether or not the guards remained in the informers' bedrooms while the witnesses slept. And there were conflicting stories about the results of the autopsy, not to mention the startling fact that Reles's body landed over twenty feet from the side of the hotel, Turkus contends, an incredible distance if he had truly fallen from his makeshift rope.

These inconsistencies and unaccountable facts, according to Turkus, led to the supposition that Reles had been murdered. And if Reles was murdered, it follows that the police on duty were accomplices. But the police did not murder Reles at their own discretion. The motivation for the killing, if such it was, came from others in positions of political and legal authority who wanted Reles killed to prevent him from testifying against Albert Anastasia. Turkus writes: "When Kid Twist hit that extension roof … none breathed a more lusty sigh at the Kid's finale than Albert Anastasia, his boss". Turkus finishes his account by accusing O'Dwyer of failing to prosecute a "perfect murder case" against Anastasia for which Reles would have been the key witness, although not the only one. The implication is clear: O'Dwyer and high members of his administration in concert with Anastasia arranged to have Reles thrown out the window.[12]

Albert Anastasia

So compelling and indeed important is the death of Reles that the September 1951 Brooklyn Grand Jury considered it necessary to attempt to determine the real story and end speculation. Their *Presentment* notes: "Recently the Kefauver Committee highlighted this occurrence. Limitation of time and other important phases of that Committee's investigation left the Abe Reles death more a riddle than ever."[13] It states that Reles, 37 years old, "fell to his death as a consequence of his attempting to escape from his room".[14] The Grand Jury goes on, however, deploring "the lack of proper investigation and the loose manner in which this important occurrence was investigated by the reponsible agencies concerned".[15] Nevertheless, it contends unequivocally that Reles "did not meet with foul play and that he did not die by suicide".[16]

As one might guess, however, the Grand Jury investigation and *Presentment* did not end speculation or suspicion. In fact, in one area it materially increases doubt concerning O'Dwyer's honesty and involvement with Anastasia. According to a number of writers and stories, it was

O'Dwyer's claim that the most important reason why Anastasia had not been indicted during his tenure as District Attorney (up to the time he left for military service) was that Reles was his key witness. With Reles dead the so-called "perfect murder case" was lost. This claim, of course, has fed much of the speculation which places O'Dwyer in the middle of a murder to protect Anastasia. In response to this issue the Grand Jury states:

> Much of the speculation that was indulged in concerning Reles' death centered about the theory that Abe Reles was the corroborating witness against one Albert Anastasia in the killing of one Morris (Moish) Diamond, on May 25, 1939.
> This is the murder which former District Attorney O'Dwyer characterized as "the perfect case" which "went out the window with Reles".
> Our investigation has disclosed that Abe Reles was not a corroborating witness in that killing. On the contrary, as a matter of law, he was only one of several accomplices. In view of the availability of the other accomplices, it follows that Reles was not even an essential witness. The prosecution of Anastasia required corroboration and Reles could not have supplied it.[17]

The Grand Jury's conclusion, then, is that the death of Reles could not support O'Dwyer's reluctance to press a murder indictment against Anastasia. O'Dwyer is, therefore, left in this precarious position: if Reles was murdered to protect Anastasia then the District Attorney was involved in either the murder or cover-up; if Reles died attempting to escape and was not necessary for a successful prosecution of Anastasia then O'Dwyer was criminally negligent in not pressing forward with an investigation and indictment.

None of this material became a public issue until O'Dwyer returned from military service and resigned as District Attorney in order to run for Mayor. At that time Governor Dewey appointed George J. Beldock, Jr., District Attorney to complete O'Dwyer's term. In what was clearly a bid to undermine O'Dwyer's candidacy as well as to enhance Beldock's campaign for election as District Attorney, Beldock initiated a Grand Jury probe into the O'Dwyer office. Among the issues investigated was the Anastasia "perfect murder case". As part of their work the Grand Jury examined a "Confidential Memorandum" concerning Anastasia prepared for O'Dwyer by Burton B. Turkus and dated April 8, 1942. The gist of the memorandum is that the investigation into the affairs of Albert Anastasia "has failed to adduce a scintilla of available competent evidence aside from or in corroboration of the testimony of accomplices".[18] And, the memorandum continues, "The corroboration supplied by Reles as set forth in the supplemental report of the Chief Investigator, likewise attached hereto, expired with Reles. Thus as the investigation now stands, no successful prosecution of Anastasia may be had."[19] The Turkus report concludes with the plea that the "matter of corroborative evidence should proceed with re-doubled effort and every lead in such direction followed through exhaustively".[20]

Upon first glance this memorandum appears to submarine the Turkus claim advanced in his book, *Murder, Inc.*, that O'Dwyer and certain members of his administration had been protecting Anastasia, as well as the 1951 Grand Jury *Presentment* that Reles could not have supplied corroboration for an Anastasia murder. But as Turkus points out in *Murder, Inc.* his memorandum was a summary of a report by "Chief Investigator Frank C. Bals dealing with the status of the investigation as to Albert Anastasia". It is the Bals' report which furnished the pessimistic conclusions contained in the memorandum. This particular report notes that according to Reles the "following killings were committed by Anastasia, either in person or by direction":[21]

Name of Victim	*Date of Killing*
Giuseppe Peraino, alias	
"Clutching Hand"	March 27, 1930
Carlo Bonacurso	June 24, 1930
Guiseppe Massaria, alias	
"Joe-the-Boss"	April 15, 1931
Angelo Simonelli,	
Charles Martura and	
Joseph Barberi	August 14, 1931
Rocco Morganti	October 16, 1932
Joseph Amberg and	
Morris Kessler	September 30, 1935
Frank Keenan	September 19, 1937
Antonio Siciliana and	
Cesare Lattaro	February 6, 1939
Felice Esposito	February 9, 1939

Morris (Mersh)
Diamond   May 25, 1939

Irving Penn (Bronx
County)   July, 1939

Irving (Puggy) Feinstein   September 5, 1939

Michael Spataro   December 14, 1939

Bals added that for all the murders (and there were others which will be discussed later) involving Anastasia there is no corroboration. With the death of Reles, who, Bals notes, "was under police guard in the Half Moon Hotel, Brooklyn",[22] the State was deprived of his testimony and information. It was this report which was the source of the Turkus memorandum. And it is the character of Frank C. Bals, Chief Investigator of the Special Investigation Squad of the District Attorney's Office, Kings County, which is of immediate interest. Bals, it turns out, was the Commander of the special police guard at the Half Moon Hotel. Despite the Reles plunge, Bals enjoyed the complete confidence of O'Dwyer who, when he won the Mayoralty, appointed Bals to the post of seventh deputy police commissioner in charge of a special squad to investigate various aspects of organized crime. While in charge of this squad, Bals is alleged to have received substantial protection payments from bookmaker Harry Gross the subject of the 1949 investigation mentioned earlier into police corruption and gambling.

The complicated Anastasia case and its repercussions on the public career of O'Dwyer does not end with the speculations concerning the death of Reles and the role of Captain Bals. There are other individuals whose mysterious actions were also scrutinized by the Beldock Grand Jury. Among them none was more prominent and indeed important than the Chief Clerk of the District Attorney's office, James J. Moran. According to Turkus, Moran, O'Dwyer, Bals, and Assistant District Attorney Heffernan were "in charge of the investigation into the activities of Anastasia" which prompted his memorandum which closed with the plea to keep the investigation going. But the " 'wanted' card on Anastasia was removed from the files of the Police Investigation Bureau!"[23] The removal of the wanted card had the effect, Turkus states, "of a formal announcement to the police that the District Attorney no longer is seeking that particular man".[24] The order to remove the Anastasia card came from Chief Clerk Moran shortly after the Bals report. The Moran order was transmitted to Police Sergeant Elwood

Divvers, who, Turkus relates, is "the same sergeant who was second in command of the guards who slept so soundly the morning Reles jumped, fell or was thrown from the Half Moon Hotel".[25] The cast of characters allegedly aiding Anastasia includes O'Dwyer, Moran, Bals, Divvers, and Heffernan.

Campaign Talk and the 1945 Grand Jury

Albert Anastasia was not the only notorious gangster named as a virtual ward of the Brooklyn District Attorney's office in the fall of 1945. Also prominently discussed by Beldock during that remarkably tumultuous campaign was Vito Genovese. Public attention was first aroused by Beldock on October 18, 1945, when he broadcast over WOR Radio a talk entitled "Mystery in the D.A.'s Office".

> Tonight let us consider the mystery of the two men indicted for murder in the first degree and the strange paralysis which fell upon the District Attorney's Office of Kings County when the case broke. The two men were key figures of the New York underworld with international connections, Mike Mirandi and Vito Genovese.
>
> The official paralysis of the District Attorney's Office persisted for twelve months. It terminated last August when the head of that office, William O'Dwyer, resigned. The murder victim in this case was one "Bocchia", known as "The Shadow". He was shot down in Brooklyn some years ago by hired killers.[26]

Beldock states that the killers and the men who hired them, Mirandi and Genovese, were arrested but almost immediately discharged. And then in 1944 almost a decade after the murder, the case broke open with a confession by one of the participants. Subsequently, a Brooklyn Grand Jury indicted Mirandi, Genovese and four others. However, by that time all six men were fugitives. And then nicely timing his remarks, Beldock announces that Chief Clerk James J. Moran knew and had known exactly where Genovese was. Genovese, it turns out, was "acting as interpreter for the Allied Military Government in Italy".[27] In addition to this position, Genovese was charged with being the "boss of the black market" in Italy. In fact, he "had been arrested by the Military Police on August 22, 1944 which was only two weeks after his indictment for murder in Brooklyn".[28] In charge of the Genovese investigation was Assistant District Attorney Heffernan who, Beldock charges, did nothing to have Genovese extradited although he also was aware that Genovese was in Italy and being held by the Military Police. And finally, William O'Dwyer not only knew where Genovese was but had seen him in Italy, where O'Dwyer was stationed, in the custody of the Military Police. Moran knew, Heffernan knew, and most importantly O'Dwyer knew where Genovese was, that he was indicted for murder, and they did nothing to secure his return. Beldock ends his talk with a blast:

O'Dwyer knew Genovese was in Italy. Surely he knew about this case. Why? He knew the people in it. He knew the actual killers. The triggermen who shot down Bocchia, "The Shadow," were old clients of O'Dwyer's before he became the Brooklyn Prosecutor.

Yes, Mr. O'Dwyer had come a long way too and if his memory is long dimmed and if it needs refreshing on these old associations, I can give him these docket numbers.[29]

Almost all of Beldock's information concerning Genovese and O'Dwyer in Italy came from Agent Orange C. Dickey, Criminal Investigation Division of the U.S. Army. Dickey whose previous job was as a campus patrolman at Pennsylvania State College had been investigating "black market activities in olive oil and wheat in Italy".[30] Working with an informer named Francesco Traisci, Dickey learned that Genovese was the "leader of a large contraband ring".[31] On the 22nd of August, 1944, Dickey arrested Genovese and ordered him held in the Military Police jail in Naples. Dickey next contacted an informant "whose name is Julius Simonelli, a former resident of New York City".[32] From Simonelli he received a copy of Craig Thompson and Raymond Allen's *Gang Rule in New York* (1940) which tells that "Genovese was a former gunman of New York City, and associated with Lucky Luciano's gang".[33] Dickey pursued his growing interest in Genovese and subsequently found out that he had been indicted for homicide in Brooklyn. But for the next six months or so, Dickey had an enormous amount of trouble locating anyone in the U.S. military who cared to pursue the Genovese black marketeering case.

To try and find someone to take Genovese off his hands, Dickey went to Rome to see Colonel Charles Poletti the commander of the American Military Government in Italy. Poletti had been a New York State Supreme Court Justice and then a successful candidate for Lieutenant Governor serving under Herbert Lehman. He left that position shortly after Governor Lehman resigned in December 1942. Poletti then joined the Army and assumed command of the military government. It was while attempting to speak with the allegedly constantly drunk and usually incoherent Poletti that Dickey met General O'Dwyer. In relating this meeting Dickey recounts:

We spoke casually about the type of work C.I.D. did, and I mentioned the fact that I had in custody a man whom the District Attorney of Brooklyn was interested in, and of course, I already knew that General O'Dwyer was District Attorney here.

I told him it was Vito Genovese, and I asked him what Mr. Hughes (Assistant District Attorney Thomas C. Hughes nominally in charge of the Brooklyn office while O'Dwyer was in the Army) intended to do with the man ... He answered that the case didn't concern him.[34]

It seemed to Agent Dickey that he was the only person in either Italy or New York who was concerned with Genovese. Rumors of extradition proceedings had reached Dickey, but they were exceptionally vague at best. He, therefore, took the initiative of obtaining the necessary orders from the Executive Officer of the Criminal Investigation Division, Major Orcutt, and proceeded to bring Genovese back to New York himself. He notified the District Attorney's Office of Kings County by cable that he was departing Italy with Genovese and asked to be met "at the boat with warrants and with an escort". On June 1, 1945, they arrived in New York and as Dickey says, "Nobody met me at the boat".[35] Dickey then took Genovese to the District Attorney's office and placed him in the custody of Assistant District Attorney Edward A. Heffernan who, Dickey reports, was very surprised.

The Genovese story was far from over, however. Beldock in his broadcast points out that between the time the District Attorney's office was officially notified that Genovese was being held in Italy and Agent Dickey's voyage, "a tragic thing happened". The key corroborating witness in the murder case, Pete LaTempa, was poisoned while being held as a material witness.

> ... LaTempa pleaded and he begged to be held elsewhere than in the Raymond Street jail. He was scared. He said something was wrong there. Other witnesses in Brooklyn, including killers had been kept in other jails and even in hotels. His last request to Heffernan for transfer from this jail was made on January 15, 1945. The very next morning LaTempa was found dead, poisoned under very mysterious circumstances.[36]

With LaTempa dead, the possibility of convicting Genovese appears to have died also. Nevertheless, Genovese was brought to trial, for reasons that are not all clear, and secured a directed verdict of acquittal. On June 11, 1946, Judge Samuel Leibowitz faced with no other choice freed Genovese with these parting words: "I cannot speak for the jury, but I believe if there was even a shred of corroborating evidence you would have been condemned to the chair".[37] The other five men involved in the murder were never brought to trial on the premise that if there was no corroboration in the Genovese case it would be fruitless to pursue the others. This is, of course, a totally indefensible proposition given that among the others were the gunmen who shot Bocchia and there were plenty of witnesses to the actual shooting.

Clearly a number of exceptionally strange and suspect decisions had been made concerning the whole case. First, Genovese is brought to trial with no hope of his conviction; second the other conspirators and actual gunmen are simply written off despite the availability of witnesses to the murder if not the whole conspiracy. But perhaps the most mysterious element of all (aside from the murder of LaTempa) is that according to documents found among the O'Dwyer papers in the Municipal Archives, LaTempa may not have been a corroborating witness under New York Law. In order to obtain a conviction "it is necessary to secure a second witness who had nothing to do with the commission of the crime. The law plainly specifies that a nonaccomplice must connect the defendant with the crime".[38]

On June 13, 1944, Assistant District Attorney Heffernan interrogated the key informer in the Genovese case—Ernest Rupolo. While Rupolo was totally incompetent in discussing the Purge as mentioned in the Introduction, he was one of the principals in the Bocchia affair. Rupolo's statement notes:

The "Shadow" was an outlaw according to the 'mob', taking over big shots. He 'took' TONY BENDER and the orders went out that he was to be killed and also WILLIE GALLO his stooge.

MIKE MIRANDO is good friends with the big shot "Bender" and he and "VIDONE" (VITO GENOVESE) assigned me to kill GALLO and I said I would use "SOLLY" Palmeri. They also assigned 'Blair' (GEO. SMURA), GUS FRASCA and another man named "SOLLY" to kill "SHADOW". These orders were given to BLAIR, GUS, SOLLY and myself at a Numbers Office in Mulberry St., PETE DEFEO gave the orders and MIKE MIRANDA was there and also "PETE SPATZ". SPATZ was given money to play cards with the

Peter *"Petie Spatz" La Tempa*

Michael *"Mirandi" Mirando*

Ferdinand *"The Shadow" Boccia*

George *Smurra*   Salvatore *Zappola*   Gus *Frasca*

SHADOW in his uncles Coffee Shop on Metropolitan Ave., and the others would come in and kill him. This was about two days before the killing. The last day DEFEO sent the order out to "cowboy" him, which meant any place you see him, shoot him.[39]

The individual named Pete Spatz in this account is none other than Pete LaTempa and was clearly an accomplice. He was involved in the conspiracy and was to play the important role of distracting the victim prior to the shooting. But while LaTempa was an accomplice there were, as previously noted, witnesses who could corroborate the murder. In what seems to be a Detective's notes[40] there appears a list of "Witnesses on premises night Bocchia was shot":

Benjamin Boccia	Rocco DeMartino
John Boccia	Thomas Napolitano
Patsy Caliendo	
Frank Musucci	
Angelo Rainone	
Joe Caccavillo	
Thomas Gulino	
Carmine Rizzano	
Sandolino Sotoro	

Why LaTempa was considered to be a corroborating witness, why he was murdered and by whom, why Genovese was brought to trial when he was, and finally, why the killers were never prosecuted are all unanswered questions.

When Beldock chose to campaign for District Attorney in 1945 on the issue of corruption in the O'Dwyer administration he was privy to much more information than he was able to reveal in his various pronouncements. For instance, it is obvious that James J. Moran was the major bridge between the underworld and Brooklyn criminal justice. The conclusion is inescapable given the nature of questions asked Moran in the autumn Grand Jury hearings. Although Moran denied any corrupt or criminal activities most of his denials were countered by other Grand Jury witnesses. Moran was questioned about the 1935 murders of gangsters Amberg and Kessler and whether or not Vincent Mangano had ordered the killings. He claimed total ignorance. He was asked whether or not he was instrumental in the loss of the "trial sheet in the Diamond case", and replied no. Next, the questioning turned to the Brooklyn waterfront and Moran's role in the aborted investigation which started on April 30, 1940. He admitted finding the body of insurgent longshoreman Peter Panto but denied knowing anything about the killing. Moran did state, however, that he knew both Joseph Ryan and Emil Camarda officers of the International Longshoremen's Association. Camarda along with Anastasia had been prime suspects in Panto's murder.

The interrogation of Moran moved from the waterfront to his relationships with various criminals. He acknowledged a long but intermittent friendship with Joe Adonis meeting him at Adonis's restaurant and at various local racetracks. He also recalled attending a political dinner with Adonis at Johnny Crews Sixth Assembly District political club. From Adonis, Beldock moved to Frank Costello. Moran stated that he had met Costello a number of times including once at Costello's Manhattan apartment. On this particular trip Moran was accompanied by then District Attorney O'Dwyer. Moran and O'Dwyer also visited with suspected racketeer Irving Sherman. In fact, Sherman enjoyed a close relationship with Moran who testified that Sherman called him many times on his private telephone in the District Attorney's office. Other criminals and power brokers Moran knew included racketeer Benny Steinberg and bail bondsman Al Newman. Beldock asked Moran whether he had directed the discharge of informers Sholem Bernstein and Albert Tannenbaum potential witnesses against Albert Anastasia. Bernstein and Tannenbaum were held as material witnesses along with Reles, but they were discharged by the District Attorney's office in 1942 right after Police Captain Bals had reported that there was no corroborating evidence against Anastasia. Moran denied responsibility for anything of any importance that went on in the prosecutor's office.

Q. There has been some testimony of witnesses that Mr. Heffernan worked directly under you, Mr. Moran. Does that agree with your recollection of what took place in the office?
A. It does not.

Q. You say very emphatically that Mr. Heffernan didn't work under you, do you?
A. Yes, and I disagree with Mr. Hughes and Mr. Hanley (two Assistant District Attorneys).

Q. There has been some testimony that at times you overruled the Chief Assistant in the office. Do you disagree with that?
A. That is not true.

Q. And you never gave any instructions to the Assistants how to handle their cases?
A. I did not.

Q. And you never instructed them to stop any prosecutions?
A. I did not.

According to Moran his work as Chief Clerk was almost totally clerical and he consciously avoided knowing anything about the stunning investigations into murder and organized crime even when those investigations involved his and O'Dwyer's friends and acquaintances. The only time he diverted from his studied routine of unbounded ignorance came "in the early part of 1940, when Murder-Incorporated first began". At that time Moran testified that he "took stenographic notes from witnesses *so there would be no leaks*" (my emphasis). It is simply astonishing to consider that last remark in the light of Moran's admitted relationships. If nothing else, Moran certainly had a great deal of confidence when questioned by the Beldock Grand Jury in 1945.

And in the late fall of 1945 both Moran's and O'Dwyer's confidence seems to have been well founded. On November 6, 1945, O'Dwyer won the Mayoralty in a walk. He carried every assembly district in the city except Manhattan's 9th. His total vote was 1,119,225 compared to the 434,050 of his nearest rival. This despite the fact that the Beldock Grand Jury had issued a damning Presentment only days prior to the election. For his trouble, Beldock was defeated in the race for District Attorney by Miles McDonald. As far as the organized crime issue went at this time, O'Dwyer easily surmounted it pointing always to his murder convictions of Buchalter and the others and to his military service. O'Dwyer's stock answer to suggestions that his subordinates had grossly mishandled their prosecutive responsibilities was to hold himself at more than arm's length. He was too busy fighting Nazis and Fascists to either worry about or be responsible for corroborating witnesses, etc.

One would think that the investigative Grand Jury in Brooklyn would have quietly folded its tent after O'Dwyer's victory. But it did not. With a lame duck prosecutor it continued probing the O'Dwyer administration's recent past and issued a second even more damning Presentment on December 20. This was the Anastasia Presentment which closes with the statement that

> Shocking abuses of public trust and confidence cannot go unchallenged. The consistent and complete failure to prosecute the 'overlord' of organized crime in Brooklyn, where the evidence was admittedly sufficient to warrant his conviction, is so revolting that we cannot permit these disclosures to be filed away in the same manner that the evidence against Anastasia were heretofore put 'in the files'.[41]

Before issuing the second Presentment the Grand Jury questioned Mayor-elect O'Dwyer for approximately ten hours. At one point a Grand Juror asked O'Dwyer whether he agreed with the Jury in "handing up the presentment". O'Dwyer replied, "Yes, I agree that the presentment was fully justified and I will say so at any time".[42] The duration of that sentiment lasted only until the next presentment when O'Dwyer blasted all the findings of the Grand Jury as political bunk. And then in a rather neat maneuver "Moran went to Kings County Judge Franklin Taylor and pointed out that there were technical flaws connected with the presentments". Taylor's response was to order the presentments "stricken and expunged" from the records.[43]

There is an interesting coda to the Beldock Grand Jury investigation. Even with Beldock gone and with the Grand Jury severely chastised by Judge Taylor its investigative work continued under Brooklyn's new District Attorney, Miles McDonald. Very little was accomplished but it is clear that Moran remained a central target. This time it was his connection to a gambling syndicate that was explored. This particular syndicate was a policy ring headed by none other than Abe Frosch who had played a minor but important role in the Amen investigation into the bail bond racket. As far as the Amen probe went, Frosch had not been linked to anything but corrupt bonding beginning as a runner for his mother, Lena. But it is also the case that while Frosch was in Amen's custody he was allowed to meet privately with Abe Reles while Reles was being held by O'Dwyer's office. This curious meeting was supposedly only concerned with an attempt by Reles to bribe his way out of trouble. Frosch was to serve as his liaison. It was obviously embarrassing to Amen that Frosch was a party to this scheme while in his jurisdiction and the story never appears in the Amen Report. Even more startling than the above, it appears that Frosch took over at least part of Reles's gambling operation as well as the policy operation run by Abe Babchick a murdered racketeer whose ring was exposed by Amen. In 1943 Miles McDonald was an Assistant District Attorney in the O'Dwyer office, although he was completely removed from the Murder, Inc., investigation and the machinations engaged in by Moran, Heffernan, and the others.

Abraham Frosch

McDonald broke the Frosch gambling syndicate in 1943 and sent the gambler to Sing Sing prison. In January, 1946, District Attorney McDonald brought Frosch back from prison to question him before the Grand Jury about his relationships with both Moran and bondsman Al Newman. It was McDonald's contention, although he was not able to prove it, that Moran protected the policy racket and that Newman served as the major intermediary.

This was the last gasp of what had begun as the Beldock Grand Jury. It had raised enormously important questions about the tie between politics, criminal justice, and organized crime. But it had ultimately failed to disrupt the social system. O'Dwyer's popularity and the tumult of World War II plus the absence of reform sentiment in the callous Borough of Brooklyn had all combined to chase its obsessions into an ever receding background. O'Dwyer was Mayor, Bals a Deputy Police Inspector and Moran was appointed by the Mayor to the position of First Deputy Commissioner of the New York Fire Department.

Exit O'Dwyer

The unravelling of O'Dwyer's New York political career over the issue of organized crime which had seemingly threatened in 1945 actually began in 1949 after his second triumphant campaign for Mayor. The immediate cause of O'Dwyer's growing troubles was Miles McDonald's investigation into police corruption and gambling in Brooklyn. This special investigation "officially began on December 22nd, 1949, when District Attorney Miles F. McDonald appeared in County Court and applied to Judge Samuel S. Leibowitz for an extension of the term of the regular December, 1949 Grand Jury".[44] Unofficially, the probe started somewhat earlier when Brooklyn *Eagle* reporter Ed Reid notified McDonald that he had information on gambling in Brooklyn and was about to begin a series of articles on "bookies, operating with political connections".[45] Quickly the investigation opened into one concerned with connivance between gamblers and police.

The first solid evidence that an "alliance existed between some members of the Police Department and gamblers came in a raid conducted in April, 1950". Bookmaking establishments were raided and slips were found with the word "ice" and various sums of money indicated. As the Grand Jury notes, " 'Ice' is the recognized term among gamblers and the underworld for protection money paid to the police".[46] It should be pointed out that as soon as McDonald realized where the investigation was leading he refused to use any members of the Police Department except for a select number of "rookies" straight out of the Academy. He thereby established a group loyal to the investigation without any prior commitment to the Force or at least to the systems of accommodation and corruption. From the initial raids which convinced McDonald of the scope and seriousness of the problem the inquiry moved ever closer to the largest operation of all—the Harry Gross ring.

On September 15, 1950, McDonald's special police raided Gross' "main wire room" in Inwood, Long Island, as well as all the other gambling premises which were part of the Gross operation. In all 34 individuals were arrested including Gross. That night Gross was held as a "material witness" on the promise, somewhat delayed, that he could and would "tell a story of vast overall corruption in the Police Department". In between the time of his arrest and his appearance before the Grand Jury, Gross was charged with 66 counts of bookmaking and conspiracy. The case came to trial in January, 1951, and after only a few witnesses were called Gross changed his plea to guilty. It was after his conviction but before his sentencing that Gross apparently decided to honor his initial promise to testify before the Grand Jury.

The Gross story began in the early 1940s, according to the Grand Jury summary of his testimony.

> He was operating in the area of Flatbush and Church Avenues. Two plainclothesmen apprehended him while he was making book. They told him he was operating like a small timer by "cheating" (making book without police protection), and that he should smarten up and make arrangements with the plainclothes squad in that division.... Systematic bi-monthly payments to the plainclothesmen were set up.[47]

From this somewhat modest beginning the "payoff system snowballed". Gross opened up new establishments and thereby increased the number of his patrons: "He quickly reached the point where payments to each division's plainclothes squad were insufficient." As he expanded outside neighborhood limits "he needed protection from squads having borough wide and city wide jurisdiction over gambling". This included, of course, Bals' special squad. In fact, it was the structure of law enforcement in Brooklyn that indicated the range of Gross' payments.

> On the 1st and 15th of each month he paid every division plainclothes squad in which he had a gambling spot. In addition, he paid for each telephone he used in the division. There were extra payments to precinct plainclothesmen and precinct captains. The borough wide squads were paid for each location in their jurisdiction. The Chief Inspector's squad and the Police Commissioner's squad having city-wide jurisdiction were paid for all locations. Inspectors in charge of divisions received regular payments as did lieutenants in charge of plainclothes squads.[48]

Following his Grand Jury appearance 21 officers were indicted and another 57 were named as undicted co-conspirators. The amount of money Gross is supposed to have paid annually for protection or what might better be termed extortion was around $1,000,000.

The manner in which O'Dwyer was drawn into this case displays a certain amount of brazen stupidity on his part. First of all, O'Dwyer disliked McDonald ever since McDonald had continued the original Beldock investigation. When McDonald began his 1949 probe, O'Dwyer tried several fairly low-key methods to submarine it. Aside from whatever personal pique he had against McDonald, the Mayor was keenly interested in protecting the general reputation of what many considered his Police Department, and, naturally, the careers of such close friends as Bals and Moran. Norton Mockridge and Robert H. Prall write that as early as the fall of 1949 "there were reports around town that Moran was on the take, . . . and that he had put the pressures on bookies, gamblers, and racketeers for contributions to the O'Dwyer campaign fund".[49] Still concerning Moran, they note it was common knowledge that he was deeply involved "with Louis Weber, one of the city's policy racket big shots, who was a constant visitor at Moran's office in the Municipal Building, across from City Hall".[50] From Weber to Gross must have seemed a very small and logical step to those concerned. In any case, O'Dwyer soon made his objections to McDonald's investigation public in a most sensational and damaging way.

The occasion for O'Dwyer's public stance was the suicide in July, 1950 of Police Captain John G. Flynn, Commander of the Fourth Avenue Precinct in Brooklyn. Flynn's suicide followed his appearance before the Grand Jury. And, although Flynn "left a note saying that his Grand Jury appearance had nothing to do with his death", a fast spreading rumor was "launched that he was a victim of this investigation".[51] It was therefore decided to use Flynn's funeral as a protest against the investigation and McDonald. Approximately 6,000 police attended. O'Dwyer seized the occasion to brand McDonald's work a "witch hunt, and a war of nerves made popular by Hitler".[52] In effect, O'Dwyer all but claimed McDonald as the killer of Flynn. Encouraged by O'Dwyer's statement, several police officers next "induced" Flynn's widow to confront McDonald in the County Court and there to accuse him of murder. This emotional confrontation was followed by a formal complaint against McDonald and the Grand Jury investigation placed with Judge Leibowitz. On the basis of the complaint Leibowitz ordered the Grand Jury to stop their inquiry into police corruption and to conduct an independent study of the allegations. After almost a month's work, the Grand Jury reported the complaint baseless and requested to be allowed to continue their work without hindrance "from those who felt the investigation might expose them".[53]

Within days of the Grand Jury's report O'Dwyer announced his resignation of the Mayoralty and his acceptance of the Mexican post. Eighteen years after Walker left New York first for Europe and then obscurity, O'Dwyer ambled off to Mexico. Unlike Walker, however, O'Dwyer would make one more public appearance in New York before he too could find relief. When next he appears in New York it is as one of the major targets of the Kefauver Committee. It was a disastrous appearance for O'Dwyer, as already mentioned. The wearying humiliation of his interrogation by Chief Counsel Rudolph Halley marks the end of his political career.

O'Dwyer's Guilt

Let us first talk of O'Dwyer and the strange denouement of his New York career. It is true that the immediate cause of his resignation was the McDonald imbroglio and his wildly intemperate remarks. But it is also the case that resignation had been contemplated earlier. In fact, according to Mockridge and Prall,[54] who unfortunately cite no sources, O'Dwyer was known to have come very close to resigning in the fall of 1949 right after his second victory. This apparent desire to escape from what O'Dwyer must have perceived as a dangerous, vexing and deteriorating situation came to a head on November 28, 1949. On that day O'Dwyer suffering from dizzy spells, "trembling, and sometimes incoherent" was placed in Bellevue Hospital. Mockridge and Prall claim there is no doubt that the mayor was "dangerously close to a complete nervous breakdown". He suffered from an almost paralyzing depression in addition to an acute respiratory infection. On December 4, the ill and confused O'Dwyer had had enough and supposedly wrote out his resignation. What followed next, write Mockridge and Prall, was a dramatic battle between Moran who rushed to the hospital, and the distraught Mayor. The climax of the fight occurred when Moran tore the note demanding that O'Dwyer not quit, at least not until Moran secured a more permanent sinecure than his position with the Fire Department (Moran was subsequently appointed by O'Dwyer Commissioner of the Board of Water and Supply).

If the above account is accurate, then O'Dwyer's deep dissatisfactions originated well before the McDonald investigation officially started and surely before its extent could have been known. What fed or caused O'Dwyer's personal "angst", however, is not known although there are hints and suspicions which point to several possibilities. These include the death of his first wife, his subsequent romance and marriage to Sloan Simpson, the increasingly bold criminal activities of Moran and other close associates, and, finally, continuing anguish over his own involvement with professional criminals. But, until O'Dwyer is seriously studied these and many other questions will remain unanswered.

What we are left with instead of evidence and solid interpretation, is a picture of an enigmatic politician. And this picture which is the one O'Dwyer himself paraded at his various forums most notably before the Kefauver Committee presents him as exceptionally vague in administration, the object of forces always a bit out of control; responsible but surely not accountable for the sinister activities of his associates. He was admittedly remiss in trusting others who were patently untrustworthy, pre-occupied when he should have been attentive, too loyal when he should have been calculating. In short, a decent man betrayed by others who suffered from a perilous lassitude rather than criminal intent.

Probably the most compelling reason, and it is not all that compelling, for accepting this line is that O'Dwyer was never caught with his hand in the till. With Mayor Walker, for example, there is no doubting his corruption knowing of his "wonderful box of tin". But there is no evidence of which I am aware which discloses anything similar in O'Dwyer's case. There are some broad hints in Mockridge and Prall's work which imply that O'Dwyer channelled dirty money through his brother's ranch in El Centro, California. But nothing is substantiated. The only other material which discusses his finances and the possibility of a slush fund is the disputed testimony of John P. Crane, President of Local 94 of the International Association of Fire Fighters given before the Kefauver Committee. Besides stating that he paid Moran $55,000 drawn from the Association's bank account part of which was to be used for O'Dwyer's 1949 campaign, Crane claimed that he personally gave the Mayor $10,000 on the steps of Gracie Mansion in October 1949. O'Dwyer vehemently denied the charge. And in what appears to be supporting prose, the Kefauver Committee reports that both men testified on this issue before a New York County Grand Jury and only O'Dwyer waived his immunity. The Crane testimony is the strongest allegation of O'Dwyer on the take, and it is far from convincing.

But whether or not O'Dwyer received dirty money tells us nothing about how deeply enmeshed he was in the social system of organized crime; how important a part he played in those patron–client relationships which linked the mutually supporting endeavors of politics, criminal justice and professional crime. And it is this point which Turkus, Beldock, McDonald, and the Kefauver Committee established. O'Dwyer and his closest associates were integral parts of a political and social system that brought them into negotiating positions with such professional criminals as Adonis, Anastasia, Genovese, Costello, Sherman, Weber, Gross and others, although it is not entirely clear just what the parameters of these relationships were.

Changing Symbols

I stated at the outset that one could track important changes in the perception of organized crime by focusing on O'Dwyer's career. To do so it is necessary to consider again the manner in which the issue of organized crime affected his political life. First of all, there were the Murder, Inc., cases which brought the newly-elected District Attorney almost immediate acclaim. He was a champion of the public interest, prosecuting gangsters for murder. And they were electrocuted! O'Dwyer accumulated a very large stock of political capital from those early days in office which was not dissipated for almost a decade. The first real intimations that O'Dwyer was not the fearless prosecutor and foe of organized crime came in 1945 with the Beldock campaign and investigation. But in 1945 few cared. General O'Dwyer could still dip into the capital so rapidly accumulated in 1940 and 1941 reminding New Yorkers that he broke the most infamous murder ring in history. In addition, the core of Beldock's accusation was corruption in the city, and that was an issue that had lost its urgency in the sweep of much greater affairs. And so O'Dwyer went on now as Mayor, enormously popular still riding the crest of his initial wave. It was not until 1949–1950 that O'Dwyer's capital would be exhausted. And when it was he was confronted by charges different in kind, scope and intensity than anything seen before.

Some of that change was glimpsed by historian William Moore who noted something fundamentally unfair in the Kefauver Committee's treatment of O'Dwyer. Moore writes:

> By suggesting, in its focus on O'Dwyer's career, that the existence and toleration of racketeering and gambling were the product of one man's political expediency, the Committee was not only personally unfair, but it was obscuring the fundamental truths that these conditions transcended reform cycles and that they sprang from certain basic problems in defining law and morality and perhaps government itself. In scapegoating Tammany, Costello, and O'Dwyer, moreover, the Committee fell into the old American pattern of seeing vice and crime as things set apart, imposing themselves on the broader community only through political corruption. To dramatize its case against a "Mr. Big", the Committee needed to show his influence on a political figure of some importance. By suggestion and repetition, its charges linking Costello and O'Dwyer, although never proved, gained a high level of public acceptance.[55]

Moore's complaint, rightly taken, is that the Kefauver Committee tried to fix the locus of blame for organized crime upon Costello and O'Dwyer. To accomplish this, it had resurrected in novel trappings a terribly dated criminology.

But the important point here is the novel trappings more so than the worn out criminology. By the fact that the Kefauver Committee was an arm of the Federal Government, that its investigation was nationwide, that "organized crime" was found wherever the Committee chose to look, the perception of organized crime was changed. As both cause and consequence, the Committee now understood the phenomenon as a singular entity. Moreover, through this ironic process of condensing organized crimes and criminal syndicates into Organized Crime and then expanding it into a national organization, the core meaning of organized crime was irrevocably changed. Where violence and corruption were the characteristics of organized crime before, now its essence was Conspiracy. This meant that O'Dwyer was not just the patron of Brooklyn gamblers and New York racketeers, but rather the protector of the Eastern Syndicate of Organized Crime.

The public's perception of organized crime no longer could be contained by the local figure of the Tammany Tiger. Organized crime was swept into the greatly expanded political arena that was one of the consequences of World War II. The role of the Kefauver Committee in all this was obviously central. But something else besides publicity lay behind the Committee itself. Its preoccupations, it methodology, its particular targets, and its old-fashioned criminology were framed by the prior belief that organized crime was neither local nor structural. Organized crime was instead the expression of an immoral conspiracy aimed at the vitals of American life. The Great Fear of Subversion which engulfed so many areas of American society in the post-war years worked its logic on crime also. The major characteristics of this great Conspiracy were its limitless geographical scope and its alien origin. And as the organized crime conspiracy was now more and more recognized as alien it brought back with a rush the always simmering but usually submerged issue of ethnicity. The lineal descendant of the Kefauver Committee's conclusions is La Cosa Nostra.

When organized crime was nationalized by the Kefauver Committee in 1950–1952, O'Dwyer became something much more than a local political hack operating in the world of municipal politics. He stood as the exposed link connecting the alien conspiracy to American politics. O'Dwyer then betrayed a world immensely larger than the one Mayor Walker was accountable either for or to. Is it any wonder that he chose to stay in Mexico ıf his life? Myth had once again taken over reality, and Mexico was as guuu a place as any to ponder these changes in the politics of organized crime.

NOTES

1 William Howard Moore, *The Kefauver Committee and the Politics of Crime, 1950–1952* (Columbia, Missouri, 1974), 173–174.
2 U.S. Senate, Special Committee to Investigate Organized Crime in Interstate Commerce, *The Kefauver Committee Report on Organized Crime* (New York, 1951), 91–92.
3 *Ibid.*, 125.
4 Turkus and Feder, 30–32.
5 *The New York Times,* March 25, 1940: 1.
6 People v. Maione, 284 N.Y. 423.
7 People v. Goldstein, 285 N.Y. 376.
8 See Court of Appeals—Brooklyn, New York, The People of the State of New York Against Louis Buchalter, Emmanuel Weiss, Louis Capone (May–June, 1942) 7944. Vols. 1, 2, 3, 4, 5; and People v. Buchalter, 298 N.Y. 181; 289 N.Y. 244; 44 N.Y.S. 2d 449: N.Y.S. 2d E 21.
9 The report signed by F. L. Strong on October 21, 1941 is located in William O'Dwyer, *Personal Papers* found in the New York City Municipal Archives. The section of the papers dealing with organized crime and O'Dwyer's career as District Attorney is known as the Murder, Inc., papers and are in boxes numbered 9239 through 9252. Unfortunately, the material in the boxes is not indexed and often the title of particular folders has little to do with the contents. None of this should reflect on the personnel of the Archives who have laboured under exceptionally trying circumstances directly attributable to the City's financial bind. Nevertheless, in citing material from the Murder, Inc., collection I will use the titles of the documents when I can but not Box numbers or folder titles as they are almost totally misleading. Again, let me reiterate that the Archival staff has been enormously helpful in the face of great difficulties.
10 Turkus and Feder, 435–436.
11 *Ibid.*, 436–437.
12 *Ibid.*, 443–458.
13 County Court, Kings County, In the Matter of the Investigation into the Circumstances Surrounding the Death of Abe Reles on November 12, 1941, at the Half Moon Motel in Coney Island, Brooklyn, New York, *Grand Jury Presentment* (December 21, 1951).
14 *Ibid.*, 2.
15 *Ibid.*, 10.
16 *Ibid.*
17 *Ibid.*, 17.
18 Burton B. Turkus, "Confidential Memorandum," (April 8, 1942) in *O'Dwyer Papers,* 1.
19 *Ibid.*
20 *Ibid.*, 2.
21 Frank C. Bals, "Report RE: Albert Anastasia LB–57, 939," in *O'Dwyer Papers,* 1.
22 *Ibid.*, 4.
23 Turkus and Feder, 450.
23 *Ibid.*, 481.

[25] *Ibid.*

[26] Radio Address of George J. Beldock, District Attorney of Kings County, over Radio Station WOR, "Mystery in the D.A.'s Office," in *O'Dwyer Papers* (October 18, 1945),1.

[27] *Ibid.*, 2.

[28] *Ibid.*, 7.

[29] *Ibid.*, 10.

[30] Statement Taken in the Office of the District Attorney of Kings County, Brooklyn, New York, "In the Matter of Vito Genovese," in *O'Dwyer Papers* (September 1, 1945), 2.

[31] *Ibid.*, 3.

[32] *Ibid.*, 9.

[33] *Ibid.*

[34] *Ibid.*, 23–24.

[35] *Ibid.*, 27.

[36] Radio Address of George J. Beldock, 7.

[37] Dom Frasca, *King of Crime* (New York, 1959), 127.

[38] *Ibid.*, 125.

[39] "Statement of Ernest Rupolo" alias "The Hawk," in *O'Dwyer Papers*, 1.

[40] "Homicide Case #237–1934," in *O'Dwyer Papers* (July, 1944).

[41] *The New York Times*, December 21, 1945: 1 & 15.

[42] U.S. Senate, Special Committee to Investigate Organized Crime in Interstate Commerce, 108.

[43] Norton Mockridge and Robert H. Prall, *The Big Fix* (New York, 1954) 112–113.

[44] The District Attorney of Kings County and the December 1949 Grand Jury, *Report of Special Investigation, December 1949 to April 1954* (New York February 1, 1955), 7.

[45] Mockridge and Prall, 131.

[46] District Attorney and Grand Jury, 10.

[47] *Ibid.*, 30.

[48] *Ibid.*, 32.

[49] Mockridge and Prall, 215–216

[50] *Ibid.*, 216.

[51] District Attorney and Grand Jury, 14.

[52] *Ibid.*, 14.

[53] *Ibid.*, 15.

[54] Mockridge and Prall, 216–219.

[55] Moore, 199–200.

Part 2

So that in the first place, I put for a general inclination of all mankind, a perpetual and restless desire of power after power, that ceaseth only in death. And the cause of this, is not always that a man hopes for a more intensive delight, than he has already attained to; or that he cannot be content with a moderate power: but because he cannot assure the power and means to live well, which he hath present, without the acquisition of more. And from hence it is, that kings, whose power is greatest, turn their endeavours to the assuring it at home by law, or abroad by wars: and when that is done, there succeedeth a new desire; in some, of fame from new conquest; in others, of ease and sensual pleasure; in others of admiration, or being flattered for excellence in some art, or other ability of the mind.

Competition of riches, honour, command, or other power, inclineth to contention, enmity, and war: because the way of one competitor, to the attaining of his desire is to kill, subdue, supplant, or repel the other. Particularly, competition of praise, inclineth to a reverence of antiquity. For men contend with the living, not with the dead; to these ascribing more than due, that they may obscure the glory of the other.

Thomas Hobbes
LEVIATHAN

Chapter 6
Syndicates and Vice

There are two basic types of criminal syndicates which operated in New York in the 1930s and 1940s. One is the enterprise syndicate which operates exclusively in the arena of illicit enterprises such as prostitution, gambling, bootlegging, and narcotics. The second type I call the power syndicate, its forte is extortion not enterprise. The power syndicate operates both in the arena of illicit enterprises and in the industrial world specifically in labor–management disputes and relations. Now neat categories cover a usually chaotic social world. And these are surely no exception. Syndicates of both stripes came and went, rose and fell with a great deal of rapidity making it very difficult to type them. Also, some syndicates displayed characteristics of both power and enterprise for periods of time. Others travelled the distance from one basic orientation to the other. For all the actual complexity, nevertheless, there seems little doubt that criminal syndicates can and should be seen as either enterprise or power depending on first the arena within which they functioned, and second on the issue of extortion. The heuristic value of this approach rests ultimately on its providing a key to understanding certain changes in the history of organized crime which have passed for other sorts of developments.

Let me give an example of this. In the Introduction I discussed the non-event Purge which supposedly signalled the end of one type of criminal organization and the emergence of another. Cosa Nostra scholars from the academic world are not the only ones to see some major structural change occurring in organized crime during the early 1930s. A large number of popular writers also maintain that organized crime (which they too view as a singular entity) passed from something to something else they call the National Crime Syndicate.[1] The central claim of these popular histories is that the entity was re-structured and centralized. Two further conclusions must be mentioned in this regard: the essential change in structure to centralization was inexorable, and lastly it was, of course, successful.

Primarily what these writers are really talking about are certain limited and ultimately unsuccessful attempts by several power syndicates at domination of enterprise syndicates working in policy gambling and prostitution. There was a centralization crisis in a number of illicit enterprises during the early 1930s and it was attributable to two factors: first the weakness of enterprise syndicates; second, the drive on the part of power syndicates to take them over. The social situation which resulted was a form of centralization which is better understood as a variant of extortion.

The history of centralization during this era lies then in the relationships between enterprise and power syndicates to a large extent. Within the general arena of illicit enterprises, power syndicates play several complex roles. For instance, they are often employed by enterprise syndicates as "protectors" of their operations. But protection covers a range of relationships which at one end culminates in power syndicates extorting some form of payment from enterprise ones as the price for them to stay in business. To further complicate the matter, over time power syndicates tend to move from protection to extortion in their relationships with enterprise syndicates. Having stated this much, I want to emphasize again that syndicates did change character and orientation, but that whatever their particular permutations they had to confront the entrepreneurs of violence, the leaders of power syndicates.

The intent of this chapter is primarily to consider the actions of certain criminal syndicates in the illicit enterprises of bootlegging, prostitution and policy gambling because they epitomized centralizing tendencies in organized crime in the 1930s. In explicating this history it will be clear that a great deal of it is best understood by focusing on the relationships mentioned above. But not all, however. In the first major example discussed, that of bootlegging, it is not possible to type the dominant syndicate with the precision one would like. That is because it had the characteristics of both power and enterprise. Nevertheless, this particular syndicate's history was crucially affected by its ability to deal with "protectors".

Differences between syndicates in illicit enterprises and the issue of centralization are not the only issues which concern us. At the very start of the discussion the important issue of the ethnic composition of syndicates is broached. The two ethnic groups which stand out are Italians and Jews. The presence of Italians is naturally no surprise given the success of Mafia and Cosa Nostra demonologists. But the presence of Jews does require some comment given the loss of the old Progressive stereotype mentioned in the first chapter. During the Progressive period if not earlier it was recognized that Jews were finding several niches in organized crime. But the method of presenting this material was so encrusted with anti-Semitic rhetoric that its historical significance was never appreciated. What was accurate in the Progressive reports was the claim that large numbers of professional criminals in New York were immigrant Jews and their children, especially their children. But this claim was read to mean that large numbers of Jews were professional criminals and that was a gross error. That part of the population of both Jews and Italians which became professional criminals was miniscule although that was not the message received nor perhaps intended. In any case it is absolutely true that many professional criminals in New York from at least the turn of the century were Jews and Italians, and that they represented only a small fraction of their populations. It should also be added that the stereotypic division of Jews as vice entrepreneurs and Italians as entrepreneurs of violence was not true in either the Progressive period or in the decades I am writing about. Both groups were involved in vice activities and both were well represented in the ranks of violent entrepreneurs.

The identification of particular ethnics in professional crime raises some additional questions that are addressed but which cannot be resolved in this chapter. There are three basic ones: (1) to what degree was there ethnic specialization in organized crime; (2) to what degree was there ethnic competition and cooperation in criminal syndicates and between criminal syndicates; (3) to what degree can we identify changes in the ethnic composition of criminal syndicates over time, that is, is there something called ethnic succession operating in organized crime? For now I will concentrate on marking ethnic composition in the syndicates discussed pointing out some tentative answers to the basic questions when appropriate.

Bootlegging

When Samuel Seabury opened his inquiry into the Magistrates Courts in 1930 America was entering its second decade of National Prohibition. And by this time the mechanics of manufacturing, importing, wholesaling and retailing illegal alcohol in various forms had long been established. Concerning bootlegging in general, the first point addressed is what can be determined about the backgrounds of leading bootleggers. Did they share, for example, any common national origins? The answer is rather quickly arrived at. In the New York Metropolitan area, according to a recent study by Mark H. Haller, bootlegging was principally controlled by Jewish, Italian and Irish entrepreneurs who were, he adds, relatively young and unknown men prior to their involvement in bootlegging.

Those who, by the mid-1920's, emerged as leading entrepreneurs tended to be young-born between 1892 and 1900 and thus some 20 to 28 years old when Prohibition began. Prohibition arrived just as the first generation of Eastern European Jewish and Italian young people raised in America were reaching maturity. Data on those who were leading bootleggers by the late 1920's indicate that some 50 per cent were Jewish, some 25 per cent of Italian background, the rest primarily Irish and Polish in background. Although their previous occupational experiences were frequently, but not universally, in some area of crime, the future bootleggers were by no means prominent in crime prior to prohibition. Many, indeed, graduated from juvenile gangs directly into bootlegging.[2]

In developing his material on bootlegging Haller identifies seventeen leading New York area bootleggers. And although they do not entirely support his generalizations about age and experience, their ethnicity is unequivocally clear. Their names, dates of birth and ethnicity follow:[3]

William "Big Bill" Dwyer	1883	Irish
Joseph Reinfeld	1899	Jewish
Abner "Longie" Zwillman	1904	Jewish
Jack "Legs" Diamond (John Nolan)	1896	Irish
Charles "Vannie" Higgins	1898	Irish
Frank Costello (Francesco Castiglia)	1891	Italian
Owney Madden	1892	—
Waxey Gordon (Irving Wexler)	1888	Jewish
Max Greenberg	—	Jewish
Meyer Lansky (Maier Suchowljansky)	1902	Jewish
Benjamin "Bugs" Siegel	1906	Jewish
Charles "Lucky" Luciano (Salvatore Lucania)	1897	Italian
John Torrio	1882	Italian
Arthur "Dutch" Schultz (Arthur Flegenheimer)	1902	German/Jewish
Frankie Yale (Francesco Uale)	1893	Italian

| Al Lilien | 1899 | Jewish |
| Charles J. Steinberg | — | Jewish |

The very important point about ethnicity advanced by Haller is confirmed by an unfortunately unidentified report located in the O'Dwyer papers in the New York Municipal Archives. The report titled "Breweries Operated by Jewish Syndicate 1928–1933" details a considerable amount of strife within the bootleg trade especially around the activities of Irving "Waxey Gordon" Wexler, one of the older and considerably more experienced criminals appearing in the Haller sample. Most significantly, the report is concerned with the issue of centralization in a segment of the bootleg trade during the early 1930s. In so doing it draws attention to several types of conflict which bounded centralization in this aspect of the illicit enterprise. But it would be an over-estimation of the evidence to hold that it establishes in clear form the power/enterprise conflict discussed above. There is some indication that the model holds, but for it to be a proper example would mean forcing the Gordon syndicate through a short history of change from power to enterprise that is not warranted by the report and other materials. Furthermore, the end of this centralization episode conforms to the end of the illicit enterprise in general brought about by Repeal. And this raises other historical issues that need exploration. Especially important in this regard is the material which discloses types of enterprises pursued by criminal syndicates post-Repeal.

Before discussing the Gordon syndicate and centralization in bootlegging Gordon's past criminal career is briefly presented. Born in 1888 he is an exception to Haller's generalization of "young Turks" muscling into bootlegging. In fact, Gordon was a major criminal in the predominantly Jewish underworld on New York's Lower East Side by 1910. At his trial for income tax evasion in 1933, Gordon testified that by 1910 he had already accumulated over $100,000 from gambling and assorted illicit activities.[4] During the course of the next decade he continued to be active in several criminal endeavors including strikebreaking and narcotics. There is some very fine and accurate information about Gordon's criminal career prior to Prohibition collected by a little known organization called the Bureau of Social Morals which was itself part of another organization called the New York Kehillah formed by segments of New York Jewry alarmed and dismayed by the Progressive attacks on the Jewish community. The Bureau's reports indicate that Gordon was a member of the Benjamin Fein syndicate which terrorized much of the Lower East Side in the 1910s. The Bureau's files also state that around 1914 Gordon took over Fein's activities as a power broker in the battles and disputes between garment unions and employers who banded together in trade associations.[5]

More revealing of the scope of Gordon's criminal activities prior to Prohibition is the evidence uncovered by the Bureau of Social Morals of his broad involvement in the narcotics trade by 1917.[6] At this time the major drug traded in the New York underworld was cocaine, and Gordon was a major partner in at least five different cocaine mobs. One was formed with his brother and two others to work in Harlem; another operated in Philadelphia; a third worked out of a tea room on Grand Street on the Lower East Side; the fourth was founded by Gordon and two notorious gangsters and was headquartered in the Odd Fellows Hall also on the Lower East Side; the last drug mob was made up of Gordon, his oldest associate known only as Jonesy the Wop, and six others working around 14th Street in Manhattan. Gordon was without doubt one of the major cocaine entrepreneurs in New York and probably Philadelphia during the second decade of the twentieth century.

Gordon's criminal activities continued during the 1920s, although there is little concrete information about them. Dewey alleges in his opening remarks at the tax trial that Gordon was involved in liquor smuggling and prostitution but produces no hard evidence. Apparently Gordon continued to deal in narcotics during the 1920s as he was indicted for transporting drugs from New York to Minnesota in the latter part of the decade. He was, however, acquitted in a jury trial. At the same time his criminal activities expanded, Gordon became a major investor in New York real estate. Along with Max Greenberg and several other associates, Gordon owned at least two hotels in Manhattan. Gordon's involvement in the beer business came toward the end of the decade at about the same time that his narcotics' indictment appeared. It was the beer business which ultimately was his downfall. In the early 1930s, the Federal government secured an indictment against him for evading taxes on at least one and one half million dollars earned in 1930–1931. The government's figures were modestly based on the known proceeds of just two breweries. Gordon as we will see controlled many more breweries than the two which the government concentrated on.

Let us now turn to the history proposed in the report. It begins by stating that in the latter days of Prohibition a number of large breweries located in New York, New Jersey, and Pennsylvania "were leased from their original owners by a Jewish controlled combine".[7] Nine men are identified as members of this syndicate with the leaders being Waxey Gordon, Max Greenberg, Max Hassel and Nick Delmore. Also mentioned as partners but in a very limited fashion are Murray Marks, Harry Meyers, Frenchy Dillon, and Charlie Mannie all of whom with the exception of Dillon are described as petty gamblers and racketeers who are "friends of Waxie". The last person identified as a syndicate partner is "Abe", really Abner, Zwillman "a street peddler, who by hi-jacking, muscling in still operations, rum running, made a fortune and then muscled in as a partner in the beer operation".[8] Zwillman's role in this brief and violent history, however, is much more complex and important than initially indicated. It must be added that several other individuals involved with Gordon in almost all of his criminal operations since the mid-1920s including the beer business are left out of the report. These include Louis Cohen, "alias Louis Black, alias James Henderson, alias J. B. Cowen, alias J. Alexander—one of Waxey Gordon's bookkeepers whose function was to operate bank accounts for the defendant under fictitious names and generally to assist in the management of his beer business"; Sam Gurock; Edward J. Baker; Murray Luxenburg; Joseph Leffler; J. S. S. Weisman; Joseph Aaront; and lastly Charles Gurock.[9]

The power of this syndicate resided in the large number of breweries controlled by them. Prior to forming the syndicate, the major conspirators were already in the bootlegging business operating several important breweries. In 1928–1929 they pooled their own breweries and seized control of others to emerge as the leading beer syndicate in the East if not the nation. Hassel and Delmore brought in two breweries, while Gordon and Greenberg contributed four more. The Gordon and Greenberg breweries had all been seized from bootleggers Frankie Dunn and Bugs Donovan who were murdered. At the height of its power the syndicate controlled at least thirteen breweries distributed in Pennsylvania, New York, and especially New Jersey. The breweries of the Jewish Syndicate follow:

Pennsylvania	New York	New Jersey
Lancaster Brewery Lancaster, Pa.	Middletown Brewery Middletown, N.Y.	Union City Brewery Union City, N.J.
Columbia Brewery Reading, Pa.	Elmira Brewery Elmira, N.Y.	Peter Hauck Brewery Harrison, N.J.
	Kings Brewery Brooklyn, N.Y.	Eureka Brewery Paterson, N.J.
		Peter Heidt Brewery Elizabeth, N.J.

Pennsylvania	New York	New Jersey
		Hygia Brewery Passaic, N.J.
		Rising Sun Brewery Elizabeth, N.J.
		Hensler Brewery Newark, N.J.
		Orange Brewery Newark, N.J.

According to the report the distribution of the syndicate's beer was nationwide, "shipped as far as the west coast via railroad freight cars". It also states that "The records of the Alcohol Tax Unit, U.S. Internal Revenue Bureau, Washington and N.J., will substantiate the above."[10]

With so much of the syndicate's activities centered in New Jersey it was forced to deal early on with two sets of "protectors" also called "strong arm men", and what we might call power syndicates. One group was located in Essex and Union Counties and was composed of Zwillman, James Rutkin, Bennie Zuckerman, Jerry Catena and Gyp De Carlo. The other was centered in Bergen, Passaic and Hudson Counties. It included "William Moretti (alias Willie Moore), Kid Steech, Carmine Sarbino (alias Chicago Fat), Vito Genovese, Pete LaBlanc (brother-in-law of Willie Moore), Lucky Luciano". The report notes that this last syndicate "were only small fry as far as financial rating was concerned at this time". And it adds "They were kept on the brewery payrolls to avoid trouble for the breweries."[11]

From protectors both syndicates began to extend their activities. The most significant move was carried out by Zwillman, Rutkin, Zuckerman, and a Joe Reinfeld who "went into liquor smuggling business". Illicit distilleries operated by this syndicate were located in Essex and Union counties their original base of power. This particular group rapidly achieved enormous financial returns primarily because of their connection to the Bronfman family in Canada who were the owners of Seagram Distilleries. The report states: "one of the distilleries operated by this group was an illicit distillery located in the Calco Chemical Plant, Newark, N.J. The alcohol from this distillery was shipped via tank car to the Seagram Distilleries in Canada; there the alcohol was used to cut the Canadian whiskey manufacturing and put into packages which were re-shipped and smuggled into Port Newark, N.J., into potato boats for the Reinfeld–Zwillman combine".[12] The second syndicate also entered into the distillery business on their own with Genovese reportedly providing the finances necessary to both lease and purchase distilleries.

Up to Repeal the situation was this: Gordon, Greenberg and Hassel controlled thirteen major breweries and several smaller ones. Delmore, one of the original partners, was gone a "fugitive in connection with the murder of a prohibition agent, F. Finnelli, at the Rising Sun Brewery".[13] Both protective syndicates had already achieved considerable wealth and authority in the bootleg trade on their own, especially Zwillman–Reinfeld. And then in an unexplained maneuver, the Gordon–Greenberg–Hassel syndicate turned over one of their breweries to the "protectors". The brewery handed over was the Union City one and the "protectors" in this case were "Zwillman, Lucky Luciano, Kid Steech (Bongiovani), Willie Moretti, and Chicago Fat Sarbino".[14]

With Repeal the situation changed drastically. Apparently, Max Greenberg anticipating repeal went to "Washington and arranged with a party by name of Dalrymple, who was Commissioner of the Alcohol Licensing Dept., and for an alleged payment of $100,000 received permits to operate the breweries under the Jewish Syndicate's control".[15] Either by design or mistake the only brewery for which Greenberg did not secure a permit was the Union City Brewery. This was a greivous error as the "protective group was highly incensed". What followed next was the elimination of the Gordon–Greenberg–Hassel syndicate. As the report puts it: "Their anger resulted in killing by Kid Steech Bongiovani of two members of the syndicate, namely Max Hassel and Max Greenberg at the Elizabeth–Cateret Hotel, Elizabeth, N.J. Waxie Gordon, who was also to be killed, escaped because he was in another part of the hotel at the time."[16]

Wexler barely escaped death but his career was rapidly ending in any case. He had been indicted on tax evasion and was arrested shortly after the murders of his partners. Tried by Federal Attorney Dewey he was convicted and sentenced to a long prison term.

To continue this brief history, it is obvious that the bootleg business at least in beer was in considerable turmoil in the weeks and months following repeal. And then in a rather neat maneuver which has not been emphasized nearly enough, "the original owners of the breweries prior to prohibition stepped in and obtained their options back and started to operate".[17] It must be added here that there is every reason to believe that the original owners had probably been receiving a share of the illegal profits from their breweries in the form of leases throughout Prohibition. It might indeed be argued that the original entrepreneurs rather comfortably waited out Prohibition sustained by their share of the profits obtained by their lessees—the infamous bootleggers.

Among the individuals mentioned so far, none were as successful as Zwillman and Reinfeld. The basis of their continuing importance was the liquor not beer business. After repeal their syndicate operated under the corporate names of "Reo Distilleries and Reinfeld Distributors and Brown Vinters, N.Y." It also appears that Zwillman became one of the major criminal entrepreneurs in Union, Essex and Middletown Counties, New Jersey. He exerted considerable influence in other adjacent New Jersey counties through his ties with members of the second protective syndicate. Beyond the New Jersey/New York area Zwillman had other interests. For instance, the report states in 1936 "Longie Zwillman, Niggie Rutkin, Meyer Lansky, with Jack Dempsey, formed a partnership and purchased a hotel in Miami Beach, later known as the Dempsey–Vanderbilt Hotel. With Dempsey as the front, the group operated a gambling casino in the hotel."[18]

Angelo "Gyp" De Carlo

Zwillman's move into casino gambling was only one of several developments in the early and mid-1930s which saw bootleggers and "protectors" moving into various types of gambling. While still working as protectors and minor distributors of beer, "Willie Moretti, Chicago Fat, Vito Genovese, started to go into the gambling racket in Bergen and Passaic Counties, namely numbers".[19] This syndicate also expanded into slot machines and in 1935 they were indicted for their gambling activities in Passaic County. Apparently nothing much happened because, the report continues, the slot machine enterprise rapidly expanded all over the country. Much of this growth is attributed to the expertise of Moretti's cousin Frank Costello who "came in from New York and started to organize the pinball and slot machine business".[20] Along with these gambling enterprises other members of the Zwillman combine namely Gyp De Carlo, Jerry Catena, Vincent DeLava, and the now returned Nick Delmore began operating "dice, bookmaking and numbers" in Union, Essex and Middletown Counties.

What this short history of bootlegging syndicates indicates is revealing. It substantiates that overall the trade in and around New York was dominated by Jews and somewhat secondarily Italians from the late 1920s to Repeal. It suggests that between these groups there was both cooperation and competition, although there is no evidence which indicates that the sources of either were brought about by ethnic concerns. It is not insignificant that Greenberg and Hassel were murdered by the North Jersey Italian "protectors", and for that matter that the "Jewish Syndicate" came to power after murdering the leaders of a smaller Irish one. But, as there are numerous reasons either given or that can be surmised for these events which have nothing to do with ethnicity it would be foolhardy to go beyond description. Other fruitful avenues which this history points to includes the importance of north-eastern New Jersey as the hub of the bootleg trade in the East. Given that, it is not surprising that local New Jersey criminals such as Zwillman and Moretti achieved prominence in the New York, now metropolitan, underworld, and that some professional criminals from Brooklyn and Manhattan moved their residences and part of their activities to New Jersey during the 1930s and 1940s. Probably the central reason for these moves is a combination of the small size and large number of municipalities in this area making law enforcement grossly inefficient overall. That, in conjunction with the patterns of influence already established by bootleggers and "protectors" combined to form "havens" for professional criminals especially when the political climate in New York City shifted under La Guardia and Dewey. One further point to mention is that Repeal not only reinstated the original legitimate brewers, but it also provided for the legitimation of some bootleggers through such companies as Reinfeld

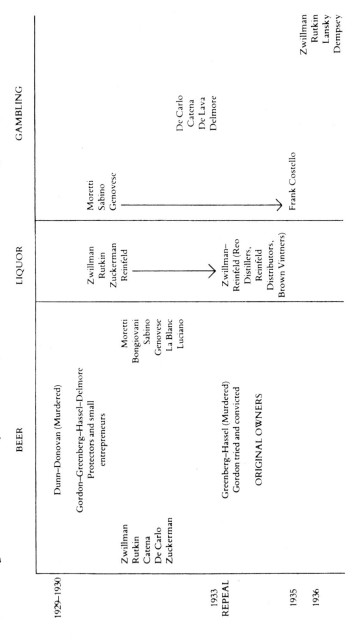

Table 1. Changes in selected illicit enterprises 1928–1936, associated with the rise and fall of Irving "Waxey Gordon" Wexler.

	BEER	LIQUOR	GAMBLING
1929–1930	Zwillman Rutkin Catena De Carlo Zuckerman		
	Dunn–Donovan (Murdered)		
	Gordon–Greenberg–Hassel–Delmore Protectors and small entrepreneurs		
	Moretti Bongiovani Sabino Genovese La Blanc Luciano	Zwillman Rutkin Zuckerman Reinfeld	Moretti Sabino Genovese
			De Carlo Catena De Lava Delmore
1933 REPEAL	Greenberg–Hassel (Murdered) Gordon tried and convicted		
	ORIGINAL OWNERS		
1935		Zwillman– Reinfeld (Reo Distillers, Reinfeld Distributors, Brown Vintners)	Frank Costello
1936			Zwillman Rutkin Lansky Dempsey

140

Distributors and Brown Vintners.

More than anything else, however, this history validates the general notion of centralization in bootlegging. Can there be any doubt that Gordon–Greenberg–Hassel centralized aspects of the beer business? They pooled together resources either developed on their own or murderously seized from others into one domineering operation. But, in doing so, they expanded the organization's scope and brought into it in some fashion local entrepreneurs of violence like Zwillman and Moretti who were part of different power syndicates. The major problem in understanding this development lies in not knowing precisely the fashion in which these power syndicates were incorporated. This is especially difficult to determine as the report also claims Zwillman as one of the partners in the primary syndicate. The most reasonable explanation is that both of the local power syndicates were probably paid to protect the Gordon syndicate from rivals as well as themselves. In one sense, the payment to the "protectors" was a form of extortion. Presumably this was agreeable for some time, although the potential for conflict must have been always present. In addition, the development by members of the "connected" power syndicates of discrete gambling and liquor smuggling businesses coterminous with the beer business strongly suggests that the centralization which went on was tenuously maintained. There were surely not stable patterns of hierarchy encompassing all the constituent elements in the beer business. Relations between the centralizing syndicate and the local power ones appears to have been federal after a short time.

Finally, it is surely the case that the extremely violent history of the Gordon bootlegging syndicate emerged from the cantankerous dealings with the ill-named protectors. Not quite a neat power/enterprise conflict but suggestive enough of the predisposition to conflict between different types of syndicates and the potentialities of extortion.

Prostitution: From Organization to Centralization

Questions about the structure and function of criminal syndicates and the centralization of illicit enterprises which are of cardinal significance for criminologists also concerned prosecutors in the 1930s and none more so than Dewey. Now it seems very likely that Dewey's views on these issues changed radically from his days as a Federal Attorney when he prosecuted Gordon to his tenure as Special Prosecutor when he tried Luciano who he called the "Czar of organized crime". In the Gordon case there is no suggestion of organized crime as a singular conspiracy with bootlegging one of its parts. But, by the time Dewey was Special Prosecutor and actively pursuing an investigation into Luciano's affairs he was much more inclined to be a conspiracy theorist. Abandoning Dewey as a theoretical guide, let us see just what was established during the Luciano trial for compulsory prostitution about organized prostitution and centralization, and power and enterprise syndicates.

The historical charge found in Dewey's opening was that Luciano and the other defendants were "going to organize prostitution into a great industry in this city, and they did so".[21] What he meant to say and should have said was that Luciano and the others were going to centralize organized prostitution in New York or more modestly some of it. In fact, his real point is that organized prostitution in brothels had developed into a fairly centralized enterprise prior to 1933 and that Luciano and the others had then conspired to carry this centralization to an extreme. Consider Dewey's following remarks:

> A few years ago a system of organization began to grow up in prostitution, what is known as the bookie or booker of women appeared on the scene. Now a bookie or booker, or as he is sometimes called, a book, is a man who knows a number of prostitutes, or gets to know them in one way or another, and a number of Madams, and he gets a business of sending these girls from house to house, where they work a week at a time ... three years ago there were a number of so-called big bookers of women in New York City. By that I mean there were at least four, ... men who ran a book in this business. That means that they had a large chain of houses of prostitution, and a great number of girls who used to call them on the telephone each Sunday or Monday, and ask where to go to work, and the booker would then book them into a house .... And these bookers would run a sort of Orpheum circuit in the business of booking women.[22]

Obviously, some significant segment of prostitution had first been organized into brothels and then been partially at least centralized by the system described above. But for Dewey centralization meant only the Luciano syndicate as he repeated his opening definitions in the *Respondent's Brief* where he names the principal bookers and their assistants.[23]

Nichola Montana

Booker	*Assistant*
"Cockeyed" Louis Weiner	Al Weiner (his son)
"Nick" Montana	Jack Ellenstein, alias Eller
David Marcus, alias Dave Miller	Andrew Attardi, alias Andy Coco
Peter Balitzer, alias Peter Harris	Joseph Weintraub, alias Jo Jo Red Healey
Charlie Spinach	Sam Green, alias Spike Green
James Frederico, alias Jimmy Fredericks	Danny Brooks and Billy Peluso

The problem in Dewey's remarks is one of terminology: prostitution in brothels had been centralized by the methodology of booking; what was done next was to centralize the booking and that is where the Luciano conspiracy begins.

Actually the move to take over the independent bookers was preceded by an important but rather confusing development in the organized trade. This is the bonding issue which must be seen within the already extant structure of the trade. In this case bonding is tied to the economic relationships among prostitutes, madams and bookers. Before bonding the way money was made and dispersed went something like this:

> Prices varied depending on the type of house. In $2 houses, the weekly earnings of the girls, as disclosed record, averaged $200, and sometimes amounted to $300 or more. The madam of the house, who customarily left the place in charge of a maid, would have a weekly settlement with her inmates. From the $200, using that as an illustration, one half would be immediately deducted for the madam's "percentage." Ten per cent of the girl's share, in this case $10, was deducted for the booker. This money was usually paid directly by the madam to the booker, his assistant, or one of his collectors or subordinates. Five dollars was then deducted by the madam for a so-called doctor's "examination".[24]

In this "average" case the prostitute was left with $85 for a week's work. Bonding was another charge added onto the prostitute's remaining earnings. It was presented as a form of insurance in case of arrest. For a mandatory $10 weekly fee the prostitute was assured that she "would go free if arrested". Presumably the bonding money was to be held in a kitty for use when arrests were made.

143

What is confusing about this issue is first of all who was responsible for initiating this new fee. In Dewey's opening he remarks that in 1933 "various groups of individuals began to get the idea and act on it, that it might be profitable to try and organize houses of prostitution from another angle",[25] this being the bonding issue. Dewey goes on: "So there were two or three groups which were actually started up in that way; and then about that time ... this group of defendants started to come in."[26] But there is no indication that the structure of the trade was to be disturbed at all. A new service was to be provided and paid for by the prostitutes and that is all. It is inconceivable that bonding could be looked upon as a new rival way of organizing the trade. Moreover, there is absolutely no indication that the bonders were looked upon as interlopers by the bookers. After all, the service they offered could have been valuable and came out of the pockets of the prostitutes and not the bookers or madams. In fact though, bonding was significant in the history of the trade because it was apparently the bonders who were first driven from business by the Luciano gangsters. Dewey states: "late in the later summer or early fall of 1933, the people who had been engaged in the business of taking $10 a week from prostitutes for so-called bonding were called downtown for a meeting".[27] These individuals were placed in a "rest room" and there waited the arrival of "Charles Luciano". It was then that Luciano announced that the bonders were out of business and that segment of the organized prostitution business would now be run by his mob. Is it any wonder that Seabury, Blanshard, Dewey and Amen focused so much time and energy on the bail bond business?

The elimination of the bonders, whoever they were, was but the prelude to taking over the system of booking which was the structure of prostitution. Moreover, the bookers, madams and prostitutes formed enterprise syndicates which were complementary. That bonding had nothing structurally to do with the trade was made clear when the Luciano mobsters again "in the late summer or early fall of 1933", began their drive to organize "prostitution into a single syndicate". To accomplish this they terrorized booker Dave Miller with threats of murder unless he paid $10,000. He did not pay but prudently left New York for about two years and then returned to the business as a syndicate booker. Pete Harris was similarly threatened and told he must pay $250 a week to "a 'mob' being formed to 'protect' the bookers".[28] Harris settled his problem by paying $100 a week to stay in business. The other major bookers including Weiner, Charlie Spinach, and Montana were also "taken over". The last of the major bookers was Jimmy Fredericks who apparently gave up his business and in December, 1933, became a member of the new "combination" being "placed in charge of the bonding arrangements".[29] By the end of 1933 then the bonders had been totally replaced and the bookers were now employees of the Luciano prostitution syndicate.

The names, aliases and particular functions of this syndicate, according to Dewey, follow:[30]

Name	*Alias*	*Function*
Charles Luciano	Charlie Lucky	Principal
Thomas Pennochio	Tommy Bull	Treasurer
David Betillo	Little Davie	General Supervisor
Abraham Wahrman	Abie	Head of strong arm men and collectors
Benny Spiller	—	Investor who provided capital, and assistant supervisor
James Frederico	Jimmie Fredericks	General Manager
Ralph Liguori	—	Strong arm man
Jesse Jacobs	—	Bondsman
Meyer Berkman	—	Bondsman
Peter Balitzer	Pete Harris	Booker
Jack Ellenstein	Jack Eller	Booker
David Marcus	David Miller	Booker
Al Weiner	—	Booker
Louis Weiner	Cockeyed Louis	Booker
Nick Montana	—	Booker
Anthony Curcio	Binge	Telephone and office man
Santos Scalfani	Chappie	Collector
Yeddy	Teddy	Collector
Yoke	—	Collector
Joseph Weintraub	Jo-Jo	Assistant to Pete Harris
Andrew Lecoco	Andy Coco	Assistant to Jack Eller
Charles Pisano	Charlie Spinach	Booker
Spike Green	—	Booker
Daniel Caputo	Danny Brooks	Assistant to Jimmie Fredericks
William Peluso	—	Assistant to Jimmie Fredericks
Joe Levine	—	Strong arm man
Abraham Karp	—	Disbarred lawyer and coach of witnesses

Name	Alias	Function
Max Rachlin	—	Lawyer
Vito	—	Assistant Supervisor

It is not clear, however, what new financial arrangements solidified the takeover. In some instances, it is testified that bookers were put on a salary turning over the remainder of their moneys to the syndicate's treasurer Thomas Pennochio. In other testimony all that was required was the bonding fee of $10 per prostitute coming either from the prostitute or the booker. And finally, it seems in some cases that the booker paid a weekly fee to the syndicate for protection. In fact, the most obvious changes that took place were in the form of bonding and the arena of violence. This despite the statement made by Dewey in his opening which claims:

> Gradually, as I say, the thing grew tighter and tighter and tighter. Everybody in it was put on a salary till the whole organized underworld in connection with this business were servants of the men at the top, and we will prove to you that Luciano said on one occasion, "We are going further; we are going to put every madame in New York on a salary, and then the whole city will be working for us, and we will raise the prices: two dollar houses will become four dollar houses; four dollar houses, six dollar houses," and so forth.[31]

Discounting Luciano's dream or vision let us consider first the bonding operation under the new syndicate. The key man in the system was Anthony "Binge" Curcio in charge of first keeping tabs on the brothels within the syndicate, and second acting as the "clearing house for arrests". When someone was arrested Binge would be notified and he then would telephone the bonding office, which was run by Jesse Jacobs. After bailing the defendant, illegally I should add, she was then brought to the bonding office and "coached" in how to testify. In almost all the cases of arrests of "protected" prostitutes they were either acquitted or charges were dismissed. There is no doubt that almost overwhelmingly the bonding system did provide the protection it claimed. And yet there was constant turmoil around the bonding issue. This was caused by a singularly greedy twist to bonding introduced by the syndicate. In posting bail the syndicate decreed that they would only put up half the bond "for the $10 a week they get from all the women". The other half must come from the particular madam affected. In the vast majority of cases the bail was returned when the defendant came to trial. And here was the new catch: the syndicate kept the total bail money returning none of it to the madam.

In this way the syndicate rapidly alienated one of the most important segments of the trade. For their recalcitrance madams faced two similar modes of discipline. They would either be robbed by Ralph Liguori who "was the stick-up man for the combination", or beaten up by Jimmie Fredericks and several others. Nevertheless, the exploitation of madams was one of the key disruptive issues under the new syndicate. Apparently, as time went on most of the syndicate's management was handled by the vicious Fredericks and cheating was rampant. As noted the madams were more and more reluctant to cooperate with the syndicate seeing that it was costing them more and more money. In collusion with some of the madams their bookers tried to conceal at least some of the brothels from the syndicate. The situation was such that Dewey states: "I think the testimony will probably indicate that practically everybody in the entire case was cheating somebody else."[32] So disruptive had the trade become that a series of meetings were held in 1934 and 1935 by the top leaders of the syndicate including Luciano considering little else than disciplinary actions. And in October 1935 Luciano reportedly wanted to give up the business as "there wasn't enough money in it for the 'headache'".[33]

The Luciano syndicate in prostitution lasted from the fall or winter of 1933 until February 1936 when Dewey's agents arrested the participants. What had it accomplished? It took a fairly centralized operation, the booking system, and subjected it to intense pressures which threatened to disrupt the entire trade. It turned on the key personnel in the trade with the exception of the prostitute herself who was already cruelly exploited, and initiated various methods of financially squeezing both bookers and madams who resorted to cheating and ultimately to testifying against their bosses. It provided a service, bonding, but one that was already in the works in any case. It was clearly an effort at extreme centralization that attacked what was already a stable system of organized prostitution. The survival of the Luciano syndicate in this operation was based solely on terror. This forced centralization was an exercise in extortion carried out by a power syndicate upon four to six enterprise syndicates. Unlike the bootlegging operations centralized by Gordon–Greenberg–Hassel there were no economies of scale to be exploited into increased profits. As neither the price structure nor the volume of trade changed under the Luciano syndicate profits for the entrepreneurs of violence could only come from the pockets of the formerly independent syndicate leaders and the madams. Indeed, one might want to argue that without substantial changes in the economics of organized prostitution, it had about all the centralization it could take by 1933.

There are two final points to consider in this brief discussion of organized prostitution. The first deals with ethnicity. That the segment of organized prostitution which has concerned us was controlled by Italians and Jews is obvious on the face of it. What must be emphasized, however, is that even with the takeover by Luciano's syndicate, key leadership roles were played by Jews such as Abraham Wahrman, Benny Spiller and Jesse Jacobs. This was an Italian–Jewish syndicate under Luciano's direction with no traces of ethnic rivalry or competition. The second point is that what I have called extreme centralization was a failure. If for no other reason, it was a conspiracy successfully prosecuted. It was brought to an end by Dewey and the celebrated conviction of Luciano. Organized prostitution, of course, went on, but never under the centralized direction of a power syndicate. Far from inexorable extreme centralization was not even sensible.

Gambling: Focus on Policy

The material on organized gambling in and around New York during the 1930s and 1940s is much greater than any corresponding information on either bootlegging up to Repeal or prostitution. One particular type of gambling enterprise will be examined. This is policy and the discussion will follow the line developed in the analysis of prostitution. An important portion of policy gambling, that centered in and around the Manhattan neighborhood of Harlem, experienced many of the same pressures as did organized prostitution. In this case, the leader of the centralizing power syndicate was Arthur "Dutch Schultz" Flegenheimer.

Dutch Schultz was one of the most infamous professional criminals in New York by the beginning of the 1930s. He had gained notoriety initially as a bootlegger where his activities were enhanced by his association with the remnants of the Dunn–Donovan mob. Members of that mob had left New Jersey after the murder of the leaders and set up a modest operation in Yonkers just north of the Bronx. And then sometime in 1931, according to Dewey, Schultz "saw this disorganized policy field" and decided to take it over.[34] Actually, Schultz and several of his associates including George Weinberg, Moe Levy and Harry Schoenhaus had an earlier fling in policy in 1929 that was financially disastrous. Let me also highlight again Dewey's tendency to claim disorganization and/or decentralization in illegal enterprises prior to the machinations of his particular targets. As will be clear, policy gambling was no more disorganized than prostitution prior to the Luciano conspiracy. There is another factor to ponder before getting to policy. In the same year that his policy racket begins, Schultz became a major target of the United States Attorney's office. From that time on all his illegal activities especially policy would be played out against a background of legal problems.

Following a long and intensive investigation Schultz was indicted for income tax evasion "charged with evading payment of $92,103 in federal income taxes on an estimated income of $481,000".[35] In response Schultz went into hiding. His fugitive status did not end until the summer of 1934. Meanwhile, his attorney and others attempted to reach a settlement with the government offering $100,000 in June, 1933. The offer was rejected, and then over a year later Schultz finally surrendered in Syracuse, New York. From the time of his arrest in November, 1934, until his death Schultz would not return to New York City. His trial took place in April, 1935, and resulted in a hung jury. About three months later he was tried again in Malone, New York. To the consternation of the government and the surprise of nearly everyone else the Malone jury found him innocent. From Malone Schultz went to Connecticut and then Newark, New Jersey. He carefully avoided New York where he was still wanted on certain inexplicable charges. In addition, the federal government came up with another set of tax charges and on October 9, 1935, indicted him. Schultz surrendered to New Jersey authorities, posted bond and prepared to fight extradition to New York. Within two weeks he and several of his associates were gunned down in the Palace Chop House and Tavern in Newark. The effects of Schultz's legal tribulations meant basically two things for policy: he would need more and more money from the racket as time went on and his legal bills piled up and there was no more bootlegging; and, he would exercise less and less personal control over policy the longer he stayed out of New York.

Policy

Before discussing the Schultz conspiracy consider the mechanics of the game and the structure of the enterprise. Policy often called numbers is wagering a small amount of money, usually in the 1920s and 30s from a nickel to a quarter, that one can guess which three numbers will appear on some agreed upon standardized daily tabulation. The chances of success are 999 to 1. If one wins, however, the payoff is 600 to 1. The difference between the odds and the payoff is known as the Bank's margin. The first point to note is the standardized daily tabulation. Originally the numbers came from the New York Clearing House. But in 1931 it discovered that its figures were being used in policy and discontinued reporting the exact numbers. Policy entrepreneurs quickly turned to the New York Stock Exchange's daily quotation of stocks traded. But this new source lasted only a month until the Exchange also caught on and began publishing only approximate and rounded numbers such as 1,500,000. When this happened there was almost complete "chaos in the policy field". Until another number system could be found there was no policy betting. Within a short while in 1931 policy gamblers came up with an exceptionally complex system based on the results of pari-mutual wagering at certain race tracks. How the daily numbers were determined follows. In each race there are three results—win, place and show and depending on the pre-race odds on each horse there are three different payoffs for each race. The first policy number came from adding together the win, place and show payoffs in the first three races and then isolating the number preceding the decimal point. The second and third numbers were computed from the remaining races in a somewhat similar fashion. Table 2 using hypothetical payoffs shows the manner of deriving the three numbers.

With the number system worked out policy could once again commence. Now, obviously, policy is a high volume enterprise. One needs vast amounts of nickels, dimes and quarters to make the enterprise worthwhile. This means that there will be large numbers of employees. At the same time, as the number of bettors increases both the legal risks and the gambling risks increase. First, the problem of the law. The more bettors, the more employees the higher the chances of arrest. The enterprise's answer to this

Table 2. The method of computing the winning numbers in the policy racket beginning in 1931.

Races	1	2	3	4	5	6	7
Win	7.60	3.20	5.50	8.10	9.60	4.30	6.30
Place	8.40	6.20	8.80	3.50	4.80	6.60	7.20
Show	5.20	3.10	7.80	6.80	3.40	5.40	4.10
Total	21.20	12.50	22.10	18.40	17.80	16.30	17.60
Policy Add		55.80	→ 55.80 + 52.50 = 108.30	→ 108.30 + 17.60 = 125.90			
First Number	5						
Second Number			8				
Third Number				5			

problem was to seek protection which I will discuss shortly and to structure the business in such a manner as to minimize the possibility of important arrests. The structural response was to initiate two flows, one of information the other of money, and to keep hidden from as many people as possible the location of what was called the bank but what was really the enterprises' accounting centers. It is important to keep in mind that the bank and the banker are not synonymous. The bank is again the accounting center the place where the bets are tabulated and the payoffs are figured. No money ever goes to the bank only slips of betting information. The banker is the entrepreneur behind the enterprise. The banker never goes to the bank. He or she receives or dispenses money through special runners or pick-up people who use hidden drop stations or points. There are two types of workers in the policy business: first are salaried employees who are paid to be tabulators, runners and pick-up people; second, there are collectors and controllers whose money comes from a fixed percentage of every day's bets minus the payoffs. The collectors, controllers and banker form a simple pyramid structure. The collector is the individual who takes the bets. This individual receives both money and wagers. Until the day's tabulations are run the money stays with the collectors. The wagering information is sent on to the controllers who then pass it on to the bank with its tabulators. From the bank the daily results of winners and losers and the amount of money owed the operation from the collectors is sent first to the controllers and from them to the collectors. When the collectors receive this information they pay the winners, take their cut, and send the money left to the controllers. The controllers then take their cut and send the remainder to the banker. The system then looks like this:

Personnel		Information Flow	Money Flow
Percentage	*Salaried*	(Policy Slips)	
Banker		Collectors	Collectors
	Tabulators	↓	↓
		Controllers	Controllers
	Runners and		
Controllers	Pick-up People	↓	↓
		Tabulators	Banker
		(Ribbons)	
Collectors		↓	
		Controllers	
		↓	
		Collectors	

Money: I mentioned that the collectors, controllers and banker all work on a percentage of the day's bets. The collector's percentage was between 20 and 24% of the bets he or she handled. The controller's percentage was 6 to 10% of the bets handled by his or her collectors. The banker then received 70% of the bets. On any day when the winnings were less than the total amount wagered the money flow was one way. On days when winnings outpaced total wagers the money, of course, had to come from the banker. I commented earlier that the success of policy comes from the enormous number of bettors involved, but that his entailed two types of risks. The business was therefore structured in such a manner as to minimize the legal risks by hiding banks, by keeping identities unknown, by separating money and information. Policy entrepreneurs also protected themselves by retaining bondsmen and sometimes attorneys whose function was to handle the police and especially the Magistrates' Courts. But the second type of risk was financial. With so many bettors the possibility of breaking the bank increased. Even with the bank's margin, if enough people guessed the correct number on a given day the payoff could be enormous. The odds against this happening are rather large, but happen it did. In most cases losing days could and would be covered by the banker. But this was not always the case. Many times bankers were faced with an exceptionally large payoff and were either unable or unwilling to pay. They therefore closed their operations and typically left town for some time to escape the wrath of bettors. This is what happened to the original Schultz, Weinberg, Levy, Schoenhaus enterprise in 1929. Faced with a disastrous losing day they chose to close down rather than pay. Unlike other policy gamblers, however, such was Schultz's reputation for violence that they did not have to leave town or go into hiding.

The Syndicate

Now to centralization. In 1931, when Schultz decided to centralize all the policy business in Harlem there were a number of large and independent bankers. The six major ones in Harlem were Alexander Pompez, Joseph M. Ison, Henry Miro, Marshal Flores, Elmer Maloney, and Wilfred Brunder. What Schultz proposed to do was to pressure through traditional means these bankers into joining a combination under his control in which they would either receive a salary or divide the banker's percentage with him. But his associate George Weinberg advised that traditional "strong-arm methods" would not work with the bankers and indeed the controllers.[36] Instead, he advised Schultz to offer them something to induce them to join his syndicate. That something, Weinberg suggested, was increased protection from the law. If Schultz could guarantee a minimum of arrests, and those only of the lower echelons in the enterprise, then the bankers might more-or-less voluntarily join.

Apparently, conversations of this sort went on for the better part of a year during which time Schultz also let it be known that he was, one way or another, going to take over policy. Meanwhile other events took place in 1931 which also materially affected policy. First came the problems with the number system. Second, two of the largest bankers, Brunder and Miro, were in the process of being tried and convicted on gambling charges. Ison would take over almost all their business. Third, Schultz was applying pressure on the other bankers to join his syndicate. As of yet, however, the pressure was not too intense. Lastly, around Thanksgiving almost all the banks in Harlem were overwhelmed with losses. A favorite number was played by thousands of bettors and they won. Ison, for instance, owed $11,000 which he apparently did not have. For relief he went to Schultz who lent him money for 66% of the bank's daily profits. Ison agreed to the deal which would be consummated when the syndicate was organized. Clearly, Schultz was in the process of taking control of policy in 1931, but not quite prepared to implement his scheme.

There are three reasons given for the delay in founding the syndicate. For one, Schultz was involved in a dangerous gang war with Vincent Coll all during 1931 and was unable to move wholeheartedly into policy until the war was resolved. In February, 1932, Coll was finally murdered and the war ended. The second has to do with the protection side of his syndicate. It was not until the spring of 1932 that Tammany Sachem James J. Hines was brought into the syndicate. It was Hines who was the key to providing protection for the operation, although we will see it was a very difficult task. Lastly, even after the Thanksgiving debacle not all the bankers were ready to accept Schultz as their boss. For example, Alexander Pompez whose bank averaged $10,000 a day net was extremely reticent to accept Schultz's help even in the face of heavy losses. On direct examination Pompez testified about a meeting held right after Thanksgiving in which a Schultz representative, Sol Girsch, tried to get Pompez to pay for "protection". Pompez's reply was: "I told him that he had the wrong man, because I did not have the money or the business to pay any protection; and furthermore that we did not need no protection to run the number business in Harlem."[37] At this time the protection offered Pompez was of the menacing, strong-arm variety. He was guaranteed that no one would be able to quit his business, that all money owed him would be promptly collected, and that he need not fear kidnappers. Pompez held off Schultz for four months, only capitulating in February 1932 at around the same time that Coll was murdered.

Martin Krompier

By the end of the winter of 1932 the syndicate formed although the protection arm, and this in Weinberg's sense, was still being solidified. But policy was centralized under the direction of Schultz and his associates including Martin Krompier, J. Richard "Dixie" Davis, Abraham "Bo" Weinberg and his brother George, John Cooney, Sol Girsch, Harry Schoenhaus, Harry Wolf, Martin Weintraub, Lou "Lulu" Rosenkranz and Abraham Landau. What did centralization mean for policy in 1932? First of all control by the Schultz forces meant that what had been a Black/Hispanic enterprise in Harlem would now be directed by Whites. And that almost all the money taken in policy would never return to the community, but would be taken by Schultz and the others. So centralization's most immediate effect was racial. Structurally, a new top was grafted onto the traditional pyramid. Above the banker was the Schultz power syndicate. The other major development in 1932 concerned the implementation of the type of protection that Weinberg had first called for.

Tammany politician James J. Hines was brought into the syndicate in the spring of 1932 at a meeting with Schultz, "Bo" and George Weinberg, Rosenkranz and Davis. He was told that the syndicate needed protection from the police especially from the Sixth Division which covered most of Harlem. A bargain was struck and Hines was paid $1,000 and then put on a retainer averaging between $500 and $1,000 a week. The first time Hines was put to the test came in the late spring when the Sixth Division began a small drive against the collectors and runners. Hines was contacted and the drive ended. Everything seemed to be falling into place. Most importantly, the volume of business increased so that by the fall of 1932 it had "increased by half ". More bankers, controllers and collectors wanted to get under the spreading umbrella of protection. At this high point of centralization, the gross annual business figured out to around $20,000,000.

At almost the moment it reached its peak, however, problems began to undermine its position. The initial difficulties centered around protection. Hines was able to control the Sixth Division, but there were other police problems. In addition to the Sixth Division there were two special squads with jurisdiction in the Harlem area. The first was the Borough Headquarters Squad and the second the Chief Inspector's Squad. In the Borough Squad one particular detective named Terminello harassed the runners and collectors. Terminello was determined to "bust" the syndicate and was uncontrollable for awhile. Finally, Hines was able to have him transferred and reduced to uniform. That took care of the Borough Squad. Much more dangerous than the actions of one detective, however, were the activities of the Chief Inspector's Squad. This group was solely responsible to the Chief Inspector and he only to the Police Commissioner.

Just as the syndicate's business reached its point of greatest success, this squad went into action. It raided the Pompez bank (accounting center) arresting over 20 people and confiscating about one half million betting slips. Among the arrested was George Weinberg. Hines was able to place the case with Magistrate Hulon Capshaw and it was dismissed. But the squad did not desist. Between the time of the first raid and the disposition of the case, it raided the Ison–Flores banks. Again Hines was consulted and suggested it go before Magistrate Erwin. This case also was thrown out. Even though the cases were dismissed both raids were exceptionally costly. In addition, while they proved that Hines and therefore the syndicate "had" the Magistrates, the raids also established that Hines could not control the whole Police Department.

The syndicate then decided to take the banks out of New York City. They moved them to Mount Vernon north of the city. But it was still hazardous to move the slips from Harlem to Mount Vernon and then to return with the ribbons. And in the winter of 1933, "Lulu" Rosenkranz one of the major partners in the syndicate as well as one of Schultz's closest associates was arrested by the squad with slips destined for Mount Vernon. Once again, Hines reached Magistrate Capshaw and the case was dismissed.

Beginning in 1933, Schultz's expenses began to multiply. His income tax indictment came down; Repeal was in. In the face of both lost income and added expenses Schultz attempted a major change in the traditional economic relationships in policy. He decided that because "his case was costing him quite a lot of money and he needed all the money he could get and that he would like a bigger percentage out of the business"[38] to cut five per cent from the controllers' end of policy. For them to survive at all they would in turn have to cut back the collectors' percentage also. There was virtual rebellion. A meeting of the bankers was called where they were told of the cut. They thought it a very bad idea and countered with the suggestion of cutting the payoff from 600 to 500 to 1. This was turned down. The bankers' meeting was followed by a mass meeting of controllers and collectors at which some declared they would bank themselves rather than submit to the cut. A committee was chosen to meet with the syndicate. They went to 351 Lenox Avenue, the headquarters, and were there told by George Weinberg that the cut was going in no matter what. And it did a few days later.

Within days, the business of policy in Harlem began to decline. The collectors and controllers were not working. In about six weeks the entire business was down to about ten per cent of its former revenue. It had become obvious that if the business was to survive at all, the cut had to be dropped. And it was. The controllers, called by Dewey the "free agent in the game of policy",[39] had won. They could not be "muscled", although it does not appear that Schultz really tried. Almost immediately after the cut was rescinded the business picked up until in the fall of 1933 its gross was larger than ever before. But by then, Schultz's expenses were also correspondingly greater.

In fact, just as the business began to expand after the disaster of the cut, expenses were materially increased by Hines who needed large sums of money to finance the campaign of his personal choice for District Attorney, William Copeland Dodge. At around the same time, Schultz was approached by Otto "Abadaba" Berman a noted handicapper who claimed that he could fix the numbers. Berman was handicapping at the Coney Island race track in Cincinnati, Ohio. During its racing season which in 1933 lasted between ten and twelve weeks, the Cincinnati track was the one used by the syndicate to get their numbers. Now Berman was both a handicapper and a "comeback" man at the track. His job was primarily to place "lay-off" bets at the track for bookmakers. To do this he must have an open telephone line and be situated close to the wagering booths. Berman's plan was to manipulate the odds on the seventh race in order to insure that certain heavily played numbers did not appear. To do this he must have a communication system with the banks who between the sixth and seventh races, by which time the first two winning numbers were known, would tell him which are their bad third numbers. The banks would have to know as rapidly as possible after determining the second number what third numbers had to be avoided. They would then tell Berman and being an outstanding handicapper he would then bet money on certain horses in the seventh race in order to change the odds and therefore the payoff and ultimately the third number. In order to accomplish this, Berman needed $10,000 a week, part of which was his salary and part used for placing the bets. It is interesting that Berman had first broached this idea back in 1932 but had then been turned down by Schultz who wanted to keep the game "honest", according to Weinberg. But in 1933

Schultz needed all the "edge" he could get. And he accepted Berman's proposal.

A review of the consequences of centralization in policy in 1933 is instructive. The two most significant developments were the cut and the fix. The first, as we know, was an almost complete disaster. By attacking the structure of the game Schultz almost lost the business. On the other hand, by apparently fixing the numbers through Berman's absolutely astounding skill, Schultz was able to prevent any of those periodic disasters such as occured around Thanksgiving, 1931. Berman had considerably reduced the area of gambling risk. It was expensive but clearly worth it if it in fact worked. Two other developments in 1933 were also significant. Both concern Hines. He was successful in getting his man Dodge elected, and he finally was able to break the Chief Inspector's Squad. All in all it seemed to herald the continuing success of the syndicate although it had learned a bitter lesson of the limits of centralization at the hands of the controllers.

But contrary to expectations from 1934 until Schultz's death in October, 1935, the syndicate seemed to dissolve. The causes were mostly extrinsic; Schultz's money and legal problems being the most important. In addition, pressure was brought upon the syndicate by the new Commissioner of Investigations, Blanshard, through his investigation of the bail bond rackets. Soon, the Grand Jury investigating bail bonds and other rackets would engage in their famous imbroglio with District Attorney Dodge who tried to steer them away from policy. It would not work and ended up with Dewey as Special Prosecutor. As early as the spring of 1934 important bankers would leave the syndicate. Over time then, the syndicate declined until it disintegrated.

What did not decline, however, was policy. The industry in Harlem simply reverted back to its pre-Schultz structure beginning in 1934. There were still bankers, controllers, collectors, runners, bondsmen and assorted fixers. The syndicate which had been grafted onto this structure merely withered away as Schultz's problems multiplied. But let me not discount this effort at centralization and coordination. The syndicate did for a few years run policy in Harlem. And in so doing, it did address the most significant areas of risk in the enterprise. With Hines as its contact man, the syndicate did have considerable leverage in the Magistrates' Courts. But as Seabury had demonstrated earlier, the Magistrates' Courts had always been exceptionally protective of policy entrepreneurs. In fact, Schultz's attorney, "Dixie" Davis, had first come to his attention as a fixer in the Magistrates' Courts. The question then is whether the influence of Hines materially increased the corruption in the courts. And there is no way of answering that.

Furthermore, the legal problems experienced by policy were undoubtedly increased by the development of the syndicate itself. It did not take very long for law enforcement to realize that Schultz and his cronies had taken over policy thereby increasing its visibility and turning it from a gambling racket to a part of the "Schultz empire". Perhaps without the syndicate the Chief Inspector's Squad would not have been so eager. The point is that it is not certain just what the consequences were in the area of protection from the law that was supposedly one of the contributions of this centralization. In the other area of greatest risk, the possibility of bankruptcy, the Berman fix was significant. But it was also peculiar and exceptionally transient resting upon Berman's position and decidedly unique skills. It could not be duplicated by others nor could it happen at the other tracks which were used when the season at Coney Island was over. There was no way to fix the numbers all the time. In addition, it was carried out within the context of Schultz's ever increasing demands for money. The revenue increase generated by the fix was gobbled up by Schultz and Hines and did not have any trickle effect upon the rest of policy. Once again then, it is impossible to evaluate the overall effect of centralization upon the traditional risks in policy.

What is most striking about the centralization interlude in policy is first of all the issue of race. As remarked on earlier, the syndicate meant white domination of a Black/Hispanic operation. This white domination also had racial consequences for the mass of workers in policy. There is evidence that indicates Black and Hispanic tabulators, collectors and runners were replaced by whites in some of the particular banks. Also significant are two factors, the first being the rebellion of controllers and collectors, the second being the overall weakness of the policy entrepreneurs to resist the demands of the entrepreneurs of violence. The two issues are intertwined and reminiscent of the Luciano conspiracy in prostitution. Both syndicates in attempting to extend their power over key personnel ran into unexpected problems. In policy there was a rebellion while in prostitution there was "cheating". The policy people were obviously more successful in resisting inroads on traditional arrangements because Schultz decided he was not in a position to "muscle" them. The bookers and madams, on the other hand, were terrorized by the Luciano enforcers and turned to more covert forms of resistance. The point is that the enterprise syndicates in prostitution and policy were susceptible to domination by "violent expropriators". And yet there were limits to this domination and methods of expressing what they were. What finally brought an end to the "extortion" of policy and prostitution entrepreneurs were factors extraneous to the enterprises which were profound changes in aspects of New York's criminal justice system.

They could not be overcome from inside because at the top there was a monopoly of force no matter how restrained it may have been at times. Clearly though, there was nothing inexorable about extreme centralization in either illicit enterprise. For a short while in the 1930s they were seized by syndicates whose forte was violence. After the demise of these syndicates they were not again subjected to such pressures.[40]

Last Thoughts

Let us discuss, for a moment, power and weakness in the complex world of illicit enterprises. Enterprise syndicates appear to be rather precariously situated between two zones of power. The primary zone we have talked about so far is the underworld itself. It is obvious that enterprise syndicates are often preyed upon by hijackers, thieves, and extortionists. To achieve some security from this sea of potential enemies, an enterprise syndicate cannot appeal to criminal justice given that it is engaged in illegal activities itself. When the potential enemies become actual ones, it is forced to deal with underworld power brokers who may be the very ones preying upon the enterprise in the first place. In such cases the broker and his associates may be put on the payroll as protectors, or may actually take over the enterprise putting the original syndicate managers themselves upon an ever decreasing payroll.

The second zone of power is that of criminal justice. Enterprise syndicates are typically structured in such a way as to reduce the risk of significant arrests. At the same time, the syndicate attempts to purchase the passivity of law enforcement through bribes and payoffs. Police are paid not to arrest members of the syndicate, while various fixers (bondsmen, attorneys) are available to work the next level of criminal justice in case law enforcement does act. Concerning criminal justice it would seem its role in the world of illicit enterprises is either the passive one of non-interference cemented by the bond of bribery, or the active one of pursuing crooks and harassing the enterprise. Actually, of course, law enforcement being a complex of overlapping jurisdictions both roles are pursued at the same time. As we have seen with policy, the Sixth Division was passive while the Chief Inspector's squad was active; the District Attorney's office was passive, the Special Prosecutor quite the opposite. But it would be a serious mistake to hold criminal justice especially law enforcement to just these two roles in illicit enterprises. There is a third one which is that of active criminality. And in the 1940s, in the enterprise of bookmaking, in the Borough of Brooklyn, the police engaged in this third role with almost outlandish fervor, acting much like an extended power syndicate of the early 1930s. The particular example I am thinking of is the Harry Gross bookmaking syndicate discussed in Chapter five. In this instance the police moved from protection/tolerance to management/extortion. During the eight years that this enterprise operated, the police exploited Gross who in turn "cheated" his employees. In fact, in the latter years of the decade Gross worked for the police who in 1949 bankrolled the operation after Gross suffered heavy gambling losses.

The factor I want to emphasize is that enterprise syndicates tended to be weak, prone to exploitation in a variety of ways by representatives from both zones of power. In addition, when there is evidence of centralization of an illicit enterprise through either consolidation or expansion one must be extremely wary of its significance. More often than not the impetus for these developments come not from the original managers but from outside or contingent forces. And when that happens the relationship between the new managers and the original syndicate(s) is at bottom extortionary and therefore divisive as the rebellions, cheating and intra-syndicate violence reveals. The primary significance of the centralization episodes discussed lie in the conflicts generated rather than in centralization itself.

NOTES

[1] See Dean Jennings, *We Only Kill Each Other: The Life and Bad Times of Bugsy Siegel* (Greenwich; Connecticut, 1967); Jack McPhaul, *Johnny Torrio: First of the Gang Lords* (New Rochelle, New York, 1970); Messick, 1971; Sann, 1971; Ed Reid, *The Shame of New York* (New York, 1953); Martin Gosch and Richard Hammer, *The Last Testament of Lucky Luciano* (Boston, 1974).

[2] Mark H. Haller, "Bootleggers and American Gambling, 1920–1950," in Commission on the Review of the National Policy Towards Gambling, *Gambling in America: Appendix I* (Washington, D.C., 1976), 109.

[3] *Ibid.*, 110–111.

[4] *U.S. v. Wexler*, 2255. The transcript I utilized came from Governor Dewey's office.

[5] See the Bureau of Social Morals files especially stories 719 and 871. The Bureau's material is part of the collection of the New York Kehillah located in the Judah L. Magnes Archives, the Central Archives for the History of the Jewish People, Jerusalem, Israel.

[6] See Alan A. Block, "The Snowman Cometh: Coke in Progressive New York," *Criminology* 17 (1979).

[7] "Breweries Operated by Jewish Syndicate 1928–1933," in *O'Dwyer Papers*, 1.

[8] *Ibid.*

[9] The material comes from Dewey, *Personal Papers*, Series 1: Early Career, Box 10, The University of Rochester Library, Department of Rare Books.

[10] "Breweries Operated by Jewish Syndicate," 2.

[11] *Ibid.*, 3.

[12] *Ibid.*, 3–4.

[13] *Ibid.*, 1.

[14] *Ibid.*, 4.

15 *Ibid.*

16 *Ibid.*

17 *Ibid.*, 5.

18 *Ibid.*

19 *Ibid.*

20 *Ibid.*

21 Court of Appeals of the State of New York, The People of the State of New York against Charles Luciano, et al., *Record on Appeal*, 311. Once again the transcript came from Governor Dewey's office.

22 *Ibid.*, 312.

23 Court of Appeals of the State of New York, The People of the State of New York against Charles Luciano, et al. *Respondent's Brief*, 13.

24 *Ibid.*, 14.

25 *Record on Appeal*, 320.

26 *Ibid.*, 321.

27 *Ibid.*

28 *Respondent's Brief*, 16.

29 *Ibid.*, 17.

30 *Ibid.*, 14–15.

31 *Record on Appeal*, 357–358.

32 *Ibid.*, 351.

33 *Respondent's Brief*, 22.

34 Court of Appeals of the State of New York, The People of the State of New York against James J. Hines, *Case on Appeal*, 136. And again, this particular transcript was put at my disposal by Governor Dewey's office.

35 Dewey, *Twenty Against the Underworld*, 117.

36 *Case on Appeal*, 139.

37 *Ibid.*, 556.

38 *Ibid.*, 894.

39 *Ibid.*, 130.

40 For a discussion of one Harlem policy bank in the 1940s, see Department of Investigation, MR-No. 9475 "Supplemental Report" (December 20, 1944) in the *La Guardia Papers*, Municipal Archives.

This particular investigation was of an enterprise syndicate operating policy under the direction of Louis Katz, Morris Katz, Max Katz and Louis Wexler. The cover for gambling was maintained by a corporation known as the Harlem Check Cashing Corporation, 290 Lennox Avenue. The Corporation was licensed by the New York State Banking Department.

Chapter 7
Power and the Urban Economy

To begin with I want to repeat a list of industries from Chapter 3 which were acknowledged to be pervaded by "racketeers": bead, cinder, cloth shrinking, clothing, construction, flower shops, Fulton market, funeral, fur dressing, grape, hod carriers, ice, Kosher butchers, laundry, leather, live poultry, master barbers, milk, millinery, musical, night patrol, neckwear, newsstand, operating engineers, overall, paper box, paper hangers, shirt makers, taxicabs, and window cleaners. All of these industries and trades as well as others were subject in one fashion or another to racketeering which was well defined in the 1930s as organized extortion, the forte of power syndicates.

The question for researchers is how to account for such an extraordinary development in which so many of the city's key trades became the province of power syndicates. The general answer to such an inquiry lies in the often violently antagonistic relations between labor and capital, workers and bosses, in the modern era. The history of trade unionism in the United States reveals the violent methodologies adopted by employers to prevent, contain, and destroy unions.[1] Among the methodologies was the use of hired thugs to engage in strikebreaking. Very often, the services of strikebreakers were purchased by a burgeoning industry known as the private detective trade dominated by such agencies as Pinkerton, Burns and Farley. Agencies engaged in strikebreaking were not timorous in announcing their services. For example, the Journal of the National Association of Manufacturers in 1906 carried an announcement of the Joy Detective Service of Cleveland which stated: " 'WE BREAK STRIKES ... We guard property during strikes, employ non-union men to fill places of strikers.' "[2] Many of the individuals recruited by private detective agencies were local gangsters some of whom because of their "ethnic and community identification" were doubly useful to employers. Noting a complaint from a New York trades union official, Jeffreys–Jones comments: " 'The private detectives employed by these agencies are recruited from East side gangs, the same gangs that support the politicians ...', with the result that politicians persuaded the police to side with employers."[3]

Within the general social situation in which employers resorted to local power syndicates masquerading as private detective agencies for strikebreaking and labor mediation there was room for duplicity and the double-cross. Jeffreys–Jones reports on a meeting between David Silverman, an executive board member of the Neck Wear Makers' Union, and Max Schlansky, of the United Secret Service Agency in 1914.

> Schlansky entered into conversation with Silverman about the strike in progress against the business of Oppenheimer, Franc and Langsdorf. The guard business arising out of the dispute was being handled for the notorious Val O'Farrell Agency by its chief agent, Schultz. The engagement was yielding $300 weekly for Schultz, but was now coming to an end. Schlansky averred that Schultz did not know his business, for he had let slip by many opportunities to prolong the strike. Perceiving an opportunity to extract some money from the situation, Schlansky proposed to Silverman that the union leader hire some of his plug uglies to beat up Schultz's men. Schlansky pointed out that in this event, Oppenheimer and partners would probably fire Schultz, and engage Schlansky. Then, presumably for a further fee, Schlansky would ensure that the union won the strike.[4]

Having created an arena of violence by their intransigence, employers soon found that extortion could be a double-edged sword. Nevertheless, even with the machinations of some power syndicates who turned their violence against employers, it is clear that the one consistent victim throughout all this turmoil was the rank and file. Control of workers through violence and the threat of violence lined the pockets of employers first and foremost, professional criminals, and corrupt union officials. The ends to which this private violence was employed besides the immediate pecuniary ones included strikebreaking, sweetheart contracts, price-fixing, monopoly and oligopoly.

The Needle Trades

In New York during at least the first four decades of the twentieth century the garment industry was the scene of almost constant turmoil in which power syndicates played pivotal roles. In fact, in the thirty trades enumerated by Seabury as racketeer dominated in the early 1930s, nine of them were part of the garment industry: bead, clothing, cloth shrinking, fur dressing, leather, millinery, neckwear, overall, and shirt makers. Among the most significant professional criminals to work in the garment industry are Louis "Lepke" Buchalter who, along with his partner Jacob "Gurrah" Shapiro, had virtual control of aspects of the clothing industry in Manhattan from the late 1920s through most of the following decade. Their dominance of the field of criminal labor relations was not seriously challenged until the fall of 1936 when the Federal government tried them on charges of extortion in New

York's almost Byzantine fur dressing industry, one of the garment trades. To understand the roles played by Buchalter and Shapiro, and in whose interests they acted, it is important to relate something of the history of the garment industry and its corresponding trade union movements. While concentrating to a large extent on the garment trades, however, I will pursue the activities of Buchalter and Shapiro into other trades especially flour trucking.

The clothing industry provided a place for the Jewish immigrant, according to Moses Rischin, "where the initial shock of contact with a bewildering world was tempered by a familiar milieu".[5] Although the manufacture of men's clothing was already an important segment of New York's economy, the arrival of the East European immigrant Jews drastically changed the ready-made clothing industry's organizational pattern. Revived was the contractor who had been ousted in the 1870s as factories had replaced outside manufacture. This time, however, the contractor introduced a unique type of production, known as section work, which exploited new recruits through a minute and deplorable division of labor. Because loft and factory rents were so high, the contractor supplied the perfect solution to the destructively competitive economics of seasonal manufacture. Upon the contractor was placed the burdens of manufacture production risks and the responsibility for supervising and recruiting a labor force. In return, contractors attempting to lower production costs developed the task system. This meant that a work quota was set for the team engaged in section work. The system, Rischin notes, was described as " 'the most ingenious and effective system of overexertion known to modern industry' ".[6]

The changes in organization went hand-in-hand with technical improvements and innovations and the influx of cheap immigrant labor which all together were responsible for the exceptional growth of the garment trades which began in the 1880s. Most of this growth was in the area of men's clothing. The phenomenal expansion of women's ready-made clothing had to wait until the turn of the century when "labor costs fell, techniques of design improved, and women gradually emancipated themselves from the home".[7] The fur industry, in turn, emerged in conjunction with the women's clothing industry. Rischin has determined that by 1910 around 75 percent of the workers as well as the majority of manufacturers in the fur trades were immigrant Jews.[8]

Commenting on the overall importance of the garment trades, Rischin states that from 1880 to 1910, the social economy of New York was reshaped by the clothing industry. He notes that in 1880 almost 10 percent of Manhattans' factories were engaged in manufacturing clothing and that they employed over 28 percent of the industrial labor force. By 1910, the figures had changed to 47 percent of the factories manufacturing clothing and employing 46 percent of the industrial labor force. In a study of the demography of the American Jew based on the 1900 census, Ben B. Seligman finds that 36 percent of the 143,337 employed persons described as Russian, almost all of whom were Jewish living in New York, Chicago, Philadelphia, Detroit, Boston, Pittsburgh, and St. Louis were employed in the needle trades.[9] Remarking on the economic and occupational status of American Jews between the two world wars, Seligman states that "three-fourths of the New York City Jews engaged in manufacturing in 1937 were in the clothing and headwear industries, where they constituted more than one-half of the total number employed in these industries". It is also estimated for 1937 that "6 percent of the New York City Jews in industry were furriers, and they constituted about four-fifths of those in the fur industry".[10] Along with the spectacular and increasing Jewish caste of the needle trades went pitiful wages, extended hours, innumerable slack seasons, contracting and subcontracting, home work, and the lack of even rudimentary safe-guards of health and decency which made the needle trades infamous as a "sweated" industry.

As a consequence of conditions like these, and a number of other factors, a dynamic trade union movement developed. The founding institution for the Jewish labor movement was the United Hebrew Trades begun in 1888.[11] The major purpose of this group was obviously organization of Jewish workers into trade unions. In a large number of cases, the unions which were formed either with the initiative or help of the UHT were local or regional bodies that had next to be affiliated with an existing national organization. In the garment trades, however, there were no national organizations until 1891 when the United Garment Workers was started for the men's clothing industry. Will Herberg describes this group as "at bottom a coalition of men's tailors, largely radical-minded immigrant Jews and Italians, on the one hand, and conservative American overall and work clothes makers, on the other".[12]

Workers in the women's garment industry waited until 1900 for their national organization—the International Ladies Garment Workers Union (ILGWU). Although the ILGWU started well, the 1903 business depression halted its growth. Subsequently, the ILGWU suffered through a difficult period which ended in 1909 when an economic upswing provided the most important surge of trade unionism that Jewish labor experienced until 1933. In the next five years, (1909–1914) there developed what Herberg calls "a tremendous transformation in the power and status of the Jewish labor movement".[13] The major events during this period in the women's garment industry were the "uprising of the twenty thousand" and the "great revolt". In the fall of 1909, a spontaneous rebellion of almost twenty thousand shirtwaist makers in New York, mostly women, proved to be enormously successful. Part of this triumph for labor can be gauged by noting that at the time of the strike, the entire membership of the ILGWU was only 2,000; while at the end, the shirtwaist makers union itself had over 10,000 members.[14] Closely following the rebellion of shirtwaist makers was the strike of the New York cloak makers known as the "great revolt". Unlike the earlier action, this strike took place in an industry employing primarily men and in which there was a strong and deep tradition of trade unionism. The strike was called for July 10, 1910, and about 60,000 workers responded. Like the earlier strike, this one too was a victory with most of the workers' demands granted. Following the example of the women's garment workers, the furriers called a general strike which was successful and led to the formation, in 1913, of the International Fur Workers Union.

The trade union movement among the men's clothing workers during these years was hampered by a serious conflict between the leaders of the United Garment Workers and the rank and file tailors. One of the primary differences was found in the extreme reluctance of the UGW leaders to become involved in labor struggles. The militant tailors, however, had great faith in the power of the strike. Increasingly, the tailors viewed their national leaders as indifferent to their problems, primarily interested in containing their militancy. The rift in the United Garment Workers widened in 1910 and again in 1912 when a general strike was called at the instigation of the New York Brotherhood of Tailors. At first, the leaders of the UGW refused to recognize the action. Later, "behind the backs of the workers and even many of the strike leaders, the UGW officials ... tried to bring the strike to an end with an agreement that enraged the strikers because it ignored the questions of recognition and other essential demands".[15] In 1914, the conflict between the tailors, who represented a majority of the unionists, and the conservative leadership resulted in the formation of the Amalgamated Clothing Workers of America, an independent union under the leadership of Sidney Hillman and Joseph Schlossberg. The Amalgamated was almost immediately called a "dual union" and therefore a betrayal of labor solidarity by the AFL. The other Jewish unions, however, ignored the slander and viewed it as a *bona fide* union. The Amalgamated soon established itself as both an integral and significant element of the labor movement wherever men's clothing was manufactured.

During the 1920s, after a period of notable accomplishments, the Jewish labor movement, along with all of organized labor in America, entered an era of decline that was not reversed until 1933. In addition to sharing in the general reversal of trade union fortunes, the Jewish unions were beset by a factor that soon overshadowed all their other problems—"the Communist drive for power". Will Herberg writes that the Jewish unions were the ground of the best planned and most nearly triumphant Communist drive for power in American labor history and that at the end of this decade-long struggle, the Jewish unions were almost completely demoralized, if not ruined.[16] Those years of strife were characterized by declining membership, economic misfortune and internal conflicts of great magnitude at a time of increased racketeer penetration.

Labor racketeering which in its simplest form is direct extortion by the imposition of union sanctions originally developed in the needle trades out of the necessity to fight scabs and thugs hired by employers. In the early part of this century prior to World War I, gangsters such as Benjamin Fein and Irving "Waxey Gordon" Wexler who fought employer goons became semipermanent fixtures in a number of needle trade locals and the United Hebrew Trades as noted in the preceding chapter. From policing strikes it was a short step to helping in organizing workers and to domination of key locals. Continuing labor–management and internal union struggles throughout the 1920s enabled other criminals such as Buchalter and Shapiro to attain positions of influence.

Buchalter's apprenticeship in the labor–management conflicts of the 1920s is somewhat unclear. One account in *Business Week*[17] states that from about 1920 on, Buchalter was the leader of a small gang that operated both independently and under the direction of Arnold Rothstein. The article describes how, as the decade progressed, Buchalter's group aligned itself more and more with the Amalgamated Clothing Workers of America and less and less with Rothstein. John Hutchinson, relying on this article, writes that Buchalter "now entered the scene as the agent for minor Amalgamated officials".[18] Using his men as regular pickets, Buchalter had them attack the Rothstein strike breakers whenever they appeared. Other duties supposedly performed by Buchalter and his gang included arson in garment firms, destroying elevator cables in loft buildings, burning clothing stocks with acid, and of course, beating and murdering. When Rothstein was murdered in 1928, Buchalter assumed a dominant position in the rackets in New York.

In contrast to this account, Burton Turkus in *Murder, Inc.*, writes that Buchalter and his partner, Jacob Shapiro were members of Jacob "Little Augie" Orgen's gang. Beginning as strike breakers, Orgen and his men soon indicated their willingness to work for the unions also. Orgen, Turkus states, frequently had his gang work both sides in the same dispute, or would contract to provide both with guns and blackjacks. Turkus goes on to describe the murder of Orgen and the emerging dominance of Buchalter. Following a conflict between Buchalter and Orgen over whether or not to interfere in a strike among painters, Buchalter directed his partner Shapiro, to murder Orgen, which he did on October 15, 1927.[19]

Whatever Buchalter's background truly was, one fact is certainly accurate, and that is his preeminence in the men's clothing industry. Buchalter accomplished his preeminence by participating in the organization of truck owners and self-employed drivers into an employers trade association which was perhaps the most significant act in the development of what must now be called business racketeering. To make the point clearer, one of the first actions of the association was to raise the cartage costs for men's clothing followed by the sharing of the windfall profits by the members of the association.[20]

At about the same time Buchalter became what Hutchinson modestly calls "influential in the clothing drivers' local of the Amalgamated", thus completing what we will see is the classic equation of business racketeering. Finally, it was at this time that Buchalter and Shapiro bought into some clothing firms, thus moving into the arena of white collar crime.

Let us expand upon the methods by which racketeers become entrepreneurs. First consider the details of Buchalter's and Shapiro's relationship with businessman, Joseph Miller, as reported by the FBI:

> Miller has been in the coat front manufacturing business since 1907, and in 1933, the name of his firm changed to the Pioneer Coat Front Company, Inc. In that year, Miller took Shapiro and Buchalter into his business as one-third partners, following their investment of $20,000 each. In 1934, Miller sold his New York plant to Samuel Weiner for $50,000 and moved to Philadelphia. At this time Weiner ascertained that Buchalter and Shapiro were stockholders in the New York Pioneer Company and they demanded to be placed on Weiners payroll, stating even though Miller had moved to Philadelphia under an agreement not to open up in the coat front manufacturing business in New York City nor to sell to his old customers, nevertheless, he would not keep his agreement and Weiner would need the services of Buchalter and Shapiro for forcing Miller to keep his promise. At this time, Buchalter and Shapiro, without any capital investment whatsoever, were taken into the Perfection Coat Front Manufacturing Company, and received $300 each, weekly. They were not satisfied with the salaries paid them by Weiner and took additional money from the Perfection Company in the nature of loans, resulting in losses to this organization of $75,000 from April 12 to September 1, 1934. The company then could not obtain additional credit unless Joseph Miller returned to New York to take over management of the company. Buchalter and Shapiro, in an effort to force Miller to return to New York from Philadelphia, stopped him from selling coat fronts manufactured in Philadelphia to his New York customers.[21]

What seems clear from the FBI account, although not commented on by them, was that Buchalter, Shapiro and Miller had entered into a scheme to defraud Weiner. Obviously, Miller had not lived up to his part of the original agreement and was busy selling to his former New York customers. It is also apparent that both Buchalter and Shapiro knew well in advance that Miller would fail to fulfill his contract and that would provide their rationale for bilking Weiner which would cause Miller to be brought back into the business.

A further indication of the business machinations engaged in by Buchalter and Shapiro along with Miller concerns the formation in 1933 of the Leo Greenberg & Company, Inc. This corporation was founded with Nathan Borish and Joseph Miller investing $10,000 and $5,000 each. Then in 1934, Jacob Shapiro also invested in the company in sufficient amount to obtain a half interest. The company's name was changed to Greenberg and·Shapiro and Jacob Shapiro placed his brother Carl in as manager of the company. The following year the company was reorganized into the Raleigh Manufacturers Company with Nathan Borish, Carl Shapiro, Jacob Shapiro, Louis Buchalter and Louis Miller each having a 20 percent interest.

One final example of the methods by which Buchalter, Shapiro and other "union organizers" joined the ranks of owners deals with the outcome of a work stoppage called by the Amalgamated to prevent garment work from being carted out of New York to non-union firms primarily located in Pennsylvania. One of the garment trucking firms balked at the stoppage claiming that it had been "double-crossed by the Amalgamated once before".[22] Buchalter countered that argument by assuring the boss of the company, Louis Cooper, that he had nothing to worry about that he (Buchalter) was now the Amalgamated. Cooper responded that he would only agree to stop his trucks if Buchalter would become his partner. Buchalter agreed and the trucks stopped.

In 1931, Buchalter attempted to take control of the cutters' union, Local 4, of the Amalgamated and thereby precipitated what Matthew Josephson, in his laudatory biography of Sidney Hillman, terms the "terrible emergency".[23] The strategic importance of the cutters' union is described by Joel Seidman:

> The jobber-contractor system is particularly vulnerable to gangster influence. Under the system of inside production, with workers of all degrees of skills under the same rook, the superior economic power of the highly skilled worker can be utilized to help unionize the entire plant; so long as the relatively small number of skilled workers refuse to work under nonunion conditions, the plant can scarcely operate, whether or not it enjoys the protection of gangsters. Under the contracting system, however, the cutters, comprising

a large percentage of the skilled workers, may work in the jobbers' shop under union conditions. If the cut goods can then be shipped to nonunion contracting ships, anywhere within a radius of a hundred miles or even more, the enterprise can undersell its completely unionized competition. The function of the gangsters is then to protect the trucks that haul the cut goods to the contractor and bring the finished product back. Protection of trucking at or near the jobber's office is more important than safeguarding the contract shop against union organizers; the gangster may indeed perform both functions, though in many small towns, the police may stand ready to repel the union organizing drives, without extra cost to the garment manufacturer.

The two points of control are therefore the cutting room and trucking. When the union is functioning properly, it checks the volume of goods cut with the volume received by inside and authorized contract shops, and learns from the truckers where the balance is being taken. If some of the cutters can be persuaded to send false figures to the union office, however, receiving part of the net savings as their share of the loot, and if in addition, the metropolitan politicians or police are bought off so that the gangsters riding the trucks are not molested in the performance of their duties, then indeed the business that receives gangster protection will prosper, and the union tailors and the legitimate employers will suffer.[24]

Seidman adds that this was exactly the situation in the metropolitan New York men's clothing industry.

Like the story of Buchalter's early years in the garment trades, the history of his battle with Sidney Hillman and the Amalgamated over control of Local 4 has several versions. According to Hutchinson, Buchalter seized the union by striking an alliance with Philip Orlofsky, one of Hillman's opponents in the Amalgamated and the leader of Local 4. Orlofsky turned control of the local over to Buchalter. Subsequently, Buchalter went after other locals of the Amalgamated, threatening to murder several officials unless they sided with him. Buchalter and Orlofsky also established for a short time the Independent Clothing Workers Union. The rest of this story relates how Hillman put the damper on racketeering by ousting Orlofsky and his crew from Local 4 and then physically seizing the union office on the morning of August 29, 1931. The alleged maneuver broke the racketeer's hold on the men's clothing industry according to what must be seen as a conservative account.

Paul Berger

Significantly different from the above version is the story of Buchalter and the Amalgamated told by prosecutor, Burton Turkus, which was constructed from the testimony and confessions of several of the racketeers themselves and confirmed in archival documents. Buchalter gained control of the cutters, Turkus relates, by convincing certain of their leaders that it would be advantageous if his mob replaced Terry Burns and Ab Slabow, who were then Local 4's enforcers. At the same time, Orlofsky who had been a business agent for the union became the manager of the cutters' local. In the battle between Hillman and Orlofsky, Turkus contends that Buchalter used Orlofsky as a pawn, trading him off for a deal with Hillman. This maneuver was followed by the designation of Bruno Belea, the general organizer of the Amalgamated, and of two Buchalter hoods, Paul Berger and Danny Fields, as the new intermediaries between Buchalter and the union. Later, another of Buchalter's men received $25,000 from Hillman himself for delivery to Buchalter. With his position concerning the Amalgamated supposedly secured, Buchalter next turned to management. He extorted anywhere from $5,000 to $50,000 from both truckers and individual manufacturers. One of Buchalter's most important operatives, Max Rubin, states that from 1934 to 1937 he took part in shakedowns of $400 to $700 per week—and he was only one of many collectors. Turkus also notes that it had been charged "that reputable garment trucking firms alone yielded Lepke a million dollars a year for ten years".[25] Not calculated, however, was the amount of money saved by employers engaged in price fixing, restraint of trade, and wage freezes.

By 1932, Buchalter became involved in the fur dressing trade. Buchalter was approached by members of the fur dressing industry and asked if he would help in overcoming resistance to an organization of manufacturers. The request, obviously criminal in intent, called for the formation of a syndicate under Buchalter's direction which would work in concert with an earlier criminal conspiracy formed by employers. As we have already seen with the formation of an employers' association among garment truckers, so-called labor racketeering "flourishes most effectively in conjunction with trade associations formed and maintained in demoralized industries".[26] These employer associations are, of course, a device to stabilize competition and to raise commodity prices. In some cases, however, "the temptation to attract business by price cutting may be so strong, that coercion becomes necessary to compel members to remain in the association or competitors to join it". In these kinds of situations, racketeers usually through intimidation of local union leadership or as partners with corrupt trade unionists are able to threaten labor problems against those recalcitrant firms attracted by the advantages of price cutting.

The fur industry was both demoralized and exceedingly competitive, according to Hutchinson. Because fur manufacturing was a skilled trade, resistant to mechanization and performed largely by hand, access into the industry was simple. The majority of firms were small: about 25 percent had only one or two employees; and, over half employed four workers, or less. In addition, Hutchinson writes that the fur trade was highly susceptible to fashion changes, quite unstable in prices, an arena replete with business and economic failures, and finally, a kind of ethical wasteland. Also, the depression struck the fur industry harder than any of the other needle trades with fur imports dropping by 1932, to one-quarter, and exports to one-third of the 1929 base. These grave difficulties increased the employers normally competitive, secretive and suspicious behavior towards each other. They were notoriously uncooperative in facing common industry problems.

Prodded by desperate competition after three years of the Great Depression in what was probably the most cutthroat part of the fur industry, the fur dressers invented two organizations they hoped would promote both stability and profit. Formed early in 1932 were the Protective Fur Dressers Corporation (Protective) consisting of seventeen of the largest rabbit skin dressing companies in the country and the Fur Dressers Factor Corporation (Factor), which included forty-six of the largest dressers of fur other than rabbit skins. As outlined later by the Federal Bureau of Investigation, the purposes and functions of the two corporations were to eliminate from the industry all the dressing firms which were not members, to persuade all dealers to work only with firms which belonged to the corporations and/or to prevent them from dealing with non-members. The associations were to set prices and to implement a quota system insuring that the different members of the corporations received a fixed percentage of the entire business handled by the member firms. Also, the associations set up a system of credit which enforced frequent settlements and blacklisted dealers who did not pay on time.

Once the corporations were organized, all the dealers and manufacturers were notified that henceforth their business was to be given to a firm designated by the Association. They were also told that prices would be increased immediately and all accounts were to be settled every Friday in full. When the Protective was first organized, the individual members set the price for dressing the cheapest rabbit skins at five cents a piece; subsequently, prices were raised until the minimum was seven and the maximum ten cents. The FBI estimated that this association controlled about eighty to ninety percent of the trade in 1932 and around fifty percent the following year. Those dealers and manufacturers who refused to cooperate with the Protective and continued doing business with independent fur dressers were subject to first, telephone warnings, and then beatings and the destruction of their goods and plants by corrosive acids and stench bombs. In extreme cases some firms were told to permanently close down or be blown up.[27]

Buchalter and Shapiro were brought into the fur industry through the efforts of Abraham Beckerman, previously a high official in the Amalgamated and subsequently general manager of the Fur Dressers Factor Corporation and the Associated Employers of Fur Workers, Inc. Beckerman's initial problems as general manager of the Factor were organizational and accordingly, he solicited the help of Buchalter and Shapiro, both of whom he had known from the Amalgamated. Beckerman explained to Buchalter and Shapiro that there was a need for "organizational work", meaning violent coercion. Beckerman then said, according to the FBI, that before he became associated with the Factor, it had contracted with gangster Jerry Sullivan, a member of the Owney Madden gang, to handle the organizational problems.[28] Sullivan's work was unsatisfactory and Beckerman had been requested to get the association out of the deal. This he had now done by contracting with Buchalter and Shapiro.

The work performed by Buchalter and Shapiro was the obvious: informed by contact men within the industry which dealers, dressers, manufacturers and union officials were not cooperating, they directed their men to intimidate and coerce these individuals into joining the Association. The FBI concluded that all together, more than fifty telephone threats were made along with twelve assaults, ten bombings, three cases of acid throwing, two of arson, and one kidnapping.[29]

A typical example of their methods can be seen in their dealings with the firm of J. Joseph, Inc., which had been averaging over a million dollars worth of business a year from 1918 to 1932 importing rabbit skins from New Zealand and Australia. During the summer of 1932, shortly after the Protective was organized, J. Joseph, Inc., began experiencing problems. When the Protective was formed, Joseph had been parcelling out some of his work to the Waverly Fur Dressing Company in Newark, New Jersey, which he continued to do until the Waverly was bombed in the spring of 1932. Joseph later received a number of threatening communications from the Protective's enforcers. On May 14, 1933, while Joseph was sitting on a bench, an unknown individual approached him and threw acid into his face. Three days later he was told that the acid "comes from the Protective". Concerning the bombing of the Waverly Company, the FBI investigators found that at the time of the explosion the firm was negotiating membership with the Protective. The Waverly Company, which did all its business with a single customer, handled about thirty thousand skins a week. The Protective demanded that the company reduce its business to fifteen thousand a week. Because of this demand, the Waverly Company had attempted to remain outside the Protective.

Buchalter and Shapiro had a relatively short career in the fur dressing industry, they lasted from April of 1932 until the summer or fall of 1933. According to Hutchinson, the decisive factor in the termination of their activities lay in the deteriorating relationship between the Protective and the Needle Trade Workers' Industrial Union,[30] perhaps the most radical union in the garment industry.[31] It is not clear in Hutchinson's account why this turn of events was, in fact, decisive unless it displayed Buchalter's inability to control labor in the industry and, therefore, turned the employers against him. Perhaps as important was a Federal investigation which resulted in indictments of the two trade associations, Buchalter and Shapiro, and others in the fall of 1933. In any case, by the spring of 1933 something like open warfare existed between Buchalter and the Industrial Union. A telling incident that is descriptive of the fragmenting cooperation or unalterable opposition between the Protective and the union concerned Morris Langer, one of the union leaders. Langer, called by Foner a "Martyr of Labor",[32] and by Hutchinson an organizer for the Protective,[33] was told by the racketeers to organize strikes against the three companies which had refused membership in the association. Langer balked because the firms were unionized. Langer also began to talk against the Protective. Before a month had passed on March 23, 1933, Langer was blown up by a bomb placed under the hood of his car.

The event which finally ended Buchalter's and Shapiro's involvement in the fur industry came in the form of a mini-war on April 24, 1933. During the morning, thugs hired by Buchalter and Shapiro staged an armed attack on the headquarters of the Industrial Union where a meeting was in progress. Contrary to expectations and even though armed with revolvers, lead pipes and knives, the gangsters were beaten back by the union men inside the building. As word of the attack spread, more workers streamed into the building and severely beat a number of the hoodlums who had been unable to escape. When it was all over, two men were dead and many injured; another man would die months later from injuries sustained in the battle.[34]

Buchalter and Shapiro had been hired by fur dressers in an effort to achieve the benefits of monopoly or at least oligopoly through forcing competitors into trade associations which dictated prices and allocated resources and markets. Garment manufacturers including fur dressers found it exceptionally difficult to escape competition and maintain profits through expansion because the industry was typically "confronted with a continually changing product" which hampered the development of large firms and dominant plants. This meant that garment businesses usually could not "afford to accept the rigidities involved in specialization and growth".[35] Instead, manufacturers relied on subcontractors and others for operations and services which otherwise they might have considered providing from inside the firms. Also, the structure of the industry encouraged the entry of entrepreneurs with limited capital which further increased the competitiveness. In many cases, highly competitive, small size, local product businesses such as the needle trades developed illegal associations staffed by professional criminals. What all this means is that the logic of competitive capitalism in industries such as the clothing trades lead inexorably to the formation of organized crime. Consumed by the desire for profit which, it seemed, could only be achieved by the creation of illegal monopolies and the elimination or more likely neutralization of trade unions, businessmen were instrumental in establishing some of the most vicious criminal syndicates in urban America.[36] Paradoxically some employers were themselves the victims of terror campaigns waged by racketeers which sometimes rivaled those aimed at both progressive trade unionists and much of the rank and file. More often that not, however, the instigators of violence against employers were themselves employers. Finally, it must be added that the single most effective organization in combatting racketeers was the Needle Trade Workers' Union, surely the most radical trade union to confront organized crime in our sample. One might well want to argue, therefore, that the more progressive the union, the more militant the rank and file, the less likely it is to be penetrated and seduced by organized crime.

Flour Trucking

The garment industries and their corresponding trade union and radical movements are exceptionally well-documented. Doubtless, the number of histories and other accounts are at least partly attributable to the centrality of the needle trades to New York's economy and the acculturation process of Jewish immigrants and their children. Such is not the case with trucking in general, and flour trucking in particular. In dealing with Buchalter's activities in flour trucking the researcher has few sources to consult which would enable one to construct the sort of arguments presented above. Nevertheless, there are still significant issues which can be addressed by an analysis of extortion in flour trucking. Most importantly, such an inquiry reveals a great deal concerning the inner dynamics of a power syndicate; how it was structured, how it operated. The discussion which follows is based upon the transcript of Buchalter's 1940 trial for extortion. Co-defendants in the case were Max Silverman, Silverman's son Harold, Samuel Schorr and William Goldis. The key prosecution witness was Max Rubin who had been shot in the head in October, 1937, after it was discovered that he had been meeting secretly with law enforcement officers from Dewey's office. Before turning to Rubin's testimony, it is necessary to present a short history of the racket to establish the context for Rubin's remarks. This was conveniently provided in a report prepared by the New York City Probation Department, parts of which were read into the trial minutes by the judge.[37]

The report states that the foundation of the racket was the use of an employer organization, known as the Flour Truckmen's Association, organized by Buchalter and the others, "for the purpose of extorting monies and membership fees from flour trucking and baking companies". The conspiracy also involved the union activities "such as pickets, strikes and threats to call strikes of Local No.138 of the Flour, Furniture, Grocery and Bakers' Supply Drivers Union" which was affiliated with the International Brotherhood of Teamsters. The manner in which money was extorted was to force independent truckers to join the Flour Truckmen's Association, paying membership fees, dues, etc. The report notes that Buchalter gained control of Local 138 in 1929 and at the same time began to gain dominance over the Brooklyn & New York Flour Truckmen's Association which was the original name of the employer association. Buchalter's power in the union was facilitated through his association with and "influence over the late William Snyder, then president of the local". Buchalter's "man" in the employer association was Danny Richter, the business manager.[38]

With Richter and Snyder in control of the bosses and workers in the industry, the racket moved along until 1932 when legal action was initiated in the Bronx against the Brooklyn and New York Flour Truckmen's Association by one of its members. This resulted in the collapse of the racket for about two years. The reasons for this collapse stemmed from the actions of two brothers, Aaron and Isidore Held, flour truckers who resisted paying tribute. In 1930, the Helds merged their business with the M & G Trucking Company and thereafter conducted business under the name of the United Flour Trucking Corporation. Buchalter demanded $2,000 for making the merger possible, which the Held brothers refused to pay. They also refused to give Buchalter "through the association, an additional levy of one penny for every barrel of flour carted by the ... corporation which, according to Held, was then trucking approximately 25,000 barrels of flour a week".[39] Reacting to Buchalter's demands, Aaron Held resigned from the employer association, whereupon his drivers were called out on strike by Local 138 during September, 1930. Held was also told that the strike would only end when he resumed membership in the association and agreed to pay a penny a barrel. Aaron Held finally agreed, but then in 1931, he "refused to take any more orders from Buchalter and caused to be filed in the Bronx County Court an indictment charging Richter, Snyder, Buchalter, and one Matthew Cantwell, a henchman of Buchalter, with extortion".[40] Buchalter and Cantwell went into hiding, while Snyder and Richter were tried and acquitted. After the trial Buchalter and Cantwell surrendered to the authorities in the Bronx, but the indictment was dismissed.

By 1934, the report continues, Buchalter along with Snyder, Goldis, Schorr and Richter resumed their racket through Local 138 which had remained in their control, and the employer association which had been reorganized and renamed the Flour Truckmen's Association. Max Silverman soon replaced Danny Richter as Buchalter's personal representative in the association. After Richter was gone, William Snyder was disposed of: "Snyder, as president of Local 138, had grown independent and was manifesting a disinclination to cooperate fully with Buchalter or Schorr and Goldis" and thus "had become an obstacle".[41] Snyder was murdered in 1934. The probation report next turns to the role played by Max Rubin who was "commissioned" by Buchalter to hang around the headquarters of Local 138 in order to straighten out the difficulties existing between Max Silverman and William Goldis and Schorr.

Rubin's testimony can be broken down into several categories of which the two most important are the relationship between Max Silverman and the union leaders Goldis and Schorr, and different examples of extortion. Rubin also briefly describes the manner of recruitment of syndicate criminals in his account of how Max Silverman became associated with Buchalter. Apparently, Buchalter and Rubin were in Lodi, New Jersey, one day when Buchalter saw Silverman and called him over. Buchalter asked him what he was doing there and Silverman said: " 'Looking to do something,' or 'Trying to do something,' ... and Lepke said to him, 'Come over and see me.' " Rubin's own recruitment into the flour trucking racket was equally as casual. In response to the developing friction between Silverman and the union, Buchalter, late in 1934, turned to Rubin who had been a friend and associate for years, and asked him "to step in and see if I could take a load off his shoulders".[42]

Rubin's function was that of a mediator between the employer association and the union. Commenting on the divisiveness, Rubin explains that William Goldis and Schorr "would accuse Max Silverman of holding out ... money, and other times accusing him of the fact that he was encroaching too much on their powers, using pickets that they knew nothing about, and all that".

When asked to place Harold Silverman within the heated conversations among Goldis, Schorr and Max Silverman, Rubin tells a confusing but revealing story of the difficulties in the organization. He states that Harold Silverman "seemed to be connected with some outfit over in Brooklyn [later identified as the Specialty Bakers of America], and pickets were used there using 138 signs". The situation in Brooklyn started out as an embarrassment to the union leaders: They "didn't even know where the strike was, and somebody would call up to look, to straighten it out, and they wouldn't know what that party was talking about". After the initial stage of confusion, conversation reportedly got around to the subject of money. "Wolfie said that he wouldn't send any pickets over there unless he got paid for it, and so the arrangement was that Harold should compensate Wolfie for his expenses that he had in those places where he knew there were pickets," so that Goldis would be able to pay the people involved.[43]

It was Goldis's contention, according to Rubin, that by controlling the Specialty Bankers of America, the Silvermans were stealing money that really belonged to the organization. Asked if Buchalter was ever informed of these complaints, Rubin said that he was, but that he did not believe the stories. Rubin added that Buchalter did not want to be bothered by the constant disputes and wanted him to settle them. Much to Buchalter's probable annoyance, however, the feelings of mistrust were not contained by Rubin, especially when Goldis managed to get the books of the Specialty Bakers. Goldis showed the books to Rubin, pointing out that they were from the "Specialty Corporation that Harold was handling, and he pointed to certain names in the books and he said the names were phonies, were false, and that Harold was pocketing that money". Even after confronting Buchalter with his evidence Goldis received no satisfaction: Buchalter only smiled and did nothing.[44]

Another example which indicates an incipient, chronic breakdown in the organization of Buchalter's flour trucking racket is found in a conversation between Rubin and Harold Silverman. Asked whether he had ever received any money from Harold Silverman, Rubin answers: "He got $1,500 from some lawyer, ... about the Wagner Pie, and that he was giving me half, but under no conditions should I give Wolfie any of it, that Wolfie threw him out of office and wants nothing to do with him."[45] The organizational integrity of this particular syndicate was not only threatened by innumerable squabbles, but violated by outright cheating and swindling.

Turning to the subject of extortion, the first firm mentioned by Rubin was Dugan Brothers, bakers. Several conversations early in 1935 among Max Silverman, Schorr and Goldis explored the possibility of making some money from the Dugans. The talks were led by Silverman who said that there was a chance to make $10,000 if they could get rid of the union in Dugan's. Both Goldis and Schorr, according to Rubin, agreed with Silverman. The method they decided upon called for the elimination of their own union delegate to the firm. In the absence of Grady, the delegate originally appointed by Goldis and Schorr to represent Local 138, they would be able to break up the union. Consequently, Grady was charged with a number of job failures and fired.[46]

Continuing his description of extortion, Rubin comments on the case of the Gottfried Baking Company. The first person to suggest the possibilities in controlling the Gottfried Company was Max Silverman. Rubin states that "Silverman came in to Wolfie Goldis and to Sam Schorr with a proposition that they had a chance to make $25,000 in the Gottfried Baking Company." Although an "easy touch", Silverman was reluctant to become overtly involved because he was friendly with an attorney who was connected with the company, a man by the name of Sam Miller. At this point, Rubin objected to the plan because the people carting the flour for the concern was the United Trucking, which was the business of Aaron and Isidore Held. Rubin was afraid that Isidore Held was too independent to be pushed around and would cause trouble for Buchalter. The plan was brought to Buchalter who agreed with Silverman that it was a fine idea.[47]

Buchalter's decision, however, did not end the affair. Rubin was requested to meet an individual called Moey who was Gottfried's cousin. Rubin was to tell him that the strike against the Gottfried Company could be settled for $25,000. After speaking with Rubin, Moey reported back that he could not get the money. Meanwhile, Rubin had spoken to Isidore Held, telling him that he had nothing to worry about as far as the strike was concerned, that he could cart his flour to Gottfried even though the strike was going on. Rubin also told Held "that there was absolutely nothing to worry about as far as losing the concern or the account." Rubin did request Held "to do us all a favor and bring the flour in after 9:00 o'clock. In other words, when the pickets of 138 would leave the place".[48] Clearly, the determination of the Held brothers had earned them a special niche of consideration, if not influence, when it came to Buchalter's flour trucking racket. And as we will see, the Held brothers were not the only people whose stubbornness gave them the right of special consideration or were given room to bargain.

Rubin was asked how the Gottfried problem was solved. Once again, Rubin testifies about a series of meetings. "Lepke asked me to go up to Bill Solomon, ... an insurance man, and we are to meet there a man by the name of Sam Miller." Apparently, Miller had complained about Buchalter to both the District Attorney of New York County and to "Washington" on behalf of the Gottfried Company. Rubin describes the meeting which was also attended by Buchalter. "Bill Solomon got up, introduced Sam Miller to Lepke," who refused "to shake hands with him" saying, "I am not going to shake hands with you. You go out and knock my brains out, you don't even know anything about me, and you go all over and knock my brains out!"[49] With that, Rubin took over the conversation, telling Miller that Buchalter had absolutely nothing to do with the situation at Gottfried's. Rubin went on to take full responsibility for the strike, declaring "if I had known that you were such a good friend of Bill Solomon's, I never would have started it". Rubin explained that Buchalter wanted to appease Sam Miller. As far as the $25,000 was concerned, Buchalter had instructed Rubin to settle the problem at any price. Thus, when Miller offered a counter proposition of $15,000 to end the strike, Rubin eagerly accepted.[50]

Following this account of arbitration in the Gottfried case, Rubin describes another extortion scheme which became a bitter source of contention between Silverman and the union. He states: "From the time I stepped into that 138 until I left, the Messing question, the Levy and Public always came up." The three firms were in the bread baking industry in Brooklyn. The problem dividing Local 138 and Silverman was that the union wanted to organize the baking companies while Silverman was opposed. Supposedly, Silverman's opposition which was quite determined was based on the claim "that Messing was too powerful to straighten him out; if you start with Messing, you got all sorts of elements to contend with in New York".[51] Silverman also had excuses to explain why 138 could not organize the other two companies. Because Rubin was unable to reconcile the differences, the issue had to be brought to Buchalter who again sided with Silverman.

One likely explanation for Silverman's behavior is that he was extorting money from these and other businesses which were not unionized by promising to prevent Local 138 from organizing their drivers. It may also have been the case that both Silverman and Buchalter were running a parallel racket in Brooklyn, but not sharing the profits with their associates in Local 138. The possibility would illuminate one of the curiosities in Rubin's testimony. Asked by defense counsel how many members of the Flour Truckmen's Association who were not organized, "opposed organization as much as possible", Rubin replies that there were not many, "perhaps two or three". Rubin then brings up an interesting exception: "there was Meyer Luckman, who belonged to 202". As a result of being organized by Local 202, Meyer Luckman's "overhead was not as great", because the requirements of that union "were not as strenuous as Local 138". With a smaller overhead, a firm "can cart cheaper" and, being able to charge less, a company like Luckman's could "take away customers".[52] Buchalter and Silverman could have been bypassing the leaders of Local 138 while collecting money from such firms as Luckman, Messing, Levy and Public by either using the threat of organization through Local 138 or working in collusion with Local 202.

The last case of extortion discussed by Rubin came up when he was asked if he ever had a talk with Buchalter about someone named Henry Goldstone. According to Rubin, Goldstone, who lived in the same fashionable apartment house as Buchalter, had gone to Buchalter saying that a friend of his son's was having trouble with the Local 138. Buchalter arranged for Rubin to meet with Goldstone who said that his son's friend, Mickey Shalit of the Shalit Wholesale Grocery Company, was faced with a ruinous strike called by Local 138. Rubin was directed by Buchalter to have the strike called off. However, Goldis and Schorr were reluctant to give in. The difficulty was finally resolved at a meeting attended by Rubin, Goldis, Schorr, Shalit and Goldstone. Rubin states that Goldis had taken a dislike to Mickey Shalit, claiming that Shalit had gone to the District Attorney of the Bronx. Goldstone answered Goldis' objections by guaranteeing that nothing like that would happen again, and promising that if they would end the strike, there would be no repercussions. After Goldstone's promise, the conversation drifted into money with Goldis agreeing to end the strike for $1,000. Goldstone accepted and added that "he would see that Mickey would live up to every obligation".[53] Shalit, like the Held brothers, was another example of someone who went to the District Attorney when threatened with extortion and not only lived to talk about it, but seemed to have suffered only minimal consequences. What Shalit had accomplished, although not on the scale of the Helds, was to bring together new power relationships which effectively protected him.

Extortion: A Brief Coda

The power of power syndicates was, it seems, variable. While in many cases there must have been a mutuality of interests binding syndicate members together, there were enough conflicts within syndicates over a variety of issues to indicate some significant dimensions of extortion. It is important first to realize that extortion which is usually defined as the taking of something from someone by the illegal use of force or fear is an exceptionally complex social activity. Part of its complexity arises because the interacting parties are neither all powerful nor all vulnerable. Depending on time, circumstance, will and connections to other sources of power an outcome is bargained through a series of face-to-face encounters. Extortion then covers a range of bargaining behavior whose possible outcomes are many including one-time payoffs to segments of power syndicates for the purpose of buying out of the organizational nexus. The pecuniary interests of the syndicate bargainers themselves can be satisfied in a variety of ways including private arrangements hidden from other syndicate members. What ultimately allows for such variability in extortion is the primitive communication system which effectively seals off some syndicate members from knowing what others may be doing. In our example of flour trucking there was no particular method of keeping track of possible spin-off rackets; no organizational way of limiting contacts, threats and deals. There was, in retrospect, a fair amount of confusion. Indeed, this found confusion in the ranks of a power syndicate is almost as striking as the degree of strife noted in the discussion. Both, of course, are related and both point, it seems to me, to the immutable nature of competition in an environment in which dominance contests are not only the key to extortion but are waged daily within and between organizations and individuals. The predominant characteristic in the social life of professional criminals in power syndicates is coercion; it orients them in time and space; it is their job and identity. Approached from this angle, extortion is not simply a vastly under-researched crime, but a complex activity sorely needing its own "sociology of occasions". In addition, it is a compelling metaphor for a life-style of competitive individualism whose rigour ironically binds and rends so many segments of both upperworld and underworld life.

None of this subverts the argument dealing with the function of power syndicates as basically anti-labor forces in the urban economy. But it does call for the recognition of the manner in which this terribly regressive function is played-out. And that is important for it reveals how much anarchy, chaos and plain disorder prevail in organized crime and surely in those sectors of the urban economy with which it interacts.

On the Waterfront

So far our examples and indeed conclusions have been drawn from the activities of Buchalter and Shapiro whose criminal careers were deeply embedded in only certain sectors of New York's economy. Untouched, up till now, is another sector which if anything was even more completely penetrated by professional criminals representing closely-knit power syndicates than were the garment and flour trucking trades. The general area is the New York waterfront, and more specifically the Brooklyn waterfront which Judge Samuel S. Leibowitz in his charge to the December 1949 Grand Jury (whose investigative life lasted until April 1954) characterizes as "the premier port" in America.[54] This despite the claim in Daniel Bell's intriguing essay "Racket-Ridden Longshoremen" that "the hub of the port is the four to five miles of piers and landings along the west side of Manhattan".[55] To return to Judge Leibowitz he states that Brooklyn's piers handle "54% of all the seaboard traffic of the entire port of New York".[56] Which includes, all the docks on the New Jersey side of the Metropolitan region. That the Brooklyn waterfront played the most important role of any section of New York's waterfront is underscored by Leibowitz's remarks that approximately $1,660,000,000 in waterfront and waterfront related business was handled yearly in Brooklyn during the latter half of the 1940s.

As a zone of both economic and social life racketeers, the Grand Jury reports, "have acquired a complete domination over the legitimate longshoremen and others whose livelihoods depend upon the docks".[57] The Grand Jury likens the social situation on the waterfront to a form of "hopeless peonage". The factors responsible for this are two: first, the "abysmal failure" of the leadership of the International Longshoremen's Association to protect the rank and file; second, "the abject surrender of the shipping and stevedoring company owners and executives to the waterfront racketeers".[58] Concerning the union leadership the Grand Jury states:

> Far from following the elementary union maxim that "in unity there is strength" they have, on the contrary, gone out of their way to diffuse the collective strength of honest union labor in such a way as to make it easier for the criminals and gangsters to take control. This has been done so systematically and so expertly as to leave no doubt of the planned, premeditated strategy behind it.[59]

Specifically the ILA set-up 31 union locals in New York which effectively undercut the "bargaining position of labor *vis-à-vis* management". The result of this diffusion was the creation of "thirty-one semi-autonomous 'delegates' or officers who are in reality thirty-one petty kings and who in their own language are wont to describe themselves as 'owning' the thirty-one different piers".[60]

Turning to the company owners and executives, I think it significant to note the Grand Jury's opening remarks as well as subsequent ones: "This," they write, "is a phase of our investigation which time has not permitted us to pursue". Nevertheless, they do go on stating that enough information has been gathered to show in a general fashion "the extent to which the employers have been ingloriously remiss". The statement continues:

> They have shown a distinct tendency to resort to bribery as a way out of the harassments of the racketeers instead of manfully invoking the protection of the law. They have not

been known to lift a finger over all these years against the operators of the "infamous loading rackets". They have bleated much about quickie strikes but the fact is that they bear much of the direct reponsibility for these themselves, in that they have permitted the racketeers and the corrupt union leaders to violate union contracts with impunity .... They have unprotestingly permitted thieves with lengthy criminal records to occupy positions of high trust in their employ ....

These shipping and stevedore companies have attempted to justify this capitulation to the racketeers and their unfair and improper demands because of the great losses which they claim they might otherwise sustain through the tying up of their ships.[61]

They summarize by claiming that this "attitude is indefensible" as it subordinates "decent dealing between labor and management to a desire for profit".[62] It must be pointed out here, how the superlative investigative efforts of the Grand Jury were ultimately undermined by what must be their strong beliefs in the potential of a "moral" market place: decency for decency's sake is their hope for the misery and collusion on the waterfront. This despite the fact that their own evidence shows that shipping and stevedoring company owners and executives pass on to consumers the costs of racketeering,[63] while at the same time hugely augmenting company profits through the "peonage" of the labor force. I very much doubt that the owners and executives either knuckled under to racketeers or were afraid of the consequences of so-called "manly" behavior, but rather acted in ways consistent with their financial interests which meant that the city's piers would be controlled by professional criminals.

What follows is one example indicating the continuity of corruption and organized criminality on the waterfront on the part of corporate owners and executives. In the *Fourth Report* of the New York State Crime Commission concerned with the waterfront, the Commission writes that "there was collusion between steamship and stevedoring companies on the one hand and union officials on the other";[64] that it was not unusual for stevedoring companies to bribe steamship companies and/or their agents to get or continue stevedoring contracts; and last, that the accounting practices of stevedoring (and surely by implication steamship companies) were fraudulent. One of the major, in fact the largest stevedoring company in the United States, reported on by the Commission is the Jarka Corporation which engaged in all the nefarious and illegal practices mentioned above. In explaining the Jarka's illegal, secret payments to ILA officials, Jarka vice-president Yates responds:

We have necessities, especially at nighttime and weekends, to have a sufficient supply of labor for the arrival of particularly passenger ships, ... I made constant calls on them in those directions, and as I saw it they were most helpful to me in the conduct of my

185

responsibilities which was the actual handling of these ships and the operation of these piers and without that goodwill built up by virtue of these payments, which I still consider small, I felt I could not call upon these people as I required.[65]

Concerning bribes to steamship companies, Jarka president Frank W. Nolan paid $10,000 to W. W. Wells, president of the Isthmian Steamship Company; $34,000 to A. Roggeveen, managing director of the Holland–America Line; $47,200 to J. C. Bruswitz, managing director of the Calmar Lines, a subsidiary of Bethlehem Steel Corporation; and lastly, $56,200 to E. C. Koenke, operating director of Ore Steamship Company also a subsidiary of the Bethlehem Steel Corporation. Lest one think that the Jarka Corporation only paid bribes, it was added that its five major officers depleted about $500,000 in "petty cash" from corporate funds from 1947 to the summer of 1952.[66]

The New York State Crime Commission also established in their confidential *Interim Report* that Albert Anastasia's brother, Anthony Anastasia, was "presently the head stevedore for the Jarka Corp".[67] How Anastasia got his job is made clear in the testimony of Joseph P. Ryan, president of the ILA, before a Subcommittee of the Committee on Interstate and Foreign Commerce, which in 1953 was also investigating waterfront conditions. According to the testimony, both Ryan and Nolan worked out an agreement which insured Anastasia's employment.[68] The Congressional committee also noted in passing that the Jarka Corporation did an annual business of about $25,000,000.

All this is revealing enough, but it should be added that the history of the Jarka Corporation and organized criminality stretches back to at least the 1920s. In that section of the Seabury investigations which focused on the problems of the North German Lloyd steamship company in securing a pier in Manhattan (discussed in Chapter 3), the Jarka Corporation played a pivotal role in the overall extortion scheme. Major Democratic politicians and Jarka officials worked together in pressuring the Lloyd for ever-increasing payoffs. It seems, therefore, beyond the bounds of common sense to view company owners and executives (the Jarka Corporation being only one example of many) as victims of professional criminals. Equally as absurd is to consider them vulnerable to racketeer pressure because they lack "manly virtues".

Let us now turn back to the Borough of Churches and trees—Brooklyn— narrowing our focus to professional criminals on the waterfront. Specifically, the area under investigation is the Italian neighborhood known as Red Hook which encompassed almost all the important commercial piers in Brooklyn. These piers and indeed the lives of about 4,000 working longshoremen, according to the New York State Crime Commission, were under the control of six extraordinarily corrupt ILA locals which were in turn controlled to an unknown degree by a particular and changing power syndicate. The whole situation is extremely complex because of overlapping spheres of power and influence exercised by the "trade union" power syndicates, and the other one. The most significant ways in which professional criminals controlled waterfront activities both licit and illicit was first through leadership positions in the locals. In addition, several of them formed in the late 1920s a political organization known as the City Democratic Club which functioned as a major channel of political influence in the Borough. And finally, unlike most of the other professional criminals mentioned so far, many of the waterfront racketeers were related. These often complex kinship relations functioned both within and across the six ILA locals, the City Democratic Club, and into the major power syndicate. Although there are examples of kin working together in criminal syndicates mentioned previously, there is nothing which approaches the level of consanguinity found on the Brooklyn waterfront.

Consider first the ILA locals which all met in the same room at 33 President Street, Brooklyn, during the 1930s. Structurally, the most important individual was Emil Camarda, ILA vice president and Brooklyn organizer. Under his supposed direction were the six infamous "pistol" locals: 327; 903; 338; 929; 1199; 346. Camarda was supposed to be in control, but there are strong indications both from the Crime Commission and other sources that in the very early 1930s (until his murder in 1931) John Guistra was the "real" leader. Others also mentioned with much more supporting evidence than Camarda are Vincent Mangano, Sr., and Albert Anastasia. Whatever Camarda's real position, it ended on October 2, 1941, when he was murdered. His position as ILA vice president and Brooklyn organizer was taken over by Constantino Scannavino who also held the post of business agent in local 1199 from some time in the 1930s until at least 1952.

The key posts in the locals were business agent and secretary-treasurer. In the late 1930s the following were the officers:

Local 327
Secretary-treasurer   Anthony J. Camarda
Business agent   Joseph E. Camarda
Business agent   Salvatore Camarda

Local 903
Secretary-treasurer   Pietro Rossi
Business agent   Philip Mangano

187

Local 338
Secretary-treasurer   Antonio Capotumino
Business agent   Joseph Mangiameli

Local 929
Secretary-treasurer   Anthony Giustra
Business agent   Joseph Indelicato
Business agent   Anthony Romeo

Local 1199
Secretary-treasurer   Anthony (Nino) Camarda
Business agent   Costantino Scannavino
Business agent   Anthony V. Camarda

Local 346
Secretary-treasurer   John Erato
Business agent   Nicholas Delli Santi

Among those arrested and sometimes convicted from the above are Anthony Romeo, convicted of robbery and assault, and arrested three times for homicide; Philip Mangano, arrested for homicide; Anthony Giustra, arrested for extortion; Salvatore Camarda, convicted of rape, arrested for felonious assault; Joseph E. Camarda, arrested for felonious assault; Nicholas Delli Santi, arrested for felonious assault; and Joseph Indelicato, convicted for armed assault.

There are other local officers apparently pre-1940 worth mentioning. Salvatore Mangiameli, president of local 338, arrested for felonious assault; Attileo Rossi, president of local 903, convicted of gambling; Angelo Merolla, vice president of local 929, arrested for assault and robbery, felonious assault, and convicted of bookmaking and violation of liquor laws; and lastly Antonio Gennoso, a trustee of local 1199, convicted of rape in 1937.

Before turning to the almost astounding political developments concerning the waterfront in 1940–1941 (some of which have been briefly touched upon in Chapter 5), there is some information about the City Democratic Club which needs highlighting. Formed in 1929, the Club, which was fronted by the "most respected professional and business men of this Italian–American community",[69] was the headquarters of the waterfront syndicate. Active club members and officers include: Vincent Mangano, Sr.; Albert Anastasia; Anthony Romeo; Philip Mangano; Gioacchino Parisi; Anthony Anastasia; Vincent Crisalli; Joseph Adonis; Joseph Profaci; Emil Camarda, chair of the Club's Board of Directors; Constantino Scannavino, Club officer; Nicholas Delli Santi, vice chair of Board of Directors; Anthony J. Camarda, Club officer; Cosimo Caminiti; Salvatore Mangiameli; and

Michael Cosenza. To list the crimes both suspected and proven committed by the above group (not already noted) would be an exercise in tedium. Suffice it to say that every shred of evidence points unmistakenly to the fact that the above are among the most vicious professional criminals in the history of New York.

Politics and the Waterfront

Beginning in the last year or so of the 1930s, a "rank and file movement composed of some 1200 longshoremen directed against the gangster domination of the longshoremen's union and the kickback and extortion rackets which were victimizing workers on the Brooklyn waterfront"[70] was somehow started. The leader of this incredibly courageous movement was Peter Panto. In mid-July, 1939, Panto disappeared. (He was murdered by Giaocchino Parisi, or so all the evidence indicates.) The following month the New York City Department of Investigation began an inquiry into the Panto case. The investigation revealed the sinister power of Albert Anastasia, assisted primarily by Anthony Romeo and Parisi, on the Brooklyn waterfront. This material was then turned over to John Harlan Amen Brooklyn's almost Special Prosecutor (see Chapter 4). One of Amen's first moves was to subpoena the books and records of local 327, on March 15, 1940.

What followed is a most interesting maneuver; interesting for several reasons. All six of the ILA locals working together attempted to fight the validity of the subpoena upon the advice of counsel—"Paul O'Dwyer, brother of the District Attorney of Kings County".[71] The locals and Paul O'Dwyer lost, at least for the moment. On April 29, 1940, the Supreme Court upheld the Amen subpoena. The very next day, however, District Attorney William O'Dwyer launched his own "investigation" of the waterfront and the books and records of all six locals were turned over to O'Dwyer's Chief Assistant, Joseph F. Hanley, and Assistant District Attorney Edward A. Heffernan.

It is the opinion of the New York State Commission, the Kefauver Committee, and the Beldock 1945 Grand Jury that William O'Dwyer effectively squelched both the burgeoning waterfront investigation as well as the murder indictments of Albert Anastasia and other waterfront racketeers. The Crime Commission reports: "The Grand Jury heard testimony to the effect that District Attorney O'Dwyer ordered the discontinuance of the entire waterfront rackets investigation on May 15, 1940 *after a conference with Joseph P. Ryan and Emil Camarda"* [72](my emphasis). As a post hoc justification for this stunning dereliction of duty, O'Dwyer claimed that

Ryan, the notorious President of the ILA, "announced he would revoke the charters of Locals 929, 903, and 346 and order a new election in all the locals involved". But as the Crime Commission points out this meant nothing more than some paper shuffling which resulted in "changing the numerical designation of these locals".[73] Most of the optimistic and surely deliberately misleading statements about this change were issued by Assistant District Attorney Heffernan who was "satisfied that the 'union had been put back in the control of law-abiding workmen to whom their officers are responsible' and with the assurance that 'constant diligence will be exercised to prevent the return of old evils' ".[74] With that, Heffernan recommended that the investigation be concluded.

To prove what a sham the O'Dwyer investigation had been, the Crime Commission composed a telling chart listing the locals and significant officers prior to the so-called reform and after.

Local 327	*Before reform*	*After reform*
Secretary-Treasurer	Anthony J. Camarda	Anthony J. Camarda
Business agent	Joseph E. Camarda	Joseph E. Camarda
Business agent	Salvatore Camarda	Salvatore Camarda
Local 903		
Secretary-Treasurer	Pietro Rossi	Pietro Rossi
Business agent	Philip Mangano	Michael Cosenza
Local 338		
Secretary-Treasurer	Antonio Capotumino	Antonio Capotumino
Business agent	Joseph Mangiameli	Joseph Mangiameli
Local 929		
Secretary-Treasurer	Anthony Giustra	Anthony Giustra
Business agent	Joseph Indelicato	Ralph Palermo
Business agent	Anthony Romeo	Ciro Ingenito
Business agent		Gus Caminiti
Local 1199		
Secretary-Treasurer	Anthony N. Camarda	Anthony N. Camarda
Business agent	Constantino Scannavino	Constantino Scannavino
Business agent	Anthony V. Camarda	Anthony V. Camarda
Local 346		
Secretary-Treasurer	John Erato	John Erato
Business agent	Nicholas Delli Santi	Anthony Passante
Business agent		Vincent Erato

The only personnel changes occur in local 903 where Philip Mangano's *nephew* Michael Cosenza takes over as business agent; in local 929 where Anthony Romeo's *cousin* Gus Caminiti takes over as business agent, and two other individuals Palermo and Ingenito appear in the same role; and lastly, local 346 where Nicholas Delli Santi is replaced by Passante and another business agent post is created and filled by John Erato's *brother* Vincent.

And so it went. Panto was long dead; insurgency had failed miserably, betrayed by not only the ILA but more importantly the Brooklyn political and criminal justice systems which, it appears, had crawled into bed with the waterfront racketeers and had the covers tucked by O'Dwyer.

Kinship and Crime

Before leaving the waterfront two additional points need elaboration. The first is kinship one of the bonding agents mentioned earlier. Basically, there are five key families mixed into the ILA locals, the City Democratic Club, and the power syndicate: Camarda, Mangano, Anastasia, Mangiameli, and Romeo. Starting with Romeo first, the kin linkages are represented by his nephew, Joseph Indelicato, and his cousin Cosimo (Gus) Caminiti. Both Anthony Romeo and Indelicato were business agents for local 929 at the same time. Caminiti becomes a 929 business agent after "reform". The Mangiameli family line which concerns us begins with Salvatore Mangiameli, president of local 338, and hiring boss for the Barker Steamship Company. Salvatore had three sons also connected to local 338: Anthony, delegate from 338 to the New York District Council; Joseph, business agent and then secretary-treasurer of 338; and John, also a business agent for 338. When Salvatore retires his son Anthony while still a delegate from 338 takes over his father's job with Barker Steamship. The Anastasia kin group associated with the waterfront is composed of four brothers: Albert; Gerardo, a business agent for local 929; Anthony, head stevedore for the Jarka Corporation and a member of local 346; and Joseph who was a foreman for the J. W. McGrath Stevedoring Company.

The last two families, Camarda and Mangano, are best represented in the following manner:

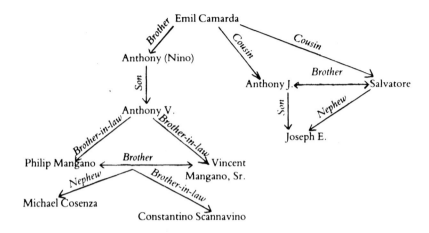

Between these two families were the ILA vice presidency (Emil Camarda and Scannavino), two of the founders of the City Democratic Club (Emil Camarda and Vincent Mangano, Sr.), and officers from locals 327, 903, and 1199.

The tenor of the Commission's "confidential" report indicates that all the union officers were grossly and constantly stealing in various fashions union money. In addition, many were also employed by Steamship and Stevedore companies in management positions. General extortion of the rank and file was literally an everyday occurrence. Beyond that, certain individuals also worked their own versions of illicit enterprises, primarily gambling and loan sharking. All of the above was supported by kin ties which meant, in effect, that certain families "owned" certain locals and indeed piers, having free rein to be as modest or outrageous in criminal activities as they wished.

Wrapping It Up

But finally, all through the Commission's report runs the theme that there was above all else one particular power syndicate which not only took a cut from the waterfront but extended its influence into non-waterfront crime which is the second point needing elaboration. The members of this syndicate appear to be: Albert Anastasia, Vincent Mangano, Sr., Anthony Romeo, Giaocchino Parisi, and Vincent Crisalli. The relationships between members of this primary power syndicate and representatives of the trade union syndicates were of course complex and not by any means pacific. A glimpse of the tension and strife can be seen in the statements of Anthony Giustra the secretary-treasurer of local 929 concerning Anthony Romeo a 929 business agent and member of the Anastasia syndicate. Giustra "confessed" to O'Dwyer in the early stages of the so-called investigation that Romeo "had extorted thousands of dollars of union funds from the local's treasury during the period 1931 to 1940".[75] Years later, Giustra was called before the Crime Commission which asked what Romeo would say during their exchanges. Giustra states: " 'Give me five hundred'—'Give me four hundred.' I say, 'Give me a chance ... This is going too fast now.' That's why I wanted to resign and the answer I got, 'What do you mean resign?' I says, 'Am I going to be bumped off?' ' "[76] Anthony Giustra was the stepbrother of John Giustra murdered presumably by Anastasia and/or Mangano, Sr., in 1931. Strife between the two overlapping zones of influence and power was fairly endemic with numerous hints throughout the Commission report of local barons being pressured by members of the primary syndicate. There is, of course, evidence of strife among the members of the primary syndicate too. The best representation of that is the murder of Romeo himself in 1942.

Top Left
Vincent Mangano

Top Right
Tony "Tony Spring" Romeo

Bottom Right
Jack Parisi

Significantly, the identified members of the primary power syndicate with the exception of Romeo held no official positions in the ILA or the City Democratic Club. Albert Anastasia, Vincent Mangano, Sr., Giaocchino Parisi, and Vincent Crisali were active in both the locals and the Club, but were not members in any official sense of either. These premier extortionists in this manner resemble Buchalter and Shapiro, and Dutch Schultz who were all free-wheeling entrepreneurs of violence active in certain zones of the city's economy but never members of particular concrete institutions such as trade associations or trade unions. Their agents, their clients, their victims composed the membership. What they possessed was clearly more important than institutional authority; they were repositories of informal power of horrifying dimensions.

The relative success of this particular power syndicate especially in comparison with the ones discussed in the garment industries and flour trucking is the last point considered. There are basically four factors which, I think, account for this. First, the ILA's corruption knew no bounds. Unlike the garment trade unions which were more contentious, more radical, more visible, waterfront trade unionism in New York was insular and isolated. The physical isolation of the waterfront surrounded by sullen working-class neighborhoods effectively removed waterfront activities from public view. As almost all the sociological literature indicates[77] the waterfront is an intensely privatized area of urban life. The second factor is the City Democratic Club itself. The Club dominated political life in both the 3rd and 8th Assembly Districts in Brooklyn. It was extraordinarily powerful, guaranteeing democratic majorities throughout the two decades under study. In addition, there was a high degree of continuity in both Districts, especially the 3rd within which all of Red Hook is situated. From at least 1928 until 1945 the leader of the 3rd was Thomas H. Cullen. It deserves noting that in this Italian–American District, the leaders were always Irish. Cullen was replaced in 1945 by Frank A. Cunningham. Perhaps this factor of political control with its interesting ethnic dimension had something to do with O'Dwyer's actions concerning the waterfront? Without more evidence, though, I am not inclined to push the line too far. But, I am not at all reticent about O'Dwyer whom I consider the third factor of success. The downfall of Buchalter, Shapiro, Schultz (although murdered), Luciano, and others came about because of changes in the politics of criminal justice. When patterns of influence in Manhattan were broken one of the inevitable results was that some of the protected would be exposed and eventually driven out of business. Even O'Dwyer was forced into action as District Attorney more by the tide of political events than anything else. And he was surely able to protect racketeers such as those his brother represented. What the waterfront racketeers had accomplished to a much greater degree than Buchalter, Shapiro, and most of the others mentioned so far, was to ground their influence in a fixed geographical area and then to create themselves a political unit of importance. Working with their political and criminal justice associates, they were able to subvert the Amen investigation which had some of the potential for criminal justice changes that Dewey embodied.

The fourth and final factor is the support for the status quo evidenced by the shipping and stevedoring companies. Conscious of both company and personal profits, the owners and executives cemented their relationships with professional criminals who, they must have seen, as "labor disciplinarians". Structurally, waterfront businesses were a world apart from the competitive, typically small capital enterprises in garments and flour trucking. This meant that even fewer waterfront enterprises could in any imaginable sense be victimized by racketeers forced into trade associations to shore up prices, etc. If anything the waterfront exemplifies even more clearly the logic of large-scale capital enterprises for whom the terror and squalor experienced by thousands of waterfront families were simply not part of the calculus of business.

NOTES

[1] Consult Sidney Lens, *The Labor Wars: From the Molly Maguires to the Sit-Downs* (Garden City, New York, 1973); Melvyn Dubofsky, *We Shall Be All: A History of the Industrial Workers of the World* (Chicago, 1969); Samuel Yellen *American Labor Struggles* (New York, 1936); Richard O. Boyer and Herbert M. Morais, *Labor's Untold Story* (New York, 1955); Leo Huberman, *The Labor Spy Racket* (New York, 1937); Philip S. Foner, *The Industrial Workers of the World, 1905–1917* (New York, 1965); Irving Bernstein, *The Lean Years: A History of the American Worker* (Baltimore, 1966); and Rhodri Jeffries–Jones, *Violence in American History; Plug Uglies in the Progressive Era*, in Donald Fleming and Bernard Bailyn, eds., *Perspectives in American History*, VII (Cambridge, Massachusetts, 1974).

[2] Rhodri Jeffreys–Jones, 524.

[3] *Ibid.*, 525.

[4] *Ibid.*, 534.

[5] Moses Rischin, *The Promised City: New York's Jews, 1870–1914* (New York, 1970), 61.

[6] *Ibid.*, 64–66.

[7] *Ibid.*, 62–66.

[8] *Ibid.*

[9] Ben B. Seligman, "The American Jew: Some Demographic Features," *American Jewish Yearbook* 51 (1950), 56.

[10] *Ibid.*, 57.

[11] "The establishment of the United Hebrew Trades brought to the force a problem that gave some concern to American labor leaders. Jewish and non-Jewish alike — the problem of the propriety of organizing separate Jewish unions .... It was not, of course, a matter of religion, but of language, culture, community ties, and the characteristic structure of the Jewish trades .... History made its own decision, considerably aided by the hostility that Jewish workers encountered when they tried to join some of the established unions. Jewish unions were formed." Will Herberg, "The Jewish Labor Movement in the United States" *American Jewish Yearbook* 53 (1952), 8.

[12] *Ibid.*, 9–10.

[13] *Ibid.*, 16.

[14] *Ibid.*, 17–18.

[15] *Ibid.*, 23.

[16] *Ibid.*, 45.

[17] "Case History: The Amalgamated," *Business Week* (August 31, 1957).

[18] John Hutchinson, *The Imperfect Union: A History of Corruption in American Trade Unions* (New York, 1970), 76.

[19] Turkus and Feder, 335–337.

[20] Hutchinson, 76.

[21] Federal Bureau of Investigation, 9.

[22] Court of Appeals—Brooklyn, New York, The People of the State of New York Against Louis Buchalter, Emmanuel Weiss, Louis Capone (May–June, 1942), 1333–1347.

[23] Matthew Johnson, *Sidney Hillman: Statesman of American Labor* (Garden City, New York, 1952), 336–339.

[24] Joel Isaac Seidman, *The Needle Trades* (New York, 1942), 190–191.

[25] Turkus and Feder, 338–343.

[26] "Legal Implications of Labor Racketeering," *Columbia Law Review* (Summer, 1937), 994–995.

[27] Federal Bureau of Investigation, 10.

[28] *Ibid.*, 11.

[29] *Ibid.*, 12.

[30] The Needle Trade Workers' Industrial Union evolved out of the battles between Communists and other trade unionists during the 1920s. Its formation signalled the end of an earlier policy of "boring from within" and the beginning of dual unionism. The original organization representing the Communist drive for dominance in the Jewish unions was the Trade Union Educational League which was formed in 1920. It was emphasized at its formation that the TUEL was not a union and neither collected dues nor issued charters. Its purpose was to coordinate communist party penetration of the American labor movement during the 1920s. While the TUEL made little headway in the Amalgamated and short-lived inroads in the Millinery Workers, its conflict with the ILGWU was almost catastrophic. The culmination of the battle in the ILGWU came in 1926, in the form of a Communist led general strike in the New York cloak industry. As the strike progressed, it became more and more chaotic and when it was alleged that the radical leadership had misused $800,000 of employers' securities deposited with the union, the ILGWU's General Executive Board assumed command of the strike and succeeded in ending it. With the termination of this strike, the influence of Communists within the ILGWU was ended. The costs for the ILGWU, however, were huge: the union itself was almost destroyed; its membership had drastically declined, and with a depleted treasury, enormous debts threatened to completely overwhelm the organization. Herberg, 39.

The single continuing success enjoyed by the TUEL was with the militant fur workers. Following a victorious general strike in the New York fur industry in 1926, it appeared that the Communists in the International Fur Workers Union under the capable and aggressive leadership of Ben Gold would almost certainly have taken over the International at its 1927 convention. To prevent this, the AFL moved to eliminate Communist leadership, but unlike what had occurred in the ILGWU after the 1926 cloak strike, the radicals continued to be supported by the majority of the membership. In 1928, a new strategy was implemented. The TUEL was changed into the Trade Union Unity League (TUUL), which started to operate as an independent center for trade unions. Subsequently, the Needle Trade Worker's Union was created, composed primarily of furriers and the so-called remnants of the left wing of the ILGWU. Bernstein, 136–141.

[31] Hutchinson, 81.

[32] Philip S. Foner, *Fur and Leather Workers' Union: A Story of Dramatic Struggles and Achievements* (Newark, New Jersey, 1950), 388–401.

[33] Hutchinson, 83.

[34] Federal Bureau of Investigation, 15–16.

[35] Edgar M. Hoover and Raymond Vernon, *Anatomy of a Metropolis: The Changing Distribution of People and Jobs Within the New York Metropolitan Region* (Garden City, New York, 1962), 61.

[36] Not all industries in which power syndicates operated were subject to the same problems. For instance the restaurant industry, a portion of which was subjected to a vicious extortion operation managed by another Dutch Schultz syndicate from 1932 to 1936 had no oligopolistic tendencies; no need or desire for price stabilization and limiting entrepreneurial entry. Clearly, though, the restaurant employers were avidly interested in resisting unionization and when that could not be avoided in negotiating "sweetheart" contracts with Schultz racketeers who had gained control of two restaurant trade union locals. Employers were forced to join the Metropolitan Restaurant and Cafeteria Association and to sign labor contracts with either Local 16 of the Hotel and Restaurant Employees International Alliance or Local 302 of the Delicatessen Countermen and Cafeteria Workers Union. In return for joining and signing wages would never have to be raised nor working conditions changed. To make the point more explicit, it has been estimated "on the basis of wage increases granted to the union in 1936 after the fall of the racket", that one employer saved about $136,000 from 1933–1936 even after paying $36,000 to the Metropolitan and signing phony labor contracts. *Columbia Law Review*, 1937: 998–999. The point here is that even in cases where businessmen may not have been instrumental in establishing rackets they would cooperate with extortionists as long as they could control the labor market. Without oligopolistic tendencies within the industry there was no necessity for a trade association which was in this case a pure extortion front unlike the trade associations in the needle trades. Taking all this into account, it seems clear that this syndicate's function was quite the same as Buchalter's even though no employers or corporations were indicted for anything in this racket. The trial transcript in the form of stenographer's minutes and the Respondent's Brief are located in Governor Dewey's law office and have been cited in Chapter 4, note 21.

[37] See Court of General Sessions of the County of New York — Part V, The People of the State of New York Against Louis Buchalter, Max Silverman, Harold Silverman, Samuel Schorr (New York, January 26, 1940), Vols. 1, 2, 3, 4. The Court's Copy 5709; added to the trial record with different pagination is the Judge's remarks on the Probation Report.

[38] *Ibid.*, 9–12.

Danny Richter was involved not only in the creation of New York & Brooklyn Flour Trucking Association, but also a garment trucking organization named the Five Borough Truckmen's Association. This group was formed in 1929 and its purpose was to fix prices and freeze accounts, according to Dewey investigator, Jacob Grumet. This organization functioned for about two years and then went into decline in 1931. Subsequently, however, it was revived early in 1932. Those responsible for its revival were Dominick Didato known as Dick Terry, John Dioguardi, and Dioguardi's uncle, James Plumeri alias Jimmy Doyle. According to Grumet's report "the association on the surface was apparently a legitimate organization in proper legal form, whose membership was composed of legitimate truckmen, but it was run and operated by Doyle, Dioguardi and Terry practically as a private enterprise of their own". Grumet goes on noting that "Doyle, in some mysterious way, became president. Terry was the secretary and treasurer. Both of them were referred to as so-called 'business organizers' in the literature of the association. Dioguardi was referred to as a solicitor." So mysterious were their actions that "most of the truckmen were surprised to learn that Doyle was president. They had not even heard of it, and some of those included members of the board of directors. One truckman, as a matter of fact, thought that he was the president and was surprised to learn that Doyle was president."

The extortionary activities of Doyle, Dioguardi and Terry were notable. Grumet notes: "Any attempt by a truckman, inside or outside the organization, to solicit business from a customer doing business with a member of the association resulted in threats of physical violence, damage to trucks and equipment. These threats were made in many cases where a manufacturer or jobber voluntarily changes from one truckman to another. These threats were usually followed by assaults, putting emery in the motor of trucks completely destroying them, and throwing of stench bombs on trucks."

The criminal activities of the three men continued until August, 1933. At that time a shooting took place in the office of the Five Borough which resulted in the death of Dick Terry and the wounding of Jimmy Doyle. This shooting which has never been investigated as far as I can determine came one month after Doyle "called on Benjamin Cohen, the president of the Garment Center Truck Owners Association, and advised him that the members of the Garment Center Truck Owners Association would have to become members of the Five Boroughs". Whether or not the shooting was in response to Doyle's demands is unknown although it appears reasonable. In any case, Dioguardi "continued the activities of the 5-Borough Truckman's Association under the name of the Allied Mutual Truckmen's Association". This association rapidly faded from the scene. Finally, Dioguardi ended up with the above mentioned Garment Center Truck Owners Association and the New York & Brooklyn Coat & Suit Trucking Association as a "labor manager". Dewey, *Personal Papers*, Series 1 — Box 90.

[39] Court of General Sessions, The People Against Buchalter, Silverman, Silverman, Schorr, 16.
[40] *Ibid.*, 17.
[41] *Ibid.*, 12–13, 15.
[42] *Ibid.*, 855–861.
[43] *Ibid.*, 863, 897–899.
[44] *Ibid.*, 953–955.
[45] *Ibid.*, 921.
[46] *Ibid.*, 873–877.
[47] *Ibid.*
[48] *Ibid.*, 871–881.
[49] *Ibid.*, 881–882.
[50] *Ibid.*, 882–883.
[51] *Ibid.*, 891–897.
[52] *Ibid.*, 1048–1053.
[53] *Ibid.*, 925–931.
[54] District Attorney of Kings County and the December 1949 Grand Jury, 99.
[55] Bell, 161.
[56] District Attorney and Grand Jury, 99.
[57] *Ibid.*, 110.
[58] *Ibid.*, 112.

[59] *Ibid.*, 110–111.

[60] *Ibid.*

[61] *Ibid.*, 112–113.

[62] *Ibid.*

[63] *Ibid.*, 116.

[64] New York State Crime Commission, *Fourth Report, Port of New York Waterfront*, Legislative Document no. 70 (1953), 12.

[65] *Ibid.*, 13.

[66] *Ibid.*, 16–18.

[67] New York State Crime Commission, *Interim Report of Evidence Adduced by the State Crime Commission Relating to Six Brooklyn Locals of the International Long-shormen's Association: Confidential* (September, 1952), 47. The material is available in Rare Books and Manuscripts, Butler Library, Columbia University.

[68] U.S. Senate, Subcommittee of the Committee on Interstate and Foreign Commerce, *Hearings of Waterfront Investigation* (Washington, D.C., 1953), 469–470.

[69] Crime Commission, *Interim Report*, 7.

[70] *Ibid.*, 21.

[71] *Ibid.*, 23.

[72] *Ibid.*, 26.

[73] *Ibid.*, 27.

[74] *Ibid.*, 29.

[75] *Ibid.*

[76] *Ibid.*, 20.

[77] See, for example, Robert C. Francis, "History of Labor on the San Francisco Waterfront," unpublished Ph.D. (University of California, Berkeley, 1934); William L. Standard, *Merchant Seamen: A Short History of Their Struggle* (New York, 1947); Joseph P. Goldberg, "American Seamen: A Study in 20th Century Collective Action," unpublished Ph.D. (Columbia University, 1951); Walter L. Johnson, "Social Adjustment of Contemporary American Merchant Seamen," unpublished Ph.D. (Yale, 1951); James W. Kelley, "Labor Problems of Longshoremen in the U.S.," unpublished Ph.D. (Boston University, 1941); Charles P. Larrowe, "The Shape-up and the Hiring Hall," unpublished Ph.D. (Yale, 1952).

Chapter 8
To Discipline and Punish

This chapter deals with several facets of that ultimate display of power—murder. Not all murders in the period 1930–1950, naturally, but a sample of that very small proportion which stemmed from the activities of professional criminals. Before getting to the data, there is a theme broached in the Introduction which should be amplified as it impinges on any discussion of violence, especially murder, in the social world of organized crime. This particular theme deals with so-called Enforcers in organized crime and most significantly with what can be inferred about the structure of organized crime once it is understood how discipline and punishment are structured. The best example of this style of argument is found in Donald Cressey's elegant and highly influential work which begins with the consequences of that magical Purge of the American Mafia discussed earlier.

What the Purge meant organizationally in the history of organized crime can be seen in the following deductions which then serve to frame Cressey's discussion of Enforcers. He states: "To use an analogy with legitimate business, in 1931 organized crime units across the United States formed into monopolistic corporations, and these corporations, in turn, linked themselves together in a monopolistic cartel." Along with corporate organization went political confederation: "To use a political analogy, in 1931 the local units formed into feudal governments, and the rulers of these governments linked themselves together into a nation-wide confederation which itself constitutes a government."[1] Cressey's sociology quickly moves to its major analytical engine. As with both business and polity, the single most important social fact of organized crime is its "division of labor" which constitutes the structure of organized crime presumably post-1931.

From the perceived division of labor, Cressey selects a particular position, the Enforcer, for analysis. The occupants of this position, he writes, arrange "for the injuring or killing of members" of organized crime as well as outsiders. Once found, discussion of this position allows him "to create information about complex governmental processes and a set of laws". The Enforcer is "one of a subset of positions existing within a broader division of labor" whose function is "to maximise organizational integration by means of just infliction of punishment of wrongdoers".[2] Moving from the area of structure to governance, he adds: "The presence of an Enforcer position ... also can be taken as evidence that members of the organization must have created some functional equivalent of the criminal law." Further inferences drawn include the "fact that punishments are to be imposed 'justly', in a disinterested manner". Building on this inference, it is then held that "the relationships between organized criminals are, to a great extent, determined by rules and expectations which insure that the consent of the governed is not lost". Finally, it is noted that when "justice prevails, the norms that govern the resort to adjudication serve to reduce conflict ..."[3]

Where all this is heading, of course, is toward the final statement on the structure of organized crime. The full-blown claim is that the structure is characterized by a more-or-less "totalitarian organization" with "rigid discipline in a hierarchy of ranks" with "permanency and form" which extend beyond the lives of particular individuals and "exist independently of any particular incumbent".[4] Cressey stands as the most forceful exponent of the view that organized crime is a bureaucracy and that syndicate criminals are at least proto-bureaucrats. It should be added, however, that in a note to his article "Methodological Problems in the Study of Organized Crime as a Social Problem" Cressey comments on another interpretation of organized crime's structure which can be inferentially drawn from his vision of the 1931 cataclysm and the position of Enforcers. He writes that the Enforcer "also makes arrangements for injuring or killing persons who are not members of La Cosa Nostra, and this fact stimulates questions about the organizational boundaries of the criminal cartel and confederation". Cressey ends stating "it is quite possible, of course, that 'organized crime' is a series of organizations, perhaps overlapping, which interact with each other and with legitimate organizations."[5] Unfortunately, this line is not pursued.

The marked propensity to view violence including murder within the social world and system of organized crime as an indicator as well as consequence of ever-increasing rationality in the Weberian sense suggests a number of problems both empirical and theoretical. The empirical evidence for the Purge as discussed in the Introduction is simply non-existent. Moreover, there is an equally significant flaw in work which posits significant changes in the early 1930s and then is totally silent about the decades following until contemporary affairs are discussed. From 1931 until the 1960s we must presume developments, an exceptionally suspect and precarious method. There are always two questions that can be asked of such interpretations: what evidence is cited for contemporary affairs, and what evidence is there that accounts for the development of current structures and functions? In grounding the contemporary sociology of organized crime upon a history of sorts, there is an obligation both to be sure of the historicity of events and to fill in the gaps. Instead we are increasingly in the realm of belief not evidence.

Nothing better exemplifies this than Mark H. Furstenberg's article, "Violence and Organized Crime", which was part of the *Staff Report* presented to the National Commission on the Causes and Prevention of Violence. At various points, this essay tries to provide evidence for the correlation of violence and rationality in the world of organized crime. The analysis starts by noting "it is true that during its period of rapid change and development, when it was consolidating its strength, organized crime was violent, sometimes wildly so".[6] Presumably as evidence for this assertion or at least part of it, Furstenberg begins his essay with the statement that "in Chicago, between 1919 and 1934, there were 765 'gang murders', an average of 48 per year. From 1935 to 1967, a period twice as long, there were 229 murders, an average of seven per year."[7] But these figures are so meaningless that no conclusions are warranted. Where are the figures year by year; what was the trend from 1919 to 1935; was murder fairly constant until 1935 and then did it decline; what criteria are used to define gang murders; what methods of gathering data were employed, and so on? The numbers are a gloss to cover what is essentially an essay of faith about violence and organized crime. This is obvious when he says that "being far more inherently rational than they are inherently violent, organized crime's leaders, ... developed and refined a system of rational alternatives to violence".[8] There is virtually nothing cited to support this conclusion. In fact, shortly after this statement in a footnote, he remarks that the "rationality of this decision can be appreciated only by realizing how inherently violent syndicate criminals really are. They come from a background in which violence is used naturally and easily to settle disputes."[9] Not only is it unclear from the text and the note whether syndicate criminals are far more inherently violent or rational, but there is no discussion of their backgrounds or any documentation for either claim.

The antithesis of violence in these accounts is rationality. As organized crime was rationalized violence declined and changed character. Theoretically what underlines these notions is the idea that organizational elaboration replaces personal violence and individual dominance with institutional authority.[10] Institutional authority is supposedly more just and disinterested than violence which springs from personal encounters. While this may be true in some general sense, there is little reason to hold that it applies to organized crime, because it has not been established that organized crime since 1931 is a highly structured cartel. With no reliable data taken from the period 1930 to at least 1960, it seems we are dealing with some variant of the old idea of progress, or the metaphysics of traditional modernization theory. The organized crime rationalists appear to accept the notion that *all* aspects of life are marching in lock-step toward ever-increasing bureaucratization. Empirically, theoretically, logically, the claimed connections among the structure of organized crime, the structure of discipline and punishment, and the process of rationality are extraordinarily suspect.

The connections discussed and disputed above are not solely nor primarily the province of academic authors. In fact, just as the history of the Purge is based on popular sources so a great deal of the discussion of Enforcers, cartelization, rationalization of violence, etc., found in contemporary criminology surfaced first in popular histories of organized crime. For instance, with just a few changes, Cressey's seemingly inferential sociology could have been lifted from the pages of *Murder, Inc.* All the categories enumerated in it, including the fixation on Enforcers as the key to the nature of the Organization, can be found in Chapter 4, "National Crime: A Cartel." This is not surprising especially when one realizes that in the historiography of organized crime no single publication has been more influential in developing the notion of Enforcers, syndicate killers, than *Murder, Inc.* The book, as we know, was constructed from information gathered in the early 1940s during the course of that astonishing investigation into murder so important for O'Dwyer's career.

The discussion of murder and violence which follows is largely based on the investigation materials—not the naive sociology of Turkus and Feder —placed in New York's Municipal Archives. The questions asked of the above materials and other primary sources as well are several: what were the general parameters of gangland murders during the 1930s and 1940s; what can be determined from calculations of known murders over the course of two decades, from some elementary typology of victims' occupations and other social data, from alleged motives of known and suspected killers, from the spatial distribution of homicides, and so on?

The Course of Murder

A list of all murders that could reasonably be attributed to professional criminals was compiled from all primary sources utilized in this study. This list was then supplemented by a search through the *New York Times* for all reported gangland slayings from 1930 through 1949. From these sources a total of 242 homicides was compiled. The vast majority of murders in the sample (78%) occurred from 1930 through 1939. Undoubtedly, the radical difference between the decades in this sample stems from the preponderance of material drawn from the Murder, Inc., investigation which was almost totally focused on the 1930s. Despite this significant bias, though, it probably is the case that many more gangland murders took place during the 1930s than in the following decade. This for such reasons as the competitive nature of much bootlegging activity and more significantly for New York because of the criminal justice and political changes and their consequences discussed in earlier chapters. The year-by-year figures for 235 murders rather than the 242 mentioned above follow. Seven murders which took place in the late 1930s are not included as their exact dates are unknown.

Table 1. The number of murders by professional criminals, 1930–1949

	1930	31	32	33	34	35	36	37	38	39
Murder Victims	40	43	11	18	8	22	10	12	3	15

	1940	41	42	43	44	45	46	47	48	49
Murder Victims	2	6	5	2	4	8	9	8	6	3

The first issue to be addressed is age and that primarily to determine if the murdered population (which was approximately 70–75% professional criminals) was in the main criminally mature or rather represented youthful professional criminals murdered as they attempted to enter established illegal enterprises. Equally as important, information about age from our sample can be compared with homicide figures compiled by the Delamar Institute of Public Health [11] for the period 1930–1938, in order to see what proportion of the murdered population in general we are dealing with. From the samples of 242 victims the ages of 138 were reported. The average age was 35, and the median 33. In the main, the victims were already established in organized crime. There is no indication that even a substantial proportion were making a transition from youthful crime to adult criminal careers. Given what is established about age for our sample we can now compare them to the total homicide figures for the age group 30–39 compiled by Emerson and Hughes. As our sample is totally male, I have only used the corresponding figures for males. First of all, the age-group 30–39 contributed about 32% of the total homicides (male) during this period. This percentage with very slight variations holds for each of the nine years although there is a marked decline in total homicides in 1936, 1937, and 1938. If we assume for the moment that all 197 victims from our sample (1930–38) fell into the age group 30–39, they would comprise 18.5% of that particular group. They do not, of course, but it is a more realistic figure than the 6% of the total male homicides which our sample represents. The point is two-fold: "gangland" murders are a very small proportion of homicides in general, but certainly not a negligible proportion in the corresponding age-group.

Ethnicity is the next issue to discuss. A substantial portion (84%) of the known victims have been ethnically identified. There are four groups represented: Italian, Jewish, Irish and Chinese. But the representation is hardly equal. Italians accounted for 116 victims, Jews for 70, Irish 9, and Chinese 8. Italians and Jews compose over 90% of the ethnically identified. More precisely, Italians account for 57%, and Jews 34.5%. Interesting as these totals are, it is more revealing to consider them year-by-year. There are 197 victims both ethnically identified and dated. At this juncture several factors stand out. First, the extraordinary number of Italian victims in 1930 and 1931; second, the large number of Jewish victims in 1935 and 1939; and third, the Chinese and Irish cluster in the first half of the 1930s. It is also obvious that the greatest percentage difference between Italians and Jews occurs in the 1940s. In the preceding decade the difference is about 12% with Italians leading. But, if the first two killing years of the 1930s are discounted then Jewish victims comprise 56.5% of the ethnically identified victims and Italians 33% over the rest of the decade.

In addition to the category of ethnicity, a fair amount of information is available concerning the occupations of victims. The most important initial distinction is that between legal and illegal ones. There are occupational data on 199 victims 60 (30%) of whom appear to have worked legal ones. The legal occupations are fairly diverse including a banker, boxer, grave digger, and journalist. There are four major trades represented: restaurant industry (11.6%); construction (13.3%); waterfront trades (15%); and the garment industry (16.6%). Cutting across these trades, however, are two other categories whose significance is more than obvious. The first is transportation especially trucking which had 18.3% of the "legal" victims. The final area in which a significant number of victims worked is trade unionism. In fact, 21.6% of the victims were employed by trade unions including the International Ladies Garment Workers (ILGWU), the International Longshoremen's Association (ILA), and two plasterer's locals.

Table 2. Victims, ethnicity in four categories, 1930–49

	1930	31	32	33	34	35	36	37	38	39	Total
Italian	21	28	3	4	1	4	4	5	1	6	77
Jewish	3	7	3	7	4	15	4	4	2	9	58
Irish	3	2		2		1		1			9
Chinese	3		1	1	3						8
Total	30	37	7	14	8	20	8	10	3	15	152

	1940	41	42	43	44	45	46	47	48	49	Total
Italian	1	2	4	2	3	7	8	5	4	1	37
Jewish		3			1		1	1	1	1	8
Irish											
Chinese											
Total	1	5	4	2	4	7	9	6	5	2	45

All 60 of the legal workers' murders have been dated and the ethnicity of 85% determined.

Considering the 60 legally employed victims the ethnic breakdown indicates that 45% were Italian, 28.3% Jews, and 10% Chinese. Comparing these figures with the entire victim pool it appears Italians had the most important percentage difference between legally employed victims and the

Table 3. Legally employed victims' ethnicity, 1930–49

	1930	31	32	33	34	35	36	37	38	39	Total
Italian	3	3		1		1	4	2		5	19
Jewish	3		2	3	1	3	2	1		1	16
Chinese	2		1		3						6
Irish		1									1
Unknown	1	1	1	2		1					6
Total	9	5	4	6	4	5	6	3		6	48

	1940	41	42	43	44	45	46	47	48	49	Total
Italian				2		2	2		1	1	8
Jewish							1				1
Chinese											
Irish											
Unknown						1		1		1	3
Total				2		3	3	1	1	2	12

total victim sample of the ethnically identified and dated (Table 2). The Italian difference figures out to 12% higher in the total sample; Jews are 6% higher in the total; and the Chinese 6% lower in the total. Although the Chinese total is very small, it is clear that the majority of murdered Chinese were legally employed. Such, of course, cannot be claimed for either Italians or Jews, although it is important to note that a larger percentage of the murdered Jews were legally employed than the murdered Italians. These points reflect upon murders which took place in the 1930s although they are based upon the figures for both decades.

In looking at occupations of murder victims the two largest divisions are between those apparently employed in legitimate endeavors and those whose only known occupations are illegal. There is, however, an intermediate category of individuals. These are victims who were legally employed and also identified as professional criminals. In the sample of 242 victims, seventeen were found to fit in this group. The legal occupations mentioned include night club owner, pool room owner, auto agency owner, fruit importer, bottling company owner, handicapper, garment manufacturers, and three officials of the International Longshoremen's Association. All seventeen victims were identified as racketeers in general which I take to mean involved in several types of criminal activities which unfortunately are not listed. In addition, three of the racketeering generalists were also bootleggers including the ones who owned the bottling company and the fruit importer, and four were primarily waterfront racketeers including the three ILA officials. Speaking of trade unions, 30% of this small group were both union officials and racketeers. It appears that trade union activity, at least in certain locals, was a hazardous undertaking whether or not one was a professional criminal. Over 23% of the murdered individuals in both parts of the sample mentioned so far were employed by trade unions.

By far the largest part of the sample are individuals whose only reported occupations are illegal. The initial point to note are the various types of professional crime or criminals indicated. There are first and foremost racketeers in general, followed by bootleggers, gamblers, narcotics traders, waterfront racketeers, loan sharks, and then a few individuals listed as alien smugglers, vice managers, black marketers, etc. There are 122 victims listed in this part of the sample. However, there are 153 occupational entries, and that because a number of victims pursued more than one identified criminal activity. In developing this line I take it for granted that those whose occupation was racketeer were involved in several distinct illegal activities as mentioned above. But in dealing with this category I recorded them in a distinct group labelled racketeer. Thus, the overlap between total individuals and total occupational entries recorded comes from individuals who combined either racketeering in general with some other category such as bootlegging, or from victims who were both gamblers and loan sharks, or bootleggers and narcotics traders, and so on. The four most significant types of illegal occupations in this part of the sample were racketeer (52%),

Table 4. Illegally employed victims' criminal occupations, 1930–49.

	1930	31	32	33	34	35	36	37	38	39	Total
Racketeer	7	10		5	4	8	2	5	2	6	49
Waterfront Racketeer	4	2									6
Gambler Racketeer	2	1	1			1					5
Gambler Loan Shark Racketeer						2			1		3
Gambler Bootlegger Narcotics	1		1						2		4
Gambler						1		1			2
Narcotics Racketeer	1					3					4
Bootlegger	5	7	3	2							17
Bootlegger Narcotics		5									5
Alien Smuggler	1	2									3

Bootlegger (14.4%), Gambler (14.4%), and Narcotics (10.5%). The percentages are computed on the figure of 153 occupational entries. I might add that the percentages remain virtually the same when the seventeen legal/illegal victims are added.

In trying to determine what occurred year-by-year to professional criminals I have arranged the victims (totalling 130 through the addition of eight individuals culled from the list of seventeen legals/criminals) in ten occupational categories which indicate some of the combining of criminal activities as well as the range.

	1940	41	42	43	44	45	46	47	48	49	Total
Racketeer		2	2			2	3	3	2	1	15
Waterfront Racketeer		1	1		1						3
Gambler Racketeer					1		1				2
Gambler Loan Shark Racketeer											
Gambler Bootleg-ger Narcotics											
Gambler		2			1	1	1	3	1		9
Narcotics Racketeer			1		1	1	1		1		5
Bootleg-ger											
Bootleg-ger Narcotics											
Alien Smuggler											

As the above table indicates nothing was quite so dangerous as being a racketeer whatever that may have meant in particular. Much more precisely it seems apparent that bootlegging alone and in conjunction with narcotics dealing was very deadly until it ended with Repeal. The murder of professional gamblers, on the other hand, was fairly constant over the course of the two decades. Because of this, gambling as an occupation in comparison with most other illegal activities was deadlier in the 1940s than in the Depression decade. Narcotics dealing was also slightly more murderous in the 1940s than previously making the same comparison. In addition, during the last half of the 1940s the only professional criminals murdered were gamblers, drug dealers and racketeers in general. Racketeering on the waterfront while not as murderous showed considerable strife in the early years of both decades. And it certainly is notable that one-half the murders of the waterfront racketeers took place in the single year of 1930. Waterfront racketeering is the only occupational category for professional criminals which by definition is similar to one of the legal categories mentioned earlier, namely legally employed waterfront workers. If one plots both categories together over time, the total of nine murders doubles to eighteen with additional killings taking place in 1930, 1933, 1935, 1937, 1945, 1947, 1948, and 1949. The murders of professional criminals and the legally employed share other similarities than those found on the waterfront. But these similarities are hidden in the ubiquitous category of racketeer which covers extortionists specializing in garments, construction, trucking, and various trade unions. The last issue to stress for the moment is that five of the categories have no victims beyond 1939. The three categories concerned with bootlegging which is hardly surprising and the one dealing with alien smuggling have no entries after 1933.

From the list of 130 murdered professional criminals the ethnic identity of 85% (82% for the 1930s, 94% for the 1940s) has been determined. The following two tables indicate the results; Table 5 uses the ten occupational categories unique to the 1930s, while Table 6 uses the five applicable categories for the next decade.

The single most important indicator that appears in these breakdowns is that once again the population concerned is overwhelming Italian and Jewish. Within this finding it is very likely that during the 1930s the risk for both populations (within the world of professional crime) was fairly even. In the following decade, however, the likelihood of an Italian professional criminal being murdered rather than a Jewish one approaches 5:1. Let me also mention the obvious concerning bootlegging, the career combination of bootlegger/drug dealer, and alien smuggling. As far as the potentialities of murder went, the population at risk in these endeavors was entirely Italian with the only exceptions being those murdered members of Waxey Gordon's beer syndicate mentioned in Chapter 6. It is also certain that among narcotics dealers those most prone to being murdered were Italian. Also of interest is the ethnicity of gamblers which shows again a marked preponderance of murdered Italians as opposed to Jews over the course of the two decades. More significantly, while there is a small cluster of murdered gamblers in 1935, just about one-half were murdered from 1944 through 1948, and with one exception they were Italians. The enterprise of narcotics during the 1940s at least, tends to show the same characteristics. There is also an interesting ethnic dimension associated with waterfront racketeering and murder. That is the shift post–1931 from Irish to Italian victims. As the waterfront is, at this time, the one racket which evokes distinct geographical areas, it is

Table 5. The ethnicity of murdered professional criminals in ten occupational categories, 1930–39 (I = Italian, J = Jewish, R = Irish)

	1930	31	32	33	34	35	36	37	38	39	Total
Racketeer	4-I 1-R	5-I 4-J		1-I 1-J	1-I 3-J	8-J	2-J	1-I 3-J	2-J	1-I 5-J	13-I 28-J 1-R
Waterfront Racketeer	3-R	2-I									2-I 3-R
Gambler Racketeer	2-I					1-J					2-I 1-J
Gambler Loan Shark Racketeer						1-I 1-I				1-J	1-I 2-J
Gambler Bootlegger			1-I								1-I
Gambler						1-R					1-R
Narcotics Racketeer	1-I					1-I 1-J					2-I 1-J
Bootlegger	4-I	6-I 1-J			2-J						10-I 3-J
Bootlegger Narcotics		4-I 1-J									4-I 1-J
Alien Smuggler	1-I	2-I									3-I

noteworthy that the 1930s murders were carried out on Manhattan's West Side piers and surrounding area which were heavily Irish, while the others were concentrated on Brooklyn's waterfront in the area known as Red Hook which was predominately Italian. But more of geography and murder shortly. Let us look at the category racketeer which encompasses over 50% of this particular sample. In the murderous 1930s racketeers accounted for a higher percentage (by 10%) of the decade's victims than in the 1940s. Turning to ethnicity, it is important that this is the one category (racketeer) in which Jewish victims outnumber Italians. Within the category itself Jews comprise almost 60% of the dead. This numerical superiority is obviously the product of severe strife during the years 1934–1939, particularly killing years for Jewish racketeers.

Table 6. The ethnicity of murdered professional criminals in five occupational categories, 1940–49 (I = Italian, J = Jew)

	1940	41	42	43	44	45	46	47	48	49	Total
Racketeer	2-J		2-I			2-I	3-I 1-J	1-I 1-J	1-I 1-J	5-J	9-I
Waterfront Racketeer		1-I	1-I		1-I						3-I
Gambler Racketeer						1-I		1-I			2-I
Gambler	1-J	1-I		1-J			1-I	1-I	3-I	1-I 2-J	7-I
Narcotics Racketeer						1-I	1-I	1-I		1-I	4-I

While those years were hard on Jewish racketeers they were also exceptionally difficult ones for Italians legally employed. It is instructive to display the yearly totals for Italians and Jews divided only by the categories of legally or illegally employed.

Table 7. Italian and Jewish victims divided into those legally employed and those illegally employed from 1930–1949.

	1930	31	32	33	34	35	36	37	38	39	40	41	42	43	44	45	46	47	48	49	Total
Legal																					
Italian	3	3		1		1	4	2		5				2		2	2		1	1	27
Jewish	3		2	3	1	3	2	1			1					1					17
Illegal																					
Italian	12	17	1	1	1	2		1		1		2	3		3	4	6	4	3		61
Jewish		5	1	3	3	11	2	3	2	6		3			1			1	1	1	43
Total																					
Italian	15	20	1	2	1	3	4	3		6		2	3	2	3	6	8	4	4	1	88
Jewish	3	5	3	6	4	13	4	4	2	7		3			1			1	1	1	58

The most substantial differences lie in the following areas. Italian professional criminals are murdered at what must be the highest rate of any professional criminals during the two decades under examination in 1930 and 1931. This is succeeded by nine years of extremely reduced risk for Italians criminals. The relative quiescence of the second half of the 1930s for Italian criminals is followed, however, by renewed violence during the 1940s with the highest concentration of murders in the years 1944–1948. The pattern for Jewish professional criminals who were murdered is quite different. Their murders are almost totally concentrated in the years 1931–1941 with the most important single year being 1935 followed by 1939 and 1931. Unlike the Italian surge of violence in the 1940s, both Jewish professional criminals and legally employed Jewish victims of gangland murders virtually disappear after 1941. For the legally employed victims there are some interesting questions raised. For instance, what explains the fact that the two worst killing years for Italians legally employed were 1936 and 1939, years when virtually no Italian gangsters were murdered? Are the murdered Italians in 1939 related in some fashion to the high number of murdered Jewish criminals in the same year?

Before turning to some of the questions about "gangland" murders raised in the preceding pages, there is one other major factor to consider: the geography of murder. In compiling the data on murder there are five major locations mentioned, four of which correspond to the Boroughs of Manhattan, Brooklyn, Queens, and the Bronx, while the fifth is the adjacent area of New Jersey. The gross distribution of murders by area over the two decades is: Brooklyn 77 (42.5%); Manhattan 71 (39.2%); Bronx 15 (8.3%); Queens 8 (4.4%); and New Jersey 10 (5.5%). Location refers to where the murders were committed and not where the victims lived although in numerous cases individuals were killed either in or near their residences. The two areas dealt with are Brooklyn and Manhattan. Before getting to them a word or two on the others. Most of the New Jersey murders (60%) were the killings of Max Hassel, Max Greenberg, Dutch Schultz, and his three associates. The individuals murdered in Queens were a diverse group: a union delegate for a bakery local, a trucking racketeer from Brooklyn, a chauffeur from Brooklyn, two potential witnesses one from the Amen investigation of paving fraud, a garment worker, a Queens racketeer, and lastly a victim whose occupation is unknown but who lived in Manhattan. In the Bronx the most discernible pattern is the six murders carried out in 1931. Five of the six were Italian, five of the six were professional criminals, and most of the murders seem to have been related to a "beer war" involving Dutch Schultz.

Brooklyn and Manhattan were the killing centers of New York. The year-by-year tallies for both Boroughs are:

Table 8. Yearly Tallies of victims in Manhattan and Brooklyn.

	1930	31	32	33	34	35	36	37	38	39	40	41	42	43	44	45	46	47	48	49
Brooklyn	21	14	3	2	1	11	3	4		3	1	1		1	1	1	3	6	1	
Manhattan	12	12	1	5	5	2	5	6	1		1	1	1	1	2	5	5	2	2	2

Plugging in the category of ethnicity limited to Italians and Jews with what is known about murder in Manhattan and Brooklyn, we find virtually no difference in Boroughs as far as Italians are concerned, but that Jews were about twice as likely to be murdered in Brooklyn.

Table 9. Ethnicity and Location of "gangland" murders.

	Italian	Jewish
Brooklyn	41	21
Manhattan	37	11

It is helpful to see the importance of Brooklyn and Manhattan in the geography of New York murders. But it is more telling to be able to find what areas within those Boroughs were the most murderous. In Manhattan there were two major areas and two minor ones. The major ones were a section of the upper East Side from about East 104th Street to 119th Street (M1). The second and most murderous section in the entire city was an area encompassing the ethnic neighborhoods known as Little Italy, Chinatown, and part of the Lower East Side (M2). The minor Manhattan areas were the garment center around 34th Street and Seventh Avenue, and the West Side piers. In Brooklyn there were three major killing zones: the first encompassed sections known as Brownsville and East New York (B1); the second was Red Hook and its waterfront extension northward (B2); the third was a large zone taking in three Brooklyn neighborhoods known as Bath Beach, Bensonhurst and Borough Park (B3). Brooklyn also had a minor killing zone situated around the section known as Williamsburg.

The following two maps with the Assembly Districts marked and numbered indicate the major killing zones in New York.

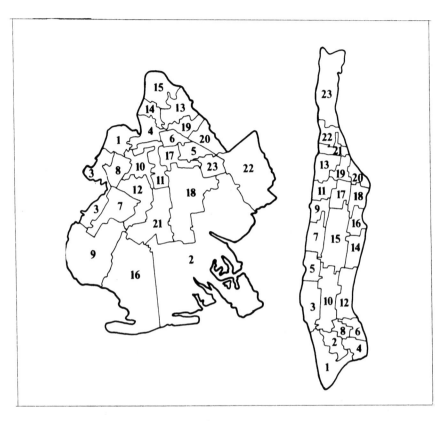

If we concentrate on these particular zones it is apparent that M1 victims were overwhelmingly Italian, and were themselves without exception professional criminals. They were bootleggers in 1930 and 1931, and then narcotics dealers after. Zone M2 presents a much more varied picture. As far as ethnicity is concerned there were five Chinese murdered, three in 1934; eleven Italians most murdered from 1942 on; six Jews five of whom were killed from 1931 to 1938; lastly, there were five victims in M2 whose ethnicity cannot be determined. The Chinese were employed as waiters with one exception, Hung Wah Hung, reported as President of a Tong Association. The Italians in M2 were bootleggers and racketeers for the most part. Of the six Jewish victims three were racketeers, one a union representative, one a trucker, and the other unknown. Besides the fact that M2 had 28 murders and M1 only 10, there is an interesting time difference between Manhattan's zones. From 1938 through 1949 M1 experienced only one murder. During that same period of time there were eight murders in M2. The major time cluster in M2 during the 1940s occurs in 1944, 1945, and 1946. In both zones there is only one murder in the period 1939–1943. As far as can be determined from the sample in Manhattan there is a localized increase in "gangland" murders of Italian professional criminals living and working in M2 beginning in 1944.

Turning to Brooklyn and area B1 to start with, Brownsville/East New York victims were Jewish with only five exceptions out of eighteen murdered. The exceptions include one Chinese, three Italians who were professional criminals, and one unknown. Almost all the Jewish victims were professional criminals. All murders of anyone from the sample in B1 took place from 1930 through 1939. The single most murderous year within B1 was unquestionably 1935 when six racketeers five of whom were Jewish were killed. The other two Brooklyn areas (B2, B3) display a very high incidence of Italian victims. And both B2 and B3 share the same time sequence with the exception of the post-war years when B3 apparently erupted with violence among gamblers. With that important exception, almost all the gangland murders in both zones were confined to 1930 and 1931.

Looking at some of the earlier tables it seems that certain factors can now be geographically set. The major killing years 1930 and 1931 had victims in all five primary areas noted above in the New York Metropolitan region, although Brooklyn, Manhattan and the Bronx predominated. The majority of victims were Italian bootleggers supplemented by Jewish racketeers, Irish waterfront racketeers, and assorted locally-employed. The 1935 murders, on the other hand, were to a much larger extent specifically confined to certain areas: Newark, New Jersey, where Dutch Schultz and three associates were shot, and Brownsville/East New York (B1) where at least five Jewish racketeers were murdered. Of all the major killing years during the two decades under investigation, the only one not geographically represented at all is 1939. The Jewish racketeers and Italian legals who comprise the bulk of 1939's murdered population (15) have not been located except for one racketeer in B1. Perhaps the most interesting, though, is how the murders in the 1940s, especially from 1944 on, are primarily concentrated in two zones —M1 and B3. Even more specifically, in the Bath Beach/Bensonhurst section of Brooklyn Italian professional gamblers were engaged in a murderous battle beginning in 1946 and peaking in 1947. Before leaving murder and geography, it should be emphasized that four of the five killing zones (M1, M2, B1, B2) roughly correspond to what were designated "high crime slum" areas in a fine study by the New York Housing Authority.[12]

Gangland murders were the most spectacular but not the most pressing social problem in these horribly impoverished areas.

Thinking About Murder: Brief Exhortations

Knowing to the best of our ability the general parameters of gangland killings let us now ask what sorts of conclusions are warranted. First, it appears that the old cliché "gangsters only kill each other" is around 70 to 75 percent valid. This points up the radically competitive nature of much professional crime. Even more so, it establishes from another angle the instability rampant in the various underworld communities. I use the plural because the spatial distribution of homicides, in effect, identifies several underworld communities, crossed or linked no doubt by partnerships and other types of networks. Nevertheless, these particular urban enclaves supported indigenous criminal cultures; their uniqueness compounded by ethnic composition as well as some economic specialization. The clearest example of this is Brooklyn's Red Hook, an overwhelmingly Italian neighborhood centered around waterfront activities. As every student of urban history and sociology knows, municipalities are changing conglomerations subject to certain uniformities and imperatives, but exhibiting vast differences in neighborhood life. The social histories of M1, M2, B1, B2, B3 and the minor killing are not the same, some indeed radically different from others. The homicide data, therefore, point researchers to the task of unravelling the social history of neighborhood crime and the mechanisms and personalities which bridge the many urban villages.

The data on murders also indicate with a fair degree of precision which trades were not only risky in comparison with others, but which were penetrated or dominated by professional criminals. As far as legitimate enterprises are concerned, restaurant, construction, waterfront and garment businesses furnished a substantial portion of the dead. And within those trades, nothing was quite so dangerous as trucking and especially trade union activity. These findings strongly support other evidence discussed in earlier chapters which all together reveal areas desperately needing attention from economic and labor historians.

Finally, while there are any number of subsidiary issues raised, there are two major ones: New York's underworlds were principally populated by Italians and Jews; and the criminal populations of both were considerably less murderous in the 1940s than in the preceding decade. The issues are, of course, more complex than stated. Italians are murdered at a fantastic rate in 1930 and 1931, while Jews were most often killed in the second half of the 1930s. In addition, the incidence of homicides varies considerably according to zone. For the social historian of organized crime the two most salient findings deal with ethnicity and the startling reduction in gangland murders in the 1940s. There is no difficulty in understanding and indeed appreciating the historical significance of the first issue given what has already been discussed in the text. What is truly puzzling, however, is the marked dimunition of homicides in the 1940s. I caution to add that there is no evidence to suggest which decade was more typical of 20th century crime, or that the reduction carried into the 1950s. The possible explanations for this found change range from (1) the effects of World War 2 on the competitiveness of certain illegal enterprises and on employment; (2) changes in the methods of dispute settlement among professional criminals; (3) changes in underworld structures brought about by the blood-letting of the 1930s; (4) grossly unreliable data; (5) changes in politics and criminal justice which materially affected the incidence of gangland murders. I will have more to say about this last point later. Any or all of the above (with the exception of grossly unreliable data) could in fact have been determinative of the reduction. But which or what combination is unanswerable. However, not being able to answer the question should not obscure the importance of being able to posit it. That there was a stunning quantitative change in killings by professional criminals seems to me indisputable and important even without specific answers to cause.

Killers

A great deal information about organized crime, and organized crime and violence can be gleaned from analyzing victims. What is needed now is the placing of as much of this mayhem as possible within the careers of particular criminals. Some murders have already been placed such as Maranzano's, Greenberg's, Hassel's, Snyder's, Drukman's, and the killing of Schultz and his associates. Another batch have been either alluded to or listed in the discussion of O'Dwyer and his famous murder investigation. And it is back to this investigation we must turn for material on killers, their motives, their methods, and their social world. A cautionary word is in order, however. The O'Dwyer investigation did not encompass the world of organized crime, but rather a particular highly important aspect; furthermore, it was concerned with events which took place in the 1930s avoiding, indeed covering up, criminal activities which were coterminous with the investigation especially when these activities dealt with waterfront racketeers.

The O'Dwyer archival material and the murder trial transcripts deal with several sets of professional criminals, their relationships, and naturally the murders they committed. A large amount of this material came from the statements of three major participants who became informers—Abe Reles, Albert Tannenbaum, and Max Rubin. There were others such as Julie Catalano, Seymour Magoon, and Sholem Bernstein, but their function and stories primarily corroborate the extended statements of the other three. For the most part I will concentrate on Reles and Tannenbaum because unlike Rubin they were professional criminals who were also killers.

Abe Reles, whose death has received so much attention was born of Austrian–Jewish parents around 1906. Shortly after, his family moved from the Lower East Side to Brownsville, Brooklyn. His father worked in one of the garment trades until some time in the Depression. The father's last known occupation was peddling knishes on the streets of Brownsville. Reles probably attended school through the eighth grade. After leaving school he "hung out" in poolrooms and candy stores in and around Brownsville. Reles had two constant companions Martin Goldstein and Harry Strauss. In 1921 he was arrested for stealing $2 worth of gum from a vending machine and sent to the Children's Village at Dobbs Ferry, New York, for four months. After leaving the quasi-reformatory, Reles and his two companions began careers as thieves and minor extortionists terrorizing small shops in Brownsville.[13]

Up until the end of the 1920s there is no doubt and disagreement about Reles's career as a Brownsville thug teamed with Goldstein and Strauss. Starting with the Depression, there are several different versions of exactly what he and his associates were doing and for whom they were acting when they murdered various individuals. Basically, the differences concern whether Reles and the others (Strauss and Goldstein, and still others to be mentioned soon) were killing people for Buchalter or Anastasia, whether they were killing people for themselves as well as Buchalter and/or Anastasia, whether they were part of either Buchalter's or Anastasia's mob, when did they begin killing for either Buchalter and/or Anastasia, and I suppose lastly to what extent their activities support the notion which began this chapter that "gangland" murder had become routinized.[14]

Among the various documents in the O'Dwyer papers are four which directly relate to Reles's activities in the late 1920s and early 1930s. They all indicate that several power syndicates were set in motion around 1930. There were primary and secondary partnerships covering various types of activities which went something like this: Reles, Goldstein and Strauss were partners in all their activities which appear at the time to have been primarily "the slot machine racket" and quickly expanded to include "shylocking, crap games and slugging in connection with union activities, the chief one being the restaurant union". This partnership was extended in late 1930 to include Harry Maione, Frank Abbandando, Vito Gurino and George De Feo. This syndicate lasted for four years until 1934. At the same time as the enlarged syndicate was formed there was also implemented secondary partnerships with Vincent Mangano, Albert Anastasia and Louis Capone. These partnerships were secondary in the sense that Mangano, Anastasia and Capone received a percentage of the syndicate's profits from certain of their activities, but not from all. In 1934, while Reles was in prison the enlarged syndicate amicably separated and when Reles returned to Brownsville late in 1935 or early 1936 his partners were Goldstein, Strauss and Louis Capone.

The term partnership needs closer scrutiny to elucidate the nature of the relationships between Mangano, Anastasia and Capone on the one hand, and Reles, Strauss and Goldstein on the other. If this is simply an economic system being described then the term might suffice. But it is not. This is a social world within which economic relations play an important part. The most precious commodity in this world is power; and individuals oriented themselves through a series of personal relationships which, if fortunate, added to their personal power and therefore their ability to successfully extort from those less fortunate. The method to secure relationships was to do "favors" for the already powerful. At the same time this social world is highly competitive and contingent with no guarantees that one's patron will remain powerful or indeed alive or that others will not be more successful in courting a patron, and so on. In this chaotic world, relationships need constant tending, and reputations especially of toughness are vitally important. Displays of personal power are constantly necessary for both personal and financial security in this most insecure world. Weakness undermines not only an individual's position but reverberates through the entire associational network which is always precarious.

In 1928 when Reles was 22 he began frequenting a cafe owned by Louis Capone and his brother which was located in the Ocean Hill neighborhood of Brooklyn immediately adjacent to Brownsville. Prior to 1928 Capone and Anastasia had formed some sort of alliance or relationship and Anastasia was a frequent visitor to the cafe. To Reles and the other young toughs such as Maione, Capone and Anastasia "were then considered advisers", which I take to mean potential patrons. Within a very short period of time, Reles did the first of a series of "favors" for Capone and Anastasia. He shot someone pointed out to him by Capone. "Thereafter Abe did a number of jobs for and at the direction of Louis Capone. These consisted of burglaries and breaking heads who incurred the displeasure of Louis Capone."

Through at least 1930 Anastasia and Capone appear to have remained as potential patrons or perhaps patrons of limited power themselves. As we have seen 1930 was the year in which Reles, Strauss, Goldstein, Maione, Gurino, Abbandando, and De Feo consolidated their fortunes while reserving part of their proceeds for Anastasia, Mangano and Capone. But 1930 was also the year when this enlarged syndicate began battling another one for control of a variety of illicit activities in and around Brownsville. And according to the major document in the archives detailing this battle,[15] Anastasia, Mangano and Capone played no role in this combat although other professional criminals did. In an exceptionally florid style the document relates that the syndicate turned its "attention to the pinball machine racket". This racket was controlled in Brownsville anyway by the "Shapiro brothers and their henchmen". The Shapiro syndicate collected $5 for every pinball machine placed in Brownsville saloons and candy stores, etc. To avoid paying the "tax" and other assorted tributes to the Shapiros, the new syndicate relied on the power of another syndicate namely the "Ben and Meyer Combination". George De Feo's brother William was supposedly "a powerful mobster, working on the East Side, Manhattan, for what was then probably the most affluent and powerful mobster organization, known and feared by the underworld ..." The leaders were Meyer Lansky and Ben Siegal. Through this kinship connection, the syndicate received a credit line on pinball machines and began actively placing them in Brownsville locations.

A number of gun fights ensued in which Meyer Shapiro, the oldest brother, was seriously wounded. The Shapiro syndicate responded by ambushing Reles, Goldstein and De Feo. The result was George De Feo dead, Goldstein and Reles wounded. When they recovered they were finally able to murder two of the Shapiro brothers in the summer of 1931 along with another of the Shapiros' mobsters. The last Shapiro brother was murdered by Maione and Abbandando in 1936.

What makes all this worth recounting is first that it explains a number of the murders of professional criminals in Brownsville (B1) in the early 1930s, and second reveals something about the complex networks active in the underworld at the time. Concerning the second it is interesting that none of the patrons such as Anastasia, Capone, or indeed William De Feo provided the syndicate with protection or help even after George De Feo was killed. In fact, the only individual protected in this whole struggle was Albert Tannenbaum who would turn out to be the other major informer in 1940. Tannenbaum worked for Buchalter at this time, and also aided the Shapiros in their struggle. As the report notes:

Louis Capone Meyer Lansky

When it was ascertained that Tannenbaum was the chauffeur of the car, the mob went looking for him to bump him off. "Little Farvel" Cohen came to them and told them that they should square things. Ben (Bugs) Siegal was present at the time and told "Little Farvel" to mind his own business, that he had no authority to straighten things out. Subsequently, a "meet" was held in "Lepke" Buchalter's headquarters on Broadway, Manhattan, when matters were straightened out, and Tannenbaum was forgiven by the Brownsville mob there represented by Reles, Louis Capone and Harry Strauss.

Lastly, it is clear that the murders of De Feo, Meyer Shapiro, Irving Shapiro, William Shapiro, along with several other Brownsville racketeers were carried out solely in the interests of the immediate combatants.

This power syndicate following their triumph over the Shapiros extended their illicit activities into various areas, most notably bookmaking. In the true spirit of extortionists "they went to the bookmakers operating in the Brownsville section of Brooklyn and 'declared themselves in' on the bookmakers' earnings. This fiat placed them on the payrolls of these bookmakers and proved a fruitful source of income to the new partnership."

From 1930 until 1935 there is very little correlation between individuals murdered at the behest of Albert Anastasia and those killed by Reles and his associates. Anastasia participated in or ordered the murder of eight individuals between 1930 and 1935 only one of whom was murdered by members of the Reles, Strauss, etc., syndicate. At the same time, the syndicate also murdered five individuals only one of whom appears to have been killed for someone outside their own group. There is no evidence that Reles and the others carried out any killings for Buchalter until 1936.

For so many reasons, 1935 was a crucial year for a number of New York professional criminals. To begin with it was the year Dutch Schultz and his associates were murdered with all the attendant confusion that produced in underworld circles. Perhaps most importantly, it was the year that Dewey would be selected as Special Prosecutor, and as far as Buchalter and the

Brownsville syndicate were concerned that was crucial. But before either Dewey's appointment became significant or Schultz's murder, several other murders took place in Brooklyn which materially affected the fortunes of the Reles syndicate as well as their patron Anastasia and partner Louis Capone. Reles was not a principal in any of the 1935 killings because he was serving time in the penitentiary, but he was kept well informed by several of his associates including "Mikie" Syckoff a loan shark working for Reles who would also become an informer living in and through the strange happenings at the Half Moon Hotel.

The first killings took place on September 15. The victims were Abraham Meer and Irving Amron both professional criminals. They were murdered in reprisal for kidnapping "one 'Bot' Silvio, who was the partner of 'Jimmy Blue Eyes', and had exacted a ransom of $8,000.00 before releasing him".[16] These murders were done at the request of "Jimmy Blue Eyes" for revenge, and carried out by Strauss and Goldstein with an eye to the future. "Blue Eyes" was a professional criminal with a large gambling operation known as "The Plantation" set up in Hollywood, Florida. The Brownsville syndicate intended to move up some of their slot machines into "The Plantation" with "Blue Eyes" permission. For an unknown reason this never came to pass. Strauss's bitter comment when he learned of this was: "If he wants us to do something, he knows where to come. Let him come down for another favor. He forgets about Meer and Amron. We had to kill them in our own neighborhood, too."

As far as the Brownsville syndicate was concerned the most momentous 1935 killings took place barely two weeks after Meer and Amron. On September 30, Joe Amberg and his driver Morris Kessler were lined up against a garage wall in Brownsville and gunned down. The killings were also revenge slayings. Amberg was a very significant racketeer with some sort of relationship to Joe Adonis and perhaps Ben Siegal. Before he could be murdered, Adonis had to be not just notified but persuaded. Apparently he was. The ostensible motive for Amberg's killing stemmed from the fact that Amberg, and two associates, Jack Elliot and Frankie Teitelbaum had murdered another professional criminal, Hyman Kasner who was connected to Anastasia in some fashion for reasons that are totally obscure. In any case, it was decided at a "conference" with Anastasia, Louis Capone, Strauss and Maione that Amberg must be killed. The killers themselves were Philip Mangano (Vincent Mangano's brother mentioned in the previous chapter), and someone known as "Red" Pulvino. Assistants in this double murder were Maione and Strauss.

Louis "Pretty" Amberg

The murder of Amberg "had repercussions in the garment industry in Manhattan, the fruit and vegetable market in Brownsville, and in other quarters".[17] This is corroborated and supplemented by a statement of Reles's which claims that after the Amberg murder: "We had the bookmaking business and a couple of unions. One union is the dress end of the garment industry in Manhattan on 35th Street. We had the fruit market union on Osborne Street. We had the van movers and we had the painters for awhile, too, and the luncheonettes and the restaurant union, and part of Local 138 of the Truckmen's Union, and the Retail Clerks and Plumbers Helpers Union."[18] A fair amount of this racketeering activity had been taken with the murder of Amberg almost automatically, it seems, by the Brownsville syndicate. It need hardly be added that Anastasia and Vincent Mangano received a significant cut from their new businesses. By this time, Louis Capone although still deeply associated with Anastasia, was considered a full partner in all the activities of the Brownsville syndicate of Reles, Strauss, and Goldstein. The associational networks were increasing, becoming more deeply layered and complex. The Brownsville syndicate had made significant inroads in both the garment industry and Local 138, both areas traditionally assigned to Buchalter. Clearly, the murder of Amberg had materially changed the status of Reles, Goldstein and Strauss, although not necessarily Louis Capone, putting them into ever closer contact with Buchalter and members of his primary power syndicate.

The high number of murders in 1935 especially among Jewish professional criminals represents the sort of violence endemic in the social world of organized crime which for strictly peculiar or idiosyncratic reasons erupted at that time in predominantly Jewish neighborhoods such as Brownsville or concerned primarily Jewish trades such as garments. That this violence included Italians such as Anastasia, Capone, and Adonis in some capacity or other merely indicates that syndicates, partnerships, and networks cut across ethnic lines with a fair amount of ease. Nevertheless, there does seem to be some bedrock of ethnic mutuality at work, although not ethnic exclusiveness. There is something else about the 1935 murders in Brooklyn which needs emphasis. The forces which brought them about were contained in the underworld itself. There were no outside issues or forces such as political upheavals or criminal justice investigations which impinged upon these murders. Meer, Amron, Kasner, Amberg and several others were murdered because professional crime is violently competitive in and of itself.

Starting in 1936, this situation would change. The Dewey investigation would loom larger and larger in the affairs of Buchalter and as it did the recently established associational network stretching from Manhattan's garment trades to Brownsville would be affected. The key event which signals this change is the murder of Joe Rosen mentioned in a different context in Chapter 5. Rosen's murder which took place early in the morning of September 13, 1936, was the result of the conjunction of several factors. Basically, Rosen who had been forced out of a garment trucking business by Buchalter in 1932, threatened to talk to Dewey. What makes this case so revealing is that Rosen annoyed, exasperated and threatened to talk to the authorities for several years before he was finally killed. What sealed his fate were the constant threats in conjunction with Dewey's burgeoning investigation. It is easy enough to track Buchalter's changing responses to the Rosen problem through Max Rubin's testimony at the murder trial.[19]

When Rosen was initially forced out of the trucking business his objection was that he was being financially ruined was countered by assurances from Buchalter that they would find him some other work. Rosen was subsequently hired by Louis Cooper the head of the Garfield Express Company. In some sense this was only fair as Garfield Express picked up all the business of Rosen's defunct company, according to one of Rosen's ex-partners, Morris Blustein.[20] In addition, Buchalter was one of Cooper's partners. A year later, however, Rosen was fired by Cooper for "stealing some hampers". Max Rubin intervened and tried to get Cooper to take Rosen back, but Cooper was adamant. Rubin went to Buchalter and exclaimed: "We cannot afford to have a woman on Fifth Avenue hollering that her husband has lost a job and been out of business; we better put him back."[21] Buchalter agreed but was unable to convince Cooper and Rosen remained out of work for about sixteen months.

Early in 1935, Rosen sought out Rubin to complain about his situation. Rubin reported to Buchalter that "we have a desperate man on our hands, that we have to get him a job; he will work for anything; he is talking a whole lot and we are liable to get into a lot of trouble".[22] Rubin suggested a solution which involved a complicated shift of personnel from several firms, but it is unclear whether this plan was ever adopted. Rubin next mentioned that Rosen had opened a candy store in Brownsville. In June, 1936, it was Buchalter telling Rubin that Rosen "was going around Brownsville, shooting off his mouth that he is going to go down to Dewey's office". At this time Buchalter was extremely anxious about the Dewey investigation going so far as to use fictitious names on the telephone which he suspected was tapped. Rubin told Buchalter that he would have various members of his local patronize Rosen's store which would satisfy him. But it did not, and Buchalter still received reports that Rosen was threatening to see Dewey. Buchalter then told Rubin to "take two bills and give it to Joe Rosen and tell him to stay out of town until I tell him to come back".[23] Rosen took the money and went to Reading, Pennsylvania, but returned within a few days.

On September 11, Rubin walked into Buchalter's office and was greeted with a barrage: "Lepke said to me, I have stood enough of that crap you have been handing me. That son of a bitch, that bastard, he is going around Brownsville and shooting off his mouth that he is going down to Dewey." Buchalter added that Rosen was not going to Dewey or any other place. Rubin pleaded for more time and left Buchalter with one last plan for controlling Rosen. It was far too late. Two days later Rosen was shot seventeen times by Emmanuel Weiss and Harry Strauss.[24]

It is obvious enough that murder in this case was more the result of criminal justice changes than anything else. And from 1936 until 1940 an increasing number of killings would be carried out in direct proportion to the legal pressures tightening around Buchalter. Additionally, as the search for both potential and actual informers went on, the pool of suspects narrowed down to encompass primarily professional criminals closely associated with Buchalter. Ironically enough, in trying to protect himself and his power syndicate by eliminating certain members, his syndicate itself disintegrated in a welter of killings. In the latter half of the 1930s, particularly in 1939, a rather cruel dialectic was revealed; one in which the peril of being a potential informer (and everyone with knowledge of Buchalter's activities qualified) drove certain criminals to police and prosecutors for self-preservation. But as they began negotiating with criminal justice agents their perfidy was all too often discovered, and murder the result. One can only imagine the fear and trembling this situation produced; the heightened violence and treacherous intrigue which must have characterized that segment of the underworld within which Buchalter had operated, including those networks which grew out of the Amberg killing.

Instability and disintegration first within that segment of professional crime concerned with the garment trades and Buchalter, and then filtering down to other syndicates which were part of the complex web of networks built during the first part of the decade partially characterize the last three years of the 1930s. In 1935 the Brownsville syndicate of Reles, Strauss, Goldstein and Capone had penetrated the garment trades through the murder of Amberg and the maneuvers of Capone. In 1936 the participants in the murder of Joseph Rosen were members of Buchalter's syndicate joined by Capone, Strauss and Sholem Bernstein a subsidiary member of the Brownsville mob. There were two factors which account for this "piecework" amalgamation: the growing mutuality of concern on the part of several syndicates over the investigation of garment racketeering; and the fact that Rosen's candy store was in East New York, part of the home territory of Reles, Strauss and the others.

From 1937 to 1939 the following individuals associated with Buchalter mostly in garment racketeering were murdered: Irving "Danny Fields" Friedman, Samuel "Tootsie" Feinstein, Albert Schuman, Harry "Big Greenie" Greenberg, Yoell Miller, Irving Penn (mistaken for Philip Orlofsky), Abraham Friedman, Leon Scharf, Hyman Yuron, Walter Sage, and Joe Weiner. Two others, Max Rubin and Joe Miller, were seriously wounded. Almost all of these killings were carried out by principals from three power syndicates which were closely allied if not intertwined at certain levels. The principals are Emmanuel Weiss, Charles Workman, and Albert Tannenbaum from Buchalter's syndicate; Capone, Reles, Strauss, and Goldstein from the Brownsville syndicate, and lastly, Parisi from Anastasia's waterfront syndicate.

Abraham "Whitey" Friedman   *Walter Sage*

Some of the developments binding these syndicates together have already been dealt with. The two important ones were the areas of mutual racketeering interest and the Capone–Anastasia partnership which resulted in the understanding of the part of the Brownsville gangsters that Anastasia was their boss and Capone their partner. Having Anastasia as their boss meant that Anastasia received a part of some of their racketeering profits, and that Anastasia had to be consulted before they murdered competitors or alleged informers. It was also understood that they were to be available for general mayhem when requested by Anastasia.

These last two points are, of course, the source of some of the more nonsensical interpretations about organized crime. The relationship between Anastasia and the Brownsville racketeers has been taken to mean that Anastasia was the boss of organized crime; that all murders of and by professional criminals were ordered by Anastasia; that the Brownsville racketeers were organized crime's Enforcers; and, that murder was therefore both rationalized and routinized. Without diminishing Anastasia's considerable importance as a professional criminal, all the above are the result of a gross inflation of the circumstances surrounding *some* "gangland" murders in the latter part of the 1930s. Anastasia was not the boss of organized crime (a term with no meaning in the sense used); very, very few of the known gangland murders were done at his request; the Brownsville group was a power syndicate making money from a variety of extortionary activities, but not a penny for murder; the individuals they killed with few exceptions were competitors or informers (actual and potential) who threatened their interests primarily in the garment trades; and lastly, the fact that Anastasia's O.K. was necessary for members of *this* syndicate when it came to murder is not proof of either rationalization or routinization. Anastasia, as far as I can determine, never vetoed any requests for murder from this syndicate which indicates the ceremonial nature of his permission not the rationalization of homicide. Furthermore, most of the information concerning informers was relayed to Anastasia by the actual killers themselves. Upon receiving word of treachery Anastasia invariably responded positively to murder requests. The executioners tended to monopolize the information process. How many personal scores were settled through deliberately false or wrong information can only be imagined.

The fact that the three power syndicates acted in concert during this period was drastically heightened by Buchalter's decision to go into hiding in the summer of 1937. Most of his time spent hiding from Dewey was passed in Brooklyn first at Louis Capone's restaurant (2780 Stillwell Avenue) and then at an apartment on Foster Avenue secured for him by Anastasia and Capone. While brought together by mutual criminal interests, by overlapping partnerships which cut across syndicate lines, by the circumstances of the Dewey investigation soon supplemented by Amen's work which must have added some degree of anxiety, and by the felt need to cooperatively eliminate as many potential and actual informers as possible, it is still unmistakenly evident that Buchalter and his syndicate viewed themselves as a distinct entity. And, over time this was reinforced as their beleagured status became even more apparent.

Evidence for this is found in MEMORANDUM OF INFORMATION GIVEN BY ALBERT TANNENBAUM, Re: Lepke and Gurrah hideouts, etc., compiled, it appears, by N. J. Higgins of the FBI. What follows are some key excerpts:

> Tannenbaum believes a conference preceded Lepke's becoming a fugitive, and that the top-notch men in the underworld then available attended, namely, Abe (Longy) Zwillman, Meyer Lansky and Ben (Bugs) Siegel, as well as the lesser characters, Moe (Dimples) Wolinsky and Tom (Kutty) Kutlow. From the usual run of conversations Tannenbaum ..., knows that Lepke first went to Newark to hideout from the authorities.[25]

Morris "Dimples" Wolinsky

Buchalter left Newark and went to Los Angeles where

> Meyer Lansky visited him there, and that both Lansky and Ben (Bugs) Siegel had demanded of Lepke that he break up his mob and that they would continue to pay the salaries of Charlie Workman and Sam Feinstein "on Ben's payroll", but the rest of the mob would have to shift for themselves.[26]

Turning to one of his visits to Buchalter in Brooklyn on Foster Avenue, Tannenbaum continues:

> Tannenbaum told Lepke that they had sufficient funds with a little money left over each week. Lepke told Mendy to try to accumulate as much money as they could and try not to go to any of the other fellows, i.e. other mobs, if Mendy and their mob could not "earn their own living", to try to be independent. Farvel at this point would say, "To hell with the other guys."[27]

On Tannenbaum's third visit to Buchalter in the early summer of 1939

Lepke started to talk about the time he was out in this high class hotel out West on the Coast and he said that it was ridiculous that Ben and Meyer had suggested breaking up the mob with Workman and Tootsie remaining on the payroll but on Ben's instead of his, and the rest of the mob being let go without provision for their upkeep.[28]

Tannenbaum's fourth visit at the end of July, 1939 found the situation extraordinarily tense. It was about a week prior to Buchalter's surrender.

Mendy said to Tannenbaum that he was glad to see him because there was trouble expected. He asked Tannenbaum if he knew where to get Workman ... Tannenbaum ... inquired what the trouble was. Weiss replied that it looked as though they were going to have a war on their hands, because Lepke got an ultimatum in a nice way to either walk in or else! ... Mendy told Tannenbaum on this occasion that they should be very careful and cautious about trusting anybody until they found out more definitely just how definite the ultimatum was. Mendy said that this alertness be extended to Abe Reles, Harry Strauss and Jack Drucker, ... until it was ascertained how they stood.[29]

Jack Drucker

That same day Tannenbaum discussed the situation with Buchalter. Tannenbaum asked

Lepke if they would do a thing like that, forcing him to surrender under pain of death. He said that if Tannenbaum had been around as much as he, he would know that they would do just that .... Lepke then said that he thought it would be the best thing "to save you kids from a lot of trouble" to walk in, adding that if they looked to harm him, they knew that his mob would put up a fight.[30]

At this point Buchalter, Tannenbaum, Weiss, and Sidney "Shimmy" Salles tried to figure out who "was who in any such fight".

Would Reles, Strauss and Anastasia be with them or against them, and they could not arrive at a satisfactory answer.[31]

The issue of how the other power syndicates would line up was resolved by Buchalter's surrender to Walter Winchell and J. Edgar Hoover.

The points I want to discuss here are structural. When the bottom line was reached Buchalter was the leader of an ever shrinking power syndicate. Shrinking because of internal strife and external circumstances brought about by the investigations and compounded by personal pique of murderous dimensions. In times of plenty, before 1936 or so, this syndicate extended its power through several types of networks with other professional criminals and thus power syndicates. These networks were not limited to those developed by Buchalter himself, but included those constructed by Workman, Weiss, Salles, and others which were most often represented by cross-syndicate partnerships in various discrete extortionary schemes. In prosperous times both group and individual interests merged so that influence and power grew at least for Buchalter exponentially. But in times of stress these networks rapidly broke down, having been changed from channels of power to ones of weakness. In Buchalter's case, the personal networks which had carried him to a position of criminal eminence disintegrated to a large extent by the time he went into hiding. The very act of hiding conveyed an already ominous loss of power in and of itself. That was certainly the message conveyed to him by Lansky and Siegel in 1937 and repeated in 1939.

Charles "Bug" Workman

Buchalter was finished in the summer of 1939 and so was what remained of his syndicate with the exception of Charles Workman. Two years earlier Workman and Sam "Tootsie" Feinstein would have been employed by other professional criminals, but Feinstein was murdered in May, 1939, in one of those internecine battles characteristic of the process of disintegration. Feinstein's murder was motivated by his reluctance "to go out and do any more work in killing people as the mob was all broken up".[32] His killer was his closest friend, fellow syndicate member, and partner in narcotics dealing, Charles Workman.

233

At the end, the only ones rallying around Buchalter must have been aware that other professional criminals viewed them as sure liabilities. Their careers in crime were almost over, their power gone. The final blow would follow rapidly Buchalter's surrender to Federal authorities. This was O'Dwyer's selective investigation of homicide which for Buchalter only represented the "coup de grace" to a life already permanently over on the streets of New York. What remained of his power syndicate when he surrendered either faced imprisonment like Workman, execution like Weiss, informing like Albert Tannenbaum, or were murdered in the early 1940s the fate of "Little Farvel" Cohen, Ben Tannenbaum and Sidney "Shimmy" Salles.

Philip "Little Farvel" Cohen   *Ben "The Boss" Tannenbaum*

Buchalter's tribulations and the attendant murders go a long way in providing a context for a number of the gangland killings discussed in the first part of this chapter. But the rise and fall of Buchalter and many of the others mentioned cannot account for even the majority of murders committed in the 1930s let alone those following their removal. The most that can be said by way of summary now is that murder is the penultimate expression of violence and that violence was endemic in the social world of organized crime which included all those sectors of urban life which either served or were serviced by professional criminals. The found differences in location, ethnicity, occupation, and the number of murder victims over the course of two decades indicate that changes were taking place in New York's underworlds. What those changes were, however cannot be determined with any precision especially when concentrating on murder. The terrible toll of victims in the 1930s compared with the next decade does deserve one or two additional comments. First of all, the early murders in 1930 and 1931 appear to be intimately related to bootlegging which was probably the most competitive and thus murderous enterprise of all. Second, there is unmistakenly a relationship between political and criminal justice changes and homicide. The more probing an investigation is, the more likely it is to be littered with dead bodies. When networks break down through the intervention of an outside agency with power, information becomes a highly important and therefore dangerous commodity. In a volatile situation the key decision is whether to buy leniency or safety through informing. Everyone, obviously, knows this and acts accordingly. Increased violence is among the inevitable results. Perhaps one explanation then for the marked decrease in murders during the 1940s is connected to O'Dwyer's ascendancy. In any case, let us finally put to rest those notions which marked the beginning of this chapter which hold that murder was rationalized and routinized becoming the expression of a consolidated underworld as of 1931. Nothing, it seems to me, could be further from the truth or more insensitive to the complexities of power and the reality of gangland murder.

NOTES

[1] Cressey, "Structure and Functions," 31.
[2] Cressey, "Methodological Problems in the Study of Organized Crime as a Social Problem," *Annals* 374 (1967), 110.
[3] *Ibid.*, 111–112.
[4] Cressey, "Structure and Functions," 58.
[5] Cressey, "Methodological Problems," 110, note 18.
[6] Mark H. Furstenberg, "Violence and Organized Crime," in National Commission on the Causes and Prevention of Violence, *Crimes of Violence: Staff Report* Vol. 13, Appendix 18 (Washington, D.C., 1969), 912.
[7] *Ibid.*, 911.
[8] *Ibid.*, 912.
[9] *Ibid.*, 932.
[10] In this vein consider Robert Bierstedt, "An Analysis of Social Power," *American Sociological Review* 15(1950).
[11] Haven Emerson and Harriet E. Hughes, *Population, Births, Notifiable Diseases, and Deaths, Assembled for New York City, 1866–1938* (New York, 1941).
[12] Irving W. Halpern, John N. Stanislaus, and Bernard Botein, *The Slum and Crime: A Statistical Study of the Distribution of Adult and Juvenile Delinquents in the Boroughs of Manhattan and Brooklyn* (New York, 1934).
[13] *New York Post*, April 8, 1940: 1 and 16; April 9, 1940: 1.
[14] For some of the popular writers consult Joseph Freeman, "Murder Monopoly: The Inside Story of a Crime Trust," *Nation* 150 (May, 25, 1940); and again Messick, McPhaul, Sann. Reid, Turkus and Feder.
[15] "Re: Killing of George De Feo," in *O'Dwyer Papers*.
[16] "Re: Killing of Abraham Meer and Irving Amron," in *O'Dwyer Papers*.
[17] "Re: Louis Capone, in *O'Dwyer Papers*.

[18] "Background of 'Buggsy' Goldstein and Harry Strauss as furnished by Abe Reles" in *O'Dwyer Papers*.

[19] Court of Appeals — Brooklyn, New York, The People Against Buchalter, Weiss, Capone.

[20] "Statement taken by Assistant District Attorney Solomon A. Klein on June 27th, 1941," in *O'Dwyer Papers*.

[21] Court of Appeals, 1341–1345.

[22] *Ibid.*, 1345–1349.

[23] *Ibid.*, 1350–1365.

[24] *Ibid.*, 1365–1376.

[25] "Memorandum of Information given by Albert Tannenbaum, Re: Lepke and Gurrah hideouts, etc.," in *O'Dwyer Papers*, 2.

[26] *Ibid.*, 4.

[27] *Ibid.*, 15.

[28] *Ibid.*, 17.

[29] *Ibid.*, 18–19.

[30] *Ibid.*, 19–20.

[31] *Ibid.*, 20.

[32] "Re: Charles Workman," in *O'Dwyer Papers*.

Conclusion

Frank Valentino

I am one of the victims of Valentino, and I cannot appear personally because if I do, they will kill me later, therefore, you have the means and the knowledge to stop the hands of these murderers.

With best wishes, I am a Plasterer.

New York City

Chapter 9
Organizing Crime

If there is one constant theme that this study of organized crime has been oriented around it is that of power. The term has been used in a variety of ways in a host of settings each hopefully refracting slightly different angles of its many manifestations. It may seem terribly banal, but power is what it was all about. Taken as a sort of limitless commodity which carries with it the promise of almost endless profit, power was at the heart of the cravings catalogued in the preceding chapters. The formal expressions of power connoted by the term authority were never enough and were continually supplanted by that extra rush which the informal arrangements promised. Power not authority was paramount. And that because in the competitive areas discussed there was a demand for the edge. In real and fictive terms one needed the gun to eliminate competitors, to discipline workers, to secure the right vote. The gun and what it signified bridged the supposed gaps between under- and upperworld. The city was staked out with for sale signs, but only the really powerful need bother to register claims. Charles Reich in a masterful essay talks about the "New Property"[1] which the administrative state dispensed. For all his insight about new property just think about all that old property still hanging about—all those permits and franchises and licenses and easements and sinecures, all that incredible patronage which was its own combination of power and profit. Out of the maw of competitive capitalism and possessive individualism marched the extortionists—the entrepreneurs of violence whose function was to mediate this state of greed while they skimmed as much as they could for themselves. This issue of power then must be seen from two primary perspectives: the first is the political world itself and corresponds to the social system of organized crime; the second is to view power as the leitmotif of the underworld, as a wedge into the social world of organized crime.

The Social System; Politics

The pursuit of power in one guise or another was the cement holding together under- and upperworlds. In many of the cases discussed throughout this book professionals from both worlds were alert and eager to form coalitions in order to pool resources and skills, to extend dominance. These coalitions encompassed the broad range of organized criminal activity and obviously penetrated such institutions and industries as the criminal justice bureaucracies, the garment, restaurant, waterfront, bakery and trucking trades. Personal alliance networks undermined the formal and legal structures of authority in the upperworld trades, institutions and bureaucracies. Power was not and could not be circumscribed by the formal and legal attributes of these institutions; there were alternate ways to achieve position then through routinized promotions; there were connections more personal than bureaucratic that could improve one's lot.

I have dealt at some length with these links in preceding chapters but still feel it necessary to discuss further the connections between municipal politics and professional crime. The major point about organized crime and politics is simple enough, although the manifestations of the relationships are complex in the extreme. The reason for such complexity is that the major and primary links lie in the social and political histories of the City's numerous Assembly Districts. The centrality of the structure of municipal politics as the key to the social system of organized crime cannot be emphasized too strongly. What McGoldrick first described back in 1928 as the "anode and cathode" of the Tammany battery—the District Leader—was proven by Seabury and those who followed the investigative trail to be the first and dominant link in the fully found system. Indeed, in many instances the rise and fall of professional criminals seems intimately related to the political fortunes of district leaders and vice versa throughout the decades under consideration. Two sets that come to mind in this regard are Schultz and Hines, and Luciano and Marinelli.

But what I want to dwell on at this juncture are the continuity of the system in general and the incessant turmoil within the system in particular. Continuity can be seen by tracking the relationships between professional criminals and district leaders from Seabury's investigations through the Kefauver Report and the findings of the New York State Crime Commission which appeared in 1953. For over two decades every investigator concentrated quite rightly on documenting relationships between district leaders and professional criminals. Turn back to the system Seabury described in his *Intermediate Report* which I suggested could be characterized in the following manner:

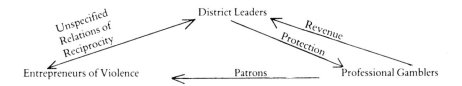

And now consider the following material from the New York State Crime Commission reported in 1953.

Alfred Toplitz was the Democratic leader of a zone of the First Assembly District for a number of years, and while he was not officially a leader at the time of the hearing there was evidence that he continued to maintain his political club and to function as leader. Years ago, Toplitz was dismissed as a Federal Prohibition Agent because of his alleged connection with the theft of liquor. Toplitz admitted to a long and close acquaintanceship with Frank Costello and to associations with other known criminals.

Clarence Neal was a Democratic assembly district leader for a period of 26 years. The proceedings in 1943, following the nomination of Supreme Court Justice Thomas A. Aureilo, and the testimony adduced at the public and private hearings of this Commission, indicate a long, close political and social relationship between Neal and Frank Costello. Irving Daniel Neustein, an attorney and former assemblyman, and a former Democratic assembly district leader, testified to Costello's influence generally among the political leaders. Neustein said he was told in 1945 by his election district captains that they would no longer support him and that Neal was primarily responsible; also, that they told him something to the effect that "the boss made you, and he is going to break you". Neustein identified the phrase "the boss" as referring to Frank Costello and as being heard frequently around Democratic headquarters.[2]

Much the same story can be gleaned from the Commission's work dealing with Samuel Kantor, leader of part of the 14th Assembly District, William J. Connolly, leader of a zone in the 8th, Angelo Simonetti of the 13th, and Sidney Moses, leader of the 6th. All the above had a variety of relationships with Frank Costello as well as other professional criminals including Buchalter, Frank Erickson and Thomas Luchese.

The Commission went on to state what must or should have been obvious to every New Yorker years before:

Any close relationship between characters of his type and political leaders is undesirable and potentially dangerous. This is clear where a relationship of this kind exists between men of generally known underworld connection such as Costello, Erickson, Rao and Stracci on the one hand, and political leaders on the other. Such connections are concealed thus permitting him to circulate freely among prominent public figures. This latter situation is illustrated by the case of Luchese, who lived a unique kind of double life. Luchese was virtually unknown to the press and public until the mayoralty campaign in the fall of 1950, in the course of which he received extensive publicity.[3]

241

The Commission's general point about relationships indicates the constantly reiterated discovery of the obvious: district leaders are linked to professional criminals and *together* they form the base of city politics and perforce the social system of organized crime. I should note that the Commission's specific remarks about Luchese whom they link forcefully to John Merli leader of the 18th South, James Bruno leaders of the 16th South, and Armand Chankalian the Administrative Assistant to the United States Attorney's Office in New York's Southern District, displays their probable belief that they had found a new grand master of organized crime.[4]

There can be no doubt that continuity marks this social system. At the same time, individuals operating within this system were subjected to severe competitive pressures. How tumultuous a world it was is described in this small part of the Kefauver Report's section on Frank Costello and his influence in politics.

> Costello denied that he had any part in defeating Paddy Sullivan in a primary campaign. He had asked Sullivan's support in 1942, when he tried to put over Fay as leader, and Sullivan had refused to commit himself on the ground that he did not wish to support anyone who had the support of Neal, one of the leaders close to Costello. Some time later, Sullivan was defeated in a primary fight. Costello did not deny that he might have offered to help Sullivan in his primary campaign in return for his support, but denied any share in Sullivan's defeat.
>
> Costello reached the height of his power in New York politics in 1942 when he unquestionably had complete domination over Tammany Hall. At that time, Costello supported Kennedy for leader of the Hall. Kennedy was Costello's second choice as Costello originally favored Neal's candidate, Fay. However, Costello and Neal decided that they could not bring about Fay's election, and then Costello brought Kennedy into the picture. Without Costello's support, Kennedy would not have had a chance. Costello being able to control the votes of Abe Rosenthal, Dr. Sarubbi, Jimmy Kelly, and Neal and being able to influence the votes of several others, provided a nucleus which he was able to use to bring about Kennedy's election.[5]

The issue here is not Costello's alleged success, but rather the turmoil of local politics.

Both the competitive nature of local politics and its function as the fulcrum of the social system of organized crime can also be seen by turning attention from Manhattan to Brooklyn, from Costello to Joseph Adonis. In a series of articles written by Edward Flynn for the *New York Post* in 1940, Flynn recounted Adonis's rise concentrating on his connections to Brooklyn politics. Flynn writes: "It was the decay of the Brooklyn Democratic organization of John H. McCooey in the early '30s which gave Joe Adonis the opportunity to make himself one of the most powerful men in the politics of the borough."[6] Principally what Adonis did was to back in 1931 Jerome G.

Ambro, a McCooey foe, in a bid for the State Assembly. Ambro was successful and the following year decided to contest the district leadership of Henry Hasenflug, a McCooey supporter, in Brooklyn's 19th Assembly District. With Adonis's backing, Ambro defeated Hasenflug. This second victory signalled that McCooey's power had declined drastically and there followed a re-shuffling of leadership positions in several Brooklyn districts during the early 1930s. Adonis played the role of broker in the primary contests of 1934 "which overhauled the Brooklyn Democratic organization".[7] Probably the key battle took place in the 23rd, where Adonis backed Dr. Maxwell G. Ross, an optometrist, in his bid to wrest leadership from the illiterate Hyman Schorenstein. Flynn notes that "Schorenstein was beaten largely because hundreds of Italian gangsters were sent to the polls to vote illegally in the Italian sections of his districts."[8] Over the next year or so Adonis, according to Flynn, consolidated his power through various means most notably by deserting his protégé Ambro who tried to oppose the nomination of Geoghan for District Attorney. When all the machinations were over Adonis reportedly held the balance of political power in one-third of Brooklyn's Assembly Districts: the 8th, 9th, 1st, 6th, 14th, 16th, 19th and the 23rd.

It is certain that in one crucial respect the manner by which one knows which professional criminals are the most powerful is to list the number of Assembly Districts they control. Surely that is the methodological message of Flynn's series on Adonis, just as it is at the heart of the Kefauver Committee's summary of Costello. Adonis controls one-third of Brooklyn's districts says Flynn and is therefore the "king of Crime", while Costello "knows, with varying degrees of intimacy, leaders, co-leaders, or both, in at least 10 districts"[9] out of 16 in Manhattan, and is therefore "the Prime Minister of the underworld". But the hold is always tenuous for these are rich prizes constantly fought over. Looking broadly at New York's political history over the two decades, the major battlegrounds both inter- and intra-party had to be the Assembly Districts. That is what political structure means; and that is how important, how fundamental, political structure is in coming to grips with the social system of organized crime. Realizing this, one sees also how micro an approach is truly necessary for researchers seriously interested in organized crime. Those over-arching networks are all grounded in real tangible neighborhoods sliced up or merged into political entities which pulse is found in clubs, saloons, restaurants, candy stores, and cafés.

The Social World: Structure

To speak of the tangible neighborhoods within which politics begins, is to move not quite imperceptibly into the other arena which has consumed the second part of this work. That arena is the underworlds themselves. More specifically, I want to discuss again some of the ways in which professional criminals structured their activities and lives. As noted many times before, to speak of mob or gang structure is to tread a dangerous path. If for no other reason than concentrating strictly on underworld groups is so seductive that it tends to obscure the much more significant groupings which bridged under- and upperworlds. The temptation is to fall into the lure of older demonologies. In addition, to find a structure or structures should not lead one to impose a sociological tyranny. Indeed, there is no general or abstract reason to make a particular structure in which an individual works a social straitjacket. With these cautions in mind there are, nevertheless, important issues to be addressed through this narrowed lens.

Many of the professional criminals we have discussed played a variety of social roles and were not in the least inhibited by either an organized hierarchy or restricted to specialized tasks. Buchalter, Schultz, Luciano, Anastasia, Capone, Reles, Weiss, Workman, Goldstein and others were all involved in a multiplicity of activities in which their positions of authority and/or responsibility varied. But these individuals were what I have called entrepreneurs of violence—leaders or members of various power syndicates in the first instance. And obviously, I think it very useful when discussing mob structure to differentiate between power and enterprise syndicates. The most telling reason is that enterprise syndicates by their very nature are more highly structured and especially routinized collectives. The social structure of enterprise syndicates replicates or takes shape from the economic stringencies of the enterprise itself including the element of risk. Individuals perform certain specialized tasks whether they be controllers or collectors in policy, bookers, madams and prostitutes in prostitution, or manufacturers and distributors of beer. There are workers in the world of illegal enterprises filling set positions. Or to put it perhaps the right way round, there are set positions in illegal enterprises with special tasks which must be performed if the enterprises are to function.

That is not the case with power syndicates whose function is to organize extortion. The social structure of power syndicates is informal in the extreme. And that is because they have no set tasks to perform except to menace and terrorize. There are, naturally, leaders and for want of a better term mobsters. But while the social structures of power syndicates is simple it must be quickly added that they often represented the top of some fairly complex structures. Successful power syndicates grafted themselves upon all sorts of enterprise syndicates as well as entrenched themselves in both employer associations and trade unions. At any given time, therefore, they appeared to be an integral part of some highly structured organizations. Even in those cases, however, it seems to me to be a mistake to view them primarily through an organizational perspective. First and foremost because the organizational perspective tends to freeze time and hence change, thereby misrepresenting the nature of power syndicates. This nature is better captured by focusing on them as fluid sets of mobile marauders in the urban landscape alert to institutional weakness in both legitimate and illegitimate spheres. They form, then, the loci of power in exceptionally competitive or unstable arenas.

Nothing better illustrates the foregoing than the following example from the career of Louis Buchalter. In 1937 the Federal authorities indicted Buchalter for conspiring to violate the narcotics laws. He was accused of leading a world-wide drug smuggling syndicate, an organization both centralized and highly structured. But, nothing could have been further from the evidence produced and, I am convinced, social reality. Indeed, so far from establishing a smooth and efficient organization run by Buchalter, the Government did not even settle such crucial questions as when and how the narcotics conspiracy started and what exactly was Buchalter's role within it. For instance, in an FBI report written soon after Buchalter's conviction (he was sentenced to fourteen years in a Federal penitentiary), it was stated that Buchalter, Jack Lvovsky, Yasha Katzenberg and Louis Kravitz became partners in a narcotics operation in 1933.[10] In contrast to this, the Federal Bureau of Narcotics reported earlier that the plan was conceived two years later in 1935, that the conspirators were known as the Lvovsky organization, and that the leaders were Lvovsky, Katzenberg, and Samuel Gross.[11] Buchalter in their construction had nothing to do with originating the syndicate or leading it.

Louis Kravitz

At Buchalter's trial in December, 1939, the major government witness was none other than Yasha Katzenberg who had earlier pleaded guilty. Katzenberg's account was that Buchalter "had abruptly invaded the racket with a simple demand for half the profits". He stated that Louis Kravitz first approached him asking if his connection hadn't been set up for Buchalter. A meeting followed during which Buchalter "demanded 50 percent". Some negotiating took place and the deal was consummated—Buchalter took half the profits.[12] The actual case developed by the Government was far removed from the speculations of both the FBI and the Bureau of Narcotics in their later reports. What the prosecution labored to show was Buchalter terrorizing Katzenberg into surrendering half the profits from an enormously profitable smuggling operation. The social situation was the familiar one of a power syndicate extorting a substantial part of the profits from an enterprise syndicate. It was Katzenberg and the others who structured a syndicate with administrators, exporters, smugglers, wholesalers, etc., not Buchalter and his power syndicate. It should be marked that this view of Buchalter as an extortionist of other criminals was affirmed, although not analytically developed, by the Kefauver Committee which stated in their report that Buchalter was not one of the originators of the scheme, "but when we heard of its success, he promptly declared himself to be entitled to one-third of the profits".[13] If Buchalter was involved in narcotics, then it was in the same spirit as Luciano in prostitution, and Schultz in policy. He labored as they did in the vineyard of extortion.

The structure of power syndicates was simple and flexible allowing members to engage in a multiplicity of illegal activities and therefore to be involved in various complex networks in addition to their primary mob. Some more discussion of narcotics and Buchalter's power syndicate will amplify this. Emmanuel "Mendy" Weiss who was executed along with Buchalter and Louis Capone in 1944 for the murder of Joe Rosen was deeply involved in drug smuggling during the 1930s. And while there is an overabundance of evidence linking Weiss to Buchalter in a number of extortion schemes and as a key member of Buchalter's power syndicate, there is no evidence that indicates their narcotics dealings were joined.

The Bureau of Narcotics Annual Report for 1941 reviewed, with accuracy this time, Weiss' career in drugs. They state that customs officers in 1937 "thought they had secured evidence against Weiss, who had long been known as an international narcotics trafficker, when at Rouses Point, N.Y., they seized a suitcase containing heroin in the posession of one Jacob Gottlieb".[14] Gottlieb implicated Weiss in the drug operation and then committed suicide in jail. Following the Rouses Point incident, which led nowhere for the moment, Weiss next encountered the Bureau of Narcotics in the summer of 1939. At that time, narcotics officers arrested Jack Langsam for possessing and selling heroin. Langsam attempted to bribe the police who reportedly pretended to go along with the offer. To secure money for the bribe, Langsam went to his brother-in-law, "Mendy" Weiss, who was promptly arrested. Apparently nothing came of this case because the next action against Weiss took place seven months later when he was indicted for his part in the Gottlieb case and for selling heroin in New York in 1937.[15] After his indictment, Weiss was released on $10,000 bond and promptly became a fugitive. Two months later in Dallas, Texas, a syndicate headquartered in New York which allegedly distributed heroin in Illinois and Texas was broken with the indictment of Weiss and 28 others.[16] Weiss was ultimately captured by narcotics officers in Kansas City, Missouri, in the spring of 1941 and returned to New York.

Jacob Gottlieb   *Jack Langsam*

The point about this exegisis on Weiss is that although he was an important member of Buchalter's power syndicate, he was well able to act independently of Buchalter in drugs. Membership in Buchalter's power syndicate, therefore, was not all consuming. Professional criminals—extortionists—were constantly participating in several syndicates at the same time, they were always alert to opportunities for forming new partnerships, new coalitions, for entering into new alliances. The claim then is that for its members the structure of a power syndicate was exceptionally flexible, displayed by their propensity toward multi-syndicate activities, and cross-syndicate partnerships.

One last example of this should suffice. The evidence this time comes from the testimony of Abe Reles at the murder trial of Irving "Knadles" Nitzberg accused of killing Albert "Plug" Schuman on January 9, 1939. Reles was asked during the trial about his gang called the Combination and its relationship with Buchalter and members of his mob. First of all, Reles identified Weiss, Charlie "The Bug" Workman, Albert Tannenbaum, and "Sheppey" Shapiro as members of Buchalter's syndicate who all had a hand in the Schuman killing. He then stated that outside of gang structure, he and Workman were partners in several extortionary activities. He also listed his own activities as "extortion, unions, shylocking, crap games, any place that was crooked". And in the same context, he added that he was "partners with the Lepke mob, our mob, whatever came up".[17] Reles was undoubtedly representing in his unique manner the fluidity of the social world.

Reles was questioned in particular about his relationship with Buchalter. Asked whether he dealt with Buchalter, he answered both yes and no. Pressed by the defense counsel to identify the business that he had with Buchalter, Reles responds "the garment industry; whatever business arose to talk". Asked again what specific activity he performed for Buchalter, he states "just talking over here, and how was things going along, and how is the business doing". The defense then asked what business Reles was talking about and was it perhaps the murder business? Reles replied that at the time he did not talk with Buchalter about murder and the business discussed was the garment industry. The Judge then interrupted and asked if Reles was manufacturing garments, to which he answers "no, we had a payroll there". Next, the Judge wanted to know if Reles was paid to protect the industry Reles replies: "the association. He was the boss of the garment industry." Defense counsel then asked "what was your business then in regard to this payroll that you are talking about?" The final answer is: "that is what it was, payroll".[18]

Reles's inability to exactly reveal what it was that he and the Combination actually did to receive their money from Buchalter was an indication that his relationship with Buchalter was not the simple commercial and organizational one assumed by the Judge and counsel. The payroll was a device for the formation of a new coalition, a new series of networks. The payroll placed Reles and his partners on call to Buchalter. Without any specific duties or responsibilities attached, Buchalter was finding himself clients for future contingencies, as well as recognizing the enhanced status of the Combination since the murder of Amberg in 1935. The Brooklyn Combination was in Buchalter's debt rather than in his mob; they were connected. Moreover individual members developed their own networks such as the one forged by Reles and Workman. One of the payoffs for developing these networks came when someone had to be murdered. "Whenever they got to kill somebody, they tell a guy from the Bronx or the East Side or Brooklyn, whoever knows the guy." In the particular case of

Schuman, Reles notes, "here Nitzberg got the contract ... He knew him. If I knew the guy, I would have got the contract. That is how it worked."[19] What is so striking about power syndicates from a strictly organizational perspective is how disorganized they appear, how informal their structure is, how many alliances and networks flow from their exceptionally flexible frame.

Albert "Plug" Schuman   *Irving "Knadles" Nitzberg*

Extortion

I have stated or alluded to this many times before, but it cannot be overstated: the specialty of criminals like Schultz, Luciano, Anastasia, Buchalter and others was political in the general sense of the word. Their success was contingent on their ability to control others, which was the manifestation of their power. Their methods ranging from persuasion to murder were all part of a politics of terror. What they were about was extortion taken to mean establishing dominance, increasing personal power. Concerning extortion we have dealt so far with the ways in which power syndicates extorted from enterprise syndicates, and the ways in which extortion manifested itself in the complex relations between labor and management. What follows is one other very long example of extortion on a personal level. Extortion is not only a complex social activity, but also a dramatic encounter. For the unknown person whose story follows the dramatic encounters were sustained for over a decade of unrelieved exploitation. The example comes from the Municipal Archives and is simply titled TO WHOM IT MAY CONCERN:

> For many years I have been in the clutches of the people whom I mention in this statement. They have extorted large sums of money from me and have kept me in constant fear of death. I have made many attempts to break away from them but they have kept me under their control with threats of death to me and my family. I am about to make a last desperate attempt to break away and I am certain that their reply will mean my death.

I am married and have a family. By profession I am an undertaker. Many years ago as a result of hard work in my profession and successful investments, I amassed a considerable fortune. Everything I earned and saved was gradually taken from me by these men. I am at the present time practically penniless.

At the funeral of a friend of mine I was approached by GUISEPPE PERAINO, whom I later came to know as the "Clutching Hand". He told me that he had a very interesting business proposition for me. When I asked him what it was all about, he told me that I would see him again and that he would tell me all about it. Some time later he came to see me. He told me that he knew I was a very popular man in the City and that I had a large acquaintance and for this reason he wanted me to join with him in the "policy Business". I told him I was earning a comfortable living in my business and that I was not interested. He said that I would stand to lose nothing, my name would be used only as a front. I refused to consent to such an arrangement. Then he stated that I was in the game whether I liked it or not because my name alone would draw a good play. He said that I did not have to worry, all payments and collections would be handled by him and his crowd and that I would stand to suffer no loss. He said that it had been decided that I was in the game and that there was no way out for me. He warned me that if I failed to keep the bargain, harm would come to me and my family. I felt that there was nothing I could do.

About one month after this meeting I began to receive telephone calls from various people demanding sums of money which they claimed they had won in the policy play. When I denied knowledge of any of this they told me that the collectors had told them that I was the boss and that they were to look to me for payment. I refused to pay anybody. Within a day or two from then I received a visit from Peraino. He told me that Little Augie wanted to see me. I asked him what he wanted to see me about and he said that Augie wanted to see me about the policy game. I told him that I would go to see no one. That same day Peraino and Augie came to my house. At first they treated me very nicely, they told me I could make a lot of money with them, that we could be very friendly and that it would be worthwhile for me to go along with them, After quite a discussion I told them that I did not dare join their band and that I did not intend to pay out any money to the people who had made demands upon me for winnings. Upon hearing this they threatened to kill me and my family. They told me that I would have the choice of paying or being destroyed. They further told me that any money I paid out would be paid back to me later. I was afraid for myself and my family and I paid and from that date to this I have paid and paid until I can no longer stand it.

Some time after I was compelled to make the first payment, I learned that the "Clutching Hand" was killed. I felt relieved because I thought that I was rid of the whole lot of them. No such thing was in store for me. Immediately after Peraino's death I was called upon by GERARDO SCARPATO. He told me that he was taking up where Peraino left off and that from then he would deal with me. He warned me that I was to continue as I did with Peraino. He came to see me very frequently and of course always made to insure the fact that I paid the sums of money which were demanded. One day he ordered me to go to see him at his restaurant known as the Villa Tamparo at Coney Island. I got there late in the afternoon, the exact time I do not remember. I drove there in my car. As soon as I reached the place another car stopped right behind me. Scarpato was outside. People got out of the car behind me and I recognized Little Augie as one of the men. Scarpato ran over to my car and asked me what I was doing there. I told him that I was there pursuant to his request. Augie came over and wanted to know what I was doing there. Scarpato wanted to know why I was there since he had phoned my home and left word for me not to go there. I told him and Augie that I did not get the message. Scarpato told me to leave right away and not to mention to anyone that I had been there that day. Augie warned me not to mention that I had seen him that day. I left. Late that night I read in the newspapers that JOE MASSARIA, Joe the Boss, was killed at the Villa Tamparo. That was my first taste of what these men were capable of.

From that day on I tried to get around Scarpato and I pleaded with him to try and get me away from these men. I kept telling him that it was no life for me and that I was gradually sinking to financial ruin. He promised to see what he could do and at the same time made me understand that the decision was not up to Augie alone. There were New York people interested in the game. The New York people were SANTINO and TONY BENDA. He told me that there would be a meeting at Augie's office on Union Street, Brooklyn, very soon. All of the principals were to be present. Scarpato told me he would explain my condition to them and try to help me out. I believed Scarpato. One day he called me and told me that the meeting was scheduled for that night. He said he was going to try to help me but that he could not do anything for me unless I got some money for him. I asked him how much money was needed and he said a few thousand. I told him I did not have that much and the best I could do was one thousand. He told me to bring the thousand that night and that everything would be all right. We arranged to meet at eight o'clock that night on the corner of Fourth Avenue and Union Street, Brooklyn, near the drug store. I went down with the money and met Scarpato on the corner. He seemed very nervous and excited. I gave him the money and he told me that he would be called up very soon. When he was to go up to the meeting I was to wait for him on the corner. A few moments later a man approached Scarpato and called him over. They talked for a few seconds. Scarpato came over to me and told me to wait for him and that he would be gone for about half an hour. I waited and in about an hour the same man who had left with Scarpato returned and was accompanied by Little Augie. They came over to me. Augie said to me "listen, no matter what happens, you never knew Scarpato. Get the hell out of here and keep your mouth shut". I went home. The man who left with Scarpato and later returned with Augie, I later found out was JAMES DEMINO. The next day I read in the newspapers that Scarpato was found killed in a car, a rope tied round his neck. A week after Scarpato was found dead, Demino came to see me. He told me that he was the representative of Augie and the New York people. He said I would not see very much of the others and that he would contact me at all times. He has been dealing with me for several years. The last time I saw him was on October 13, 1941, when he told me that Augie and Santina wanted to see me in Long Island. He told me that Augie needs help because he has been in a lot of trouble lately. Demino told me that I had to go and that he had already made an appointment for me with Augie and Santina. I told him that I had no more money and that I was afraid to go. Demino said that there was nothing for me to worry about because I was to meet them where they play golf.

I am afraid to go to meet these men. If I do I am quite sure I will meet the same fate of Massaria and Scarpato. I told Demino that I would not go to meet anyone. I further told him that I would not and could not pay anything because I am now ruined. I further told him that I did not want to see any of his crowd again.

The Little Augie I mention is Augie Pisano, whose real name is Carfano.

Since my dealings with these men I have paid them approximately forty thousand dollars. All my protests for the return of my money have been answered by threats and threats. At the present time I am not only a financial wreck, but a physical and moral one as well.

I have decided to finish this mess once and for all and I am quite certain I will meet the same end as Massaria and Scarpato.

My family is all grown up now, and are well able to take care of themselves. They know nothing of this mess.

The men I have mentioned control all the gambling in the City. Tony Benda operates a gambling place in New York. They are involved in policy, lottery, and loan shark operations.

I pray to God that this information can be used to rid society of these men. I well realize that I should have brought this to the attention of the authorities before, but I know I was too weak to do so. All the information I give is the truth and I make this statement knowing full well that I am on the way to certain death.

Power and Becoming

The manifestations and meanings of the politics of terror summed by the term extortion are still not fully catalogued. The long term decline of the physical, financial and moral wreck who penned the above appeal is one of the dramatic consequences of personalized politics. There are others. For instance, it is vital to understand that displays of power were constantly important; that individuals were continually orienting themselves in the unstable and murderous environment. Daily dramas took place which were open-ended dominance contests whose outcomes were by no means foreordained. These contests, which were often life and death ones, were carried out within the full range of power syndicates and their corresponding networks. Disputes which were endemic in such a competitive milieu energized not only the primary participants but ran up and down lines of contact. Disputes which were occasioned by and called forth the illegal use of force or fear, always had the potential to radically alter whatever temporary stability was current. The contours of disputes, of dominance contests, of extortionary culture, reveal much about the social world of organized crime—about power, rivalries and networks, about ultimately the existential quality of the underworld.

Seymour Magoon

Of all the documents I have come across nothing describes this better than the following long MEMORANDUM OF INFORMATION FURNISHED BY SEYMOUR MAGOON, In re: Jimmy Abbatamarco (called "Bat" for short).

Seymour was called "on the carpet" by Albert A. at the City Democratic Club because of trouble with "Bat" over a loan transaction. "Bat" was a cousin of Frankie Shatz. He had come to the corner of Saratoga and Livonia Avenues for a loan. Seymour had told Mikey Sycoff, who had not previously known "Bat", to make the loan and on his word Sycoff loaned "Bat" $200, repayable at the rate of $40 a week for six weeks. The first payment of $40 was made to Mikey, but nothing more was heard for five or six weeks. Thereupon, Mikey came complaining to Seymour, who went with him to the undertaker, Abbatamarco, at Fourth Avenue and Carroll Street, where "Bat", Shatz and gang hung out. There Seymour saw Jimmy "Bat" and called him out. Seymour "bawled him out" for not repaying the loan as agreed. Jimmy "Bat" replied that he had no money. Seymour said that if he had to come down again he would knock Jimmy "Bat's" brains out. He said he would have the money in a couple of days.

Two weeks later found no payments made by "Bat" to Mikey, who again came to Seymour complaining. Seymour and Mikey went looking for "Bat". Seymour went to some fellow's house on Prospect Place, where "Bat" frequented, and was told that they had gone to a barber shop on Atlantic Avenue. This was about 10.00 p.m. Arriving at the barber shop, Seymour and Mikey find it closed but see a light in back. Seymour knocks at the window. Joe Roberts opened the door. Seymour asked him if Jimmy "Bat" were there. He said yes. Out came "Bat" and two others, who "heisted" Seymour and Mikey, saying that they should get into a car. Mike was scared. Seymour said that if they were going to do anything, to do it right then and there. He said that they were not going into any car. "Bat", seeing Seymour unfazed at gunpoint, forgot about the car, told Seymour that they weren't on Fourth Avenue, and asked him whose brains he was going to knock in. Seymour did not answer him. So he said, "Get in that car." Seymour said no, that he should do what he had to do right there. Finally "Bat" forgets about the car and says to Mikey that he is on the payroll at $50 a week, payable by Seymour. "Bat", turning to Seymour, says that he has to bring down the $50 to him every week. Seymour inquired where he wanted him to bring it. He said, "You know where." Seymour said it was all right, that he would bring it down. So both of them got into the car and drove the car to the corner. Seymour was in tears. On the corner he sees Abe Reles. He asks Reles if he has any pistols. Reles says he has. Seymour tells him what has happened and asks for two pistols. Reles replied, "why two?" He said it was three, one for him too. Reles gets three guns. Seymour thinks that Mikey did not get one, however. He thinks "Buggsy" came along. Mike drove the car and Abe, "Buggsy" and Seymour with the guns went along. Seymour had told "Bat" that he would not have to wait a week for the payroll; he would have it that night. Seymour said that. knowing that they were affiliated with Albert A. anyway (the Italian end of it). So they drove to Fourth and Carroll Street. The undertaker was closed. They went to DeLeo's Bar & Grill, where "Bat", Shatz and gang were known to go. Mikey parked the car across the street, while Reles remained in the car, "Bugs" stationed himself on the curb and Seymour went into the bar. He asked for Jimmy "Bat". Maybe ten or 15 Italians are in there. They said, "Hello, Si" to him, and said he wasn't there. Somebody asked if there was anything he could do for Seymour. Seymour asked who he was and he said he was Jimmy "Bat's" brother. Seymour asked him to come outside. He asked Seymour if he couldn't do the talking there, and was told in strong terms no. The language was accompanied by a dropping here and there, a scurrying for cover. The brother thereupon walked out of the bar. Seymour asked him where his brother was, but he was so frightened he could not answer. Seymour asked where he lived, and he finally managed to tell him where. Seymour and his friends were driven by Mikey to Jimmy "Bat's" home, but couldn't find him there. They waited around for about an hour, but he did not show up. Then Seymour and his men went to various places looking for him, finally winding up in Brownsville. Then Seymour suggested they go back there again about 2.00 a.m. So his companions agreed. This time "Sholem" Bernstein went with Seymour, while Mikey drove. Some other fellow, who Seymour cannot recall at the moment, accompanied them. They went back to Fourth Avenue. Meanwhile, as Seymour later learned, Albert A. and Frankie Shatz were in Brownsville. There was a rumour on Fourth Avenue set afloat at the time they went to the bar earlier in the night, which brought Albert A. and Shatz to Brownsville. They inquired of Reles if he knew where Seymour and Mikey were. Reles, though knowing where they were, told Albert A. that he did not. Reles managed to get Albert A. off to the side and told him, so that Shatz could not overhear it, where Seymour was. As they were conversing there, Seymour returned. Albert said that they would have to go to Vince. So they had a "meet" for the following day.

The "meet" took place at the City Democratic Club. Present were Louis Capone, Abe Reles and Mendy Weiss, sent by Lepke, representing Seymour and Mikey, who were also there, and on the other side were Albert A., Frankie Shatz, Jimmy "Bat" and another cousin, and all were seated around a table there. They denied the whole thing, says Seymour, not the loan but the "heist". Albert A. suggests they forget it and shake hands. Seymour did not want to shake hands with Jimmy "Bat". Seymour called him a liar. So Albert gave Seymour the nod with his head, beckoning for him to shake hands. Seymour waved his hand. With that Louis Capone asks about the money that was loaned. Albert surprised all by saying that he would pay it. Eventually Albert paid practically all the money that was due to Mikey. Albert at that time told Seymour that they are not over friendly with Harry Fontana, a cousin of this "Bat", and that Vince said he is looking to get something on him. Seymour said O.K., he wanted him to shake hands and it's O.K. with him. That ended the "meet".

About six months prior to this, Frank Shatz and Seymour had a run in. He owed something like $700, and he thought he was "cute", because he was Tony Bender's partner. So Seymour went down to Louis C., and told him that Frank Shatz owed this money and was acting as though he didn't want to pay it. Capone asked if Seymour had been there himself. Seymour said no, that he had sent Dominick down to see him. Capone asked why he had sent that dumb fellow down. So Seymour said he wanted to tell him first, because he had gone first and had been treated as Dominick had by Frank Shatz. Capone would have asked why he hadn't come to him first. Therefore, Seymour told Capone that he was going down to Shatz from that time on.

Seymour then went to the undertaker's and saw Shatz and Joe Pitt from Coney Island as well as a couple or more of "high class ginzos", fellows who would shoot somebody and shake him down for the rest of his life, says Seymour. They greeted him. Seymour asked Shatz about the money he owed. He answered that Dominick had been bothering him. Seymour said, "What do you mean, bothering you? Do you owe the money?" He replied that he did. Seymour said that it was better in his pocket. He reminded Shatz of his undertaking to repay it every week and here it was the third or fourth week without anything having been paid. Shatz said that he would have it sometime during the week. Seymour said that undertaking would be good for his uncle, but he would have to have a definite time. Shatz asked how he could give a definite time. It wound up in an argument. Seymour finally said that if he had to come down again it would be with a bat. With that he walked out.

Seymour went to see Louis Capone to tell him about the conversation. Seymour waited patiently during the week, but no sign of Frank Shatz. So at the end of the week, Seymour went to Frank Shatz's home at about 5.00 o'clock in the morning. He banged on the doors. Awoke the house. Shatz came to the door to see what had struck the house. Seeing Seymour, he asked him in for coffee. This bit of kindness dumbfounded Seymour, who accepted the invitation. He told Shatz that Dominick was waiting in the car for him. Anyway, Shatz made coffee at that early hour and they drank. Seymour asked him, "How about the money?" He said he had a hundred and forty on him and asked if he wanted to take that. Seymour said he did. Shatz told him he didn't have to send Dominick down, that he would come down with the balance. Seymour could not understand such kindly treatment following the storming of the house.

A couple of days later Louis Capone came to Seymour and said, "Albert wants to see you". Seymour inquired, "What now?" and was told, "On account of Frankie Shatz." He continued telling Seymour that the report was that he had broken into the Shatz house at six o'clock in the morning, called his wife nasty names (real bad names), and had maligned all the Italians. Seymour set Capone straight on that, saying he had gone to the house at five o'clock and not six, had been treated nicely, and there had been no untoward incident. Capone said that was the story Shatz had given that it was necessary for Seymour to go down to Albert. Reles overheard the conversation and asked Seymour if he had done it. Seymour said no. Reles told him to go down with him, then. (Seymour is not positive if Reles went down, but believes he did). Seymour went to Albert's house. Louis Capone was also there. Seymour related the whole story to Albert, who then asked him if he had been repaid the money. He said he had not. Albert thereupon said "O.K." and Seymour walked out. The next day Seymour assumed Shatz' attitude, with Albert A.'s O.K. behind him, and walked right in and demanded the money. He got the money that next day.

The social world Magoon describes was fraught with complexities, uncertainties, frustrations, terrors. All together they gave form and substance to its evolving character. Consider how many times violence threatened, how close the individuals came to murder and what that may have done to the web of networks from which Anastasia and Capone drew some of their strength. It is also characteristic of the individuals described in the Magoon document to be deeply committed to face. This is pointed up by Magoon's frustration at one point and his tears of rage. This rancorous world was indeed extraordinarily unstable depending ultimately on the management skills of patrons who were themselves notably violent, often irrational, and devoted to personalized politics. The litany of extortionary culture reveals a social world always in motion, always in the process of becoming. Out of the endemic disputes came the possibilities of new machinations. It is a world with no end, with no surcease from the daily dangers and encounters which as often promised disaster as well as profit.

In looking at this social world, it seems to me that what professional criminals were all about was the process of organizing crime. Precisely because their domain was shaped by informal power, their associations were fluid enabling them most efficiently to respond to changing circumstances— to organizing crime. I need hardly add that looking exclusively through structural–functional lenses, the most important element of all is typically missed: the rigour of professional criminals in organizing crime because they exist within a world of rather tumultuous change. The most efficient "organized criminals" were the most individualistic, the least committed to particular structures; one of the major differences between the managers of illegal enterprises and the extortionists. And what finally can be said about the tension between continuity and turmoil, the particular and the general? It is simple enough—the stability of the social system of organized crime in general was the ground of opportunity for the residents of that world in particular. Organizing crime was the challenge offered by that civil society, that political economy. To borrow a telling phrase from another context: "the entire ensemble is part of a system that determines their conduct without uniting their will".[20]

NOTES

1 Charles A. Reich, "The New Property," *The Yale Law Journal* 73 (April, 1964).
2 New York State Crime Commission, *Second Report*, Legislative Document No. 40(1953), 9.
3 *Ibid.*, 13.
4 That Luchese was considered the most important organized crime figure by the Commission can be seen in their *Confidential Digest of Information on Certain Arrest Records* in which the activities of about 70 professional criminals are scrutinized for connections to Luchese. The Commission's evaluation of Luchese follows:
> Born in Italy and brought to this country at an early age by parents. He obtained naturalization in New Jersey while still residing in Long Island. In the 1928 homicide of Cerasula, the victim was ganged up on by Tommy Brown, Scupette Gaudio and Joe Palisades. None of the eye witnesses will identify any of the individuals who were present at the shooting of Gerasulo. Gerasulo's death-bed advices to his wife involved these three but were not sufficiently legally strong. The 1930 homicide of Pinzola was similar. Pinzola, Luchese and others were partners in a wine brick business and had a dispute. Three men were in the office with the victim; the victim got shot and all present claim they were lined face to the wall by men with badges and couldn't see anything. In 1931 he was arrested in Cleveland, Ohio, while attending the Schmelling fight with Joe Biondo and Lucky Luciano. In 1932 Brown was operating gambling machines with Costello, Luciano and others in Harlem. Rumor has it that Philly

"Rags" held out on his collections. "Rags" was found dead in the Harlem River; no arrests were made. Subsequently, Brown branched out into legitimate enterprises, particularly in the clothing industry. He became friendly with Armand Chankalian, administration assistant to the U.S. Attorney in New York. Got a certificate of good conduct and became naturalized and began attending political dinners and functions, gaining acquaintance of political figures. Although his legitimate interests are heavy, he is still considered a key man in the Mafia and of the narcotics group. His name turns up with considerable frequency on persons arrested in narcotics cases. EXAMPLE: Dragna in California and Luciano in Italy.—Brown protests his innocence. New York State Crime Commission Papers in Rare Books and Manuscripts, Butler Library, Columbia University.

5 U.S. Senate, *The Kefauver Committee Report*, 102–103.
6 *New York Post*, April 25, 1940.
7 *Ibid.*, April 26, 1940.
8 *Ibid.*, April 16, 1940.
9 U.S. Senate, *The Kefauver Committee Report*, 102.
10 Federal Bureau of Investigation, 61.
11 U.S. Department of Treasury, Bureau of Narcotics, *Traffic in Opium and Other Dangerous Drugs: Annual Report* (Washington, D.C., 1937), 20–21.
12 *The New York Times*, December 8, 1939: 26.
13 U.S. Senate, *The Kefauver Committee Report*, 148.
14 Bureau of Narcotics, *Annual Report* (1941), 16.
15 Bureau of Narcotics, *Annual Report* (1939), 33–34.
16 Bureau of Narcotics, *Annual Report* (1941), 28, 39–41.
17 Court of Appeals—Brooklyn, New York, The People of the State of New York Against Irving Nitzberg (September–October, 1941) 7760, 151–156, 201.
18 *Ibid.*, 159–161.
19 *Ibid.*
20 Raymond Aron, *History and the Dialectic of Violence: An Analysis of Sartre's Critique de la Raison Dialectique*, translated by Barry Cooper (Oxford, 1975), 52.

Index